Third Edition

BASIC REHABILITATION TECHNIQUES

A Self-Instructional Guide

Editors
Robert D. Sine, M.D.
Shelly E. Liss, M.D.
Robert E. Roush, Ed.D., M.P.H.
J. David Holcomb, Ed.D.
Georgianna Burbidge Wilson, M.Ed., P.T.

Contributors
Ruth Avidan, O.T.R.
David C. Bradshaw, M.D.
Susan Ellison Dominguez, R.N.
Mary Ellen Hayden, Ph.D.
Barbara M. Henley, C.S.W./A.C.P.
Gerald Hirschberg, M.D.
Zvi Kalisky, M.D.
Gerald Keane, M.D.
Virginia L. Kerr, O.T.R.
Linda Jean Larson, M.A., S.P./C.C.C.
Daniel Morrison, M.D.
Frances Pendergraft, C.S.W./A.C.P.
Patrick M. Plenger, Ph.D.
Mahendra Shah, O.T.R.
Franz U. Steinberg, M.D.
Stanley K. Yarnell, M.D.

Third Edition
BASIC REHABILITATION TECHNIQUES

A Self-Instructional Guide

Robert D. Sine, M.D.
Shelly E. Liss, M.D.

Robert E. Roush, Ed.D., M.P.H.
J. David Holcomb, Ed.D.
Georgianna Wilson, M.Ed., PT

AN ASPEN PUBLICATION®
Aspen Publishers, Inc.

1988

Rockville, Maryland
Royal Tunbridge Wells

Library of Congress Cataloging-in-Publication Data

Basic rehabilitation techniques: a self-instructional guide/Robert D. Sine...[et. al.].--3rd ed.
p. cm.
"An Aspen publication".
Includes index.
ISBN: 0-87189-768-7
1. Rehabilitation nursing--Handbooks, manuals, etc. I. Sine, Robert D.
RT120.R4B37   1988   615.8′2--dc19
88-14584
CIP

Editorial Services: Mary Beth Roesser

Library of Congress Catalog Card Number: 88-14584
ISBN: 0-87189-768-7

Printed in the United States of America

1 2 3 4 5

Table of Contents

Editors' Profiles

Robert D. Sine, M.D., is Director, Department of Rehabilitation Medicine at St. Mary's Hospital, San Francisco, California. He is an active teacher and is a clinical associate professor in the Department of Rehabilitation Medicine at Stanford University. His major interests are stroke rehabilitation ("The Lateralized Stroke Program," "The Callosol Syndrome: Implications for Stroke Rehabilitation," "A Double Blind Study of Stimulants in Left Hemiplegia"), chronic pain ("Non-Pharmacological Approaches to Cancer Pain," "The Quieting Response: The Evolution of Pain"), and electrodiagnosis ("Positive Sharp Wave Origins: Clinical Implications," "Experience With 250 Epidural Electrospinograms").

Shelly E. Liss, M.D., is Medical Director of the Department of Physical Medicine and Rehabilitation, Memorial Hospital, Houston, Texas; Clinical Associate Professor, Department of Physical Medicine, Baylor College of Medicine; and Clinical Assistant Professor of Family Practice, the University of Texas School of Medicine, Houston, Texas. He is an active spokesman for the field of rehabilitative medicine in numerous local, state, and national organizations and has been responsible for the development of several statewide programs utilizing rehabilitation techniques for general and patient populations. Dr. Liss's publications include papers demonstrating how the medical profession can use rehabilitation techniques to improve patient care in various diagnostic categories.

Robert E. Roush, Ed.D., M.P.H., is Director, Center for Allied Health Professions, Baylor College of Medicine. He has directed educational research on the preventive aspects of cardiovascular disease and cancer, and was the principal investigator of a recent National Science Foundation grant on improving science and math opportunities for future health professionals. Currently, Dr. Roush is the project director of one of the 31 federally-funded geriatric education centers in the United States, The Texas Consortium of Geriatric Education Centers. Dr. Roush earned his doctorate at the University of Houston, completed postdoctoral work in medical education at the University of Southern California School of Medicine, and received an M.P.H. degree from The University of Texas School of Public Health. An international allied health consultant, he teaches graduate classes on research design at Baylor and is also a member of the adjunct graduate faculties of the University of Houston and Texas A&M University.

J. David Holcomb, Ed.D., is Professor and Head, Division of Allied Health Sciences, Department of Community Medicine, Baylor College of Medicine. He is a member of the faculties of Texas A&M University, the University of Houston, and The University of Texas Health Science Center, Houston. He serves as the coordinator of Baylor's graduate program in Allied Health Education and Administration. Dr. Holcomb is the coauthor of a book on improving medical education. His current research interests are on the roles of health professionals in health promotion and disease prevention and the scholarly activities of allied health faculty. He earned his doctorate at the University of Houston and completed postdoctoral training at the University of Southern California.

Georgianna Burbidge Wilson, M.Ed., P.T., is currently Department Head, Physical Therapist Assistant Program, Houston Community College, Houston, Texas. She is a 1965 graduate of the Mayo Clinic School of Physical Therapy. She received her B.S. from Rockford College, Rockford, Illinois, in 1964, and her M.Ed. in Allied Health Education and Administration from the University of Houston and the Baylor College of Medicine in 1987. Mrs. Wilson was previously Director of Physical Therapy at Rosewood General Hospital, Houston, Texas, and worked in California at the Contra Costa County Hospital Rehabilitation Center with Dr. Gerald Hirschberg, originator of the Stand-up, Step-up Program; she was influential in the development of a Stand-up, Step-up Program at Rosewood General Hospital.

Contributors' Profiles

Ruth Avidan, O.T.R., is a registered occupational therapist trained at the Israel School of Physical Therapy in Jerusalem, Israel. Mrs. Avidan was, during the course of the initial stages of the development of the first edition of this book, Chief of Occupational Therapy at Rosewood General Hospital's Rehabilitation Unit in Houston, Texas. At this time, Mrs. Avidan resides in Israel.

David C. Bradshaw, M.D., currently is Medical Director of the Rehabilitation Service at Mt. Zion Hospital, San Francisco. He has special interests in nonsurgical management of spine pain as well as in general rehabilitation. Before medical school Dr. Bradshaw received a master's degree in electrical engineering and was a biomedical engineer in Mission Control for Apollo 11 and 12.

Susan Ellison Dominguez, R.N., was head nurse of the Rehabilitation Unit of Rosewood General Hospital, Houston, Texas, at the time of the development of the second edition of this book. She is a graduate of the Jackson Memorial Hospital School of Nursing in Miami, Florida. Mrs. Dominguez has considerable experience in the field of medical-surgical nursing. At this time, Mrs. Dominguez is utilizing her rehabilitation skills in home health nursing in rural Mississippi.

Mary Ellen Hayden, Ph.D., is a clinical neuropsychologist in private practice. She specializes in rehabilitation neuropsychology and supports the rehabilitation efforts of the teams at Medical Center del Oro Hospital and Memorial Hospital Southwest, Houston, Texas. She is also on the part-time faculty at the University of Houston, where she teaches courses in neuropsychology. Dr. Hayden's most recent publications have focused on the use of neuropsychological techniques in the rehabilitation setting.

Barbara M. Henley, C.S.W./A.C.P., is Director of Social Work at Ben Taub General Hospital, Houston, Texas; an instructor in the Department of Community Medicine, Baylor College of Medicine; and a field instructor for the Graduate School of Social Work, University of Houston. As a member of the Patient Services Council of the AHA, she participated in developing guidelines on psychosocial aspects of hospital care and has done numerous workshops on discharge planning. She is a past president of the National Society of Hospital Social Work Directors and author of numerous publications.

Gerald Hirschberg, M.D., obtained his M.D. at the University of Marseille in 1939 and has been publishing, teaching, and practicing rehabilitation medicine without a lapse ever since. Some of his work has attained the status of "classic in the field" ("Recovery of Voluntary Motion in the Upper Extremity following Hemiplegia"). He has proposed innovative treatment which has become the backbone of stroke rehabilitation ("stand-ups—step-ups"). His book *Rehabilitation* is an invaluable text full of "pearls." His most recent interest is low back pain. He continues practicing in El Cerrito, California, and teaching at U.C. Irvine, where he holds a teaching clinical professorship.

Gerald Keane, M.D., is a graduate of Brown University Medical School and served his residency at Stanford University Medical Center in physical medicine and rehabilitation. He is currently the rehabilitation consultant to the Spine Center, St. Mary's Hospital, San Francisco, California, and specializes in pain management and spinal rehabilitation.

Virginia L. Kerr, O.T.R., was formerly the head of Occupational Therapy in the Rehabilitation Unit, Rosewood General Hospital, Houston, Texas. A 1970 graduate of Texas Woman's University, Mrs. Kerr was an occupational therapist at Rosewood during the writing of the first edition of this book.

Zvi Kalisky, M.D., is Associate Director, Department of Rehabilitation Medicine at Medical Center Del Oro Hospital, and Clinical Assistant Professor, Department of Physical Medicine, Baylor College of Medicine, Houston, Texas. He has gained extensive experience in all aspects of rehabilitation of head injury patients and has contributed to the subject at scientific conferences and in the medical literature. His recent publications include "Medical Problems Encountered during Rehabilitation of Patients with Head Injury," "Comparison between the CT Scan and the MRI of Brain Injured Patients Undergoing Rehabilitation," and "Effects of Oral Physostigmine and Lecithin on Memory and Attention in Closed Head Injury Patients."

Linda Jean Larson, M.A., S.P./C.C.C., is Director of the Speech, Language and Hearing Department at Memorial Hospital in Houston, Texas, and an instructor at the University of Houston. Her extensive knowledge has been derived from years of experience as a speech pathologist with brain-injured patients in rehabilitation settings.

Daniel Morrison, M.D., is Medical Director of Rehabilitation Medicine at Medical Center Del Oro Hospital. He is an assistant professor at Baylor College of Rehab Medicine. Prior to coming to Houston he was an assistant professor at Albert Einstein College of Medicine. He helped publish a book on the anatomy of electromyography and has participated in scientific articles on head injury and spasticity. His special interests are brain injury, electromyography, and chronic pain.

Frances Pendergraft, C.S.W./A.C.P., is Director of the Social Work Department at the Institute for Rehabilitation and Research, Houston, Texas, where she has been employed for the past 23 years. Her experience in rehabilitation began in 1958 with respiratory dependent poliomyelitis and has included work with the spinal cord injured, amputees, stroke patients, and patients having various other neurological impairments. Mrs. Pendergraft has held a faculty appointment in the Department of Sociology, Texas Women's University. She is a member of the National Society for Hospital Social Work Directors and is a board member of the Texas Society for Hospital Social Work Directors. She is also a member of the American Congress of Rehabilitation Medicine. Mrs. Pendergraft has made numerous presentations on planning home care for the severely disabled as well as on psychosocial implications of disability.

Patrick M. Plenger, Ph.D., is a clinical neuropsychological intern. He has been on an interdisciplinary treatment team treating closed head injury patients for over two years. Dr. Plenger's dissertation was on the effect of treating cognitive deficits in patients with closed head injury. Other areas of interest and research include memory impairment and recovery following closed head injury as well as the use of neuropsychological predictors for return to work.

Mahendra Shah, O.T.R., has been practicing occupational therapy since 1963 at major rehabilitation centers from Bombay to San Francisco. He is presently the Chief Occupational Therapist at St. Mary's Hospital, San Francisco, where he initiated the occupational therapy program. He is a creative teacher and a coauthor of "The Lateralized Stroke Program." His current interests are the cognitive rehabilitation of stroke patients and behavioral pain control.

Franz U. Steinberg, M.D., is Director of Residency Training in Physical Medicine and Rehabilitation at the Jewish Hospital of St. Louis, Washington University School of Medicine. He is a former director of the Department of Rehabilitation Medicine at the Jewish Hospital. He is Professor of Clinical Medicine at Washington University School of Medicine. Dr. Steinberg is a member of the American Academy of Physical Medicine and Rehabilitation and chairman of the academy's Special Interest Division of Geriatric Rehabilitation. He is a fellow of the American College of Physicians and of the American Geriatrics Society. Dr. Steinberg's publications include papers in the fields of rehabilitation medicine and geriatrics. He is editor of a book, *Care of the Geriatric Patient,* and author of a monograph, *The Immobilized Patient: Functional Pathology and Management.*

Stanley K. Yarnell, M.D., is currently Program Director of the Spinal Cord Unit at St. Mary's Hospital, San Francisco, California. He received his M.D. from Ohio State University Medical School and his residency training in rehabilitation in the same institution. He has been intensively involved with spinal cord injuries in terms of clinical care, residency teaching, and research. He is also considered an authority on post-polio syndrome. He has published in the areas of intermittent catheterization and bowel training. He is an outstanding clinician and teacher and is an examiner for the physical medicine board and the rehabilitation board.

Foreword

The basic concept of medical rehabilitation is to have the healthy part of the body take over functions that the diseased part cannot handle. This is not done spontaneously by most disabled persons and usually requires intensive training by competent professional personnel. *Basic Rehabilitation Techniques* provides the necessary information for that training. The techniques described here are simple and utilize equipment that is universally available. The text is written in clear language. Excellent drawings and pictures add to comprehension of minute details of the techniques. Emphasis and attention to detail are a crucial part of effective rehabilitation care.

The editors of *Basic Rehabilitation Techniques* as well as the contributors deserve acclaim for the production of this outstanding instructional manual. It will be of great value to nurses, rehabilitation therapists, social workers, physicians, and others who are responsible for the rehabilitation of disabled persons.

Gerald Hirschberg, M.D.
November 1987

Preface

This book is dedicated to all people who, regardless of the cause of their disability, deserve the best care that can be given to them by the practitioners of modern rehabilitation medicine.

Often it is the unanticipated pleasure which is most savored. So it is with the third edition of *Basic Rehabilitation Techniques*. We are pleased that the book, which has been translated into Japanese, Spanish, and German, has found its way into the hands of so many practitioners of rehabilitation. It is an unexpected pleasure since the original text comprised a set of training manuals developed for a series of workshops held at Rosewood General Hospital in Houston, Texas. For three years, nurses with inservice responsibilities, primarily from small rural hospitals, used the manuals in workshops under the aegis of the Center for Allied Health Professions at Baylor College of Medicine. After completing the educational program, the nurse trainees were able to return home and teach others the new techniques they had learned.

We are convinced that the book's success is due to the clarity of focus that such teaching manuals require. The manuals were judged by their effectiveness in teaching rehabilitation techniques. The techniques were judged by their effectiveness in rehabilitating patients in the least time. New authors for this edition were urged to review the book and write their chapters using clarity and economy of style. The techniques described are those which have clinically withstood the test of time in terms of practical benefits and ease of application. There is great enough detail of description and little enough suggested equipment that they are easily instituted.

Of course, our approach also has its "downsides." The book is not comprehensive. There are concepts and techniques some consider "state of the art" which are simply omitted. The space and focus does not allow for presentation of controversy.

Yet we see no erosion of relevance with time. The eye to economy of practice, in fact, seems more in keeping with the economics of medicine today than ever before. Study has confirmed the value of the approach[1], and the very survival of

rehabilitation as an organized system of care may depend on recognition of the economic realities.[2]

Some of these economic realities have always been present and have inspired the writing of the original manuals. Far too often it was, and still is, the general duty nurse who must face the massive and complex needs of the patient. Without the support of the rehabilitation staff, he or she is ill-prepared to meet those needs and is overwhelmed. The manuals were designed to help. They were to provide at least a basic underpinning of knowledge. Ensuing editions have increased the depth and scope of the content, and with it the readership has expanded. We are confident the present edition will be of value to any member of the rehabilitation team, including the patient and his or her family. However, the original concerns for the nurse are still apparent in this edition wherein some chapters still address the reader under the assumption that he or she is a nurse. We hope non-nurse readers will forgive an oversight which may appear partisan and find reward in the utility of the material presented.

The third edition is organized into parts, which hopefully will facilitate reference. There have been a number of chapter "rewrites" and new chapters added to reflect evolving patterns of care, new experiences, and trends in emphasis. They make the book reflect the living, changing body of knowledge about rehabilitation.

Both the old and the new chapters occasionally make use of the masculine pronoun *he* to refer to "the patient" and, more rarely, the feminine pronoun *she* to refer to "the nurse." We fully recognize that many nurses are male and many patients are female. We are not sexist in our thinking and we do not intend to be sexist in the presentation of our material. Clarity and concision called for the use of singular pronouns and we decided to dispense with the inelegant and sometimes confusing *he or she, him or her,* etc. We are all committed to the principle that jobs or positions should be open to all equally, irrespective of their sex. We want to make this point unequivocally.

A book would not be a book without the help of many people. This one is no exception. It has been a team effort in the best rehabilitation tradition. The contributors are people who work on the wards every day. Professionals in the purest sense of the word, they wrote on their own time for an audience expected to be small but important.

The editors especially want to acknowledge the seminal roles of the original contributors. Without their contributions this book would not have been possible.

The editors also want to recognize the vital roles played by Rosewood General Hospital, Baylor College of Medicine, and the Memorial Hospital Southwest, all in Houston, and St. Mary's Hospital in San Francisco. Without the cooperation of numerous individuals in our four institutions, including our secretaries, neither this third edition nor the previous editions would ever have been completed.

Finally, Dr. Gerald Hirschberg, whose ingenious exercise program was of central importance in developing the first edition, is thanked here for having written the foreword.

In closing, we hope you, the readers, appreciate the interdisciplinary input into this effort and sense the spirit of camaraderie in team care that characterizes this book.

The Editors

NOTES

1. J. Lord and K. Hall, "Neuromuscular Reeducation vs. Traditional Programs for Stroke Rehabilitation," *Arch Phys Med & Rehabil* 67 (1986): 8891.

2. R. Sine, "Neuromuscular Reeducation," *Arch Phys Med & Rehabil* 67 (1986): 421.

Common Disability Syndromes

1 Disability Syndrome of Hemiplegia

Robert D. Sine, M.D.

INTRODUCTION AND OBJECTIVES

We have coined the phrase *disability syndrome* for two reasons: (1) to enable us to discuss in a reasonable space the common constellation of disabilities which may appear secondary to multiple etiologies and (2) to emphasize that a common therapeutic approach to these disabilities is workable. If you can recognize a major portion of the syndrome, knowing what may accompany those impairments will flesh out the syndrome and improve your understanding of it. You can direct your assessment by looking for the associated disabilities. The syndrome of hemiplegia is a good model for this approach. Look for the problems associated with the syndrome and side effected in your next patient. As with anything, what you find will depend in large part on your knowing what to look for. Upon completion of this chapter, you should be able to

1. discuss the pathophysiology of common etiologies of hemiplegia
2. discuss the common impairments associated with the syndrome of hemiplegia
3. discuss lateralized functions of the brain and how the brain's asymmetry is manifest in hemiplegia

Most rehabilitation workers find the disability most frequently encountered is hemiplegia. This is to be expected, since 1.2 percent of Americans have suffered a stroke in the past, resulting in 2.8 million stroke victims. So much contact leads to familiarity and we assume that we "know" the syndrome. The syndrome is complex, however. It occurs with injury to the sensorimotor cortex and its pathways. These are the intricate structures whose functions raise man above the other mammals. The effects of their impairment cannot be simple.

ANATOMY

The sensorimotor cortex lies along the upper middle surface of the hemisphere (Figure 1-1). The neurons in this area send forth axons which converge deeper within the hemisphere, where they can be seen as an L-shaped area of white tissue known as the internal capsule (early anatomists thought it was a capsule). Beyond the internal capsule the fibers continue through the pons to the medulla, where axons cross to the opposite side (decussate). It is because of the decussation that the right side of the brain controls the left side of the body and the left side of the brain controls the right side of the body. It is probably important, however, that all axons do not decussate.

PATHOPHYSIOLOGY

Any agent that attacks the sensorimotor cortex or its pathways can produce the hemiparetic syndrome. Included in the many possible lesions are direct trauma and trauma productive of subdural hematoma; benign tumor; malignant primary and metastatic tumor; abscess; arterio-venous malformation; hemorrhage; and infarction. The most commonly encountered pathology in the rehabilitation setting is an infarct in the middle cerebral artery distribution. The findings seen in patients suffering this injury are the model for the symptomatology discussed in the rest of this chapter.

Tissue death secondary to loss of its blood supply (infarction) is the most common cause of the syndrome. It is well known that, with aging,

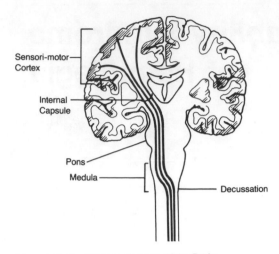

Figure 1-1 Frontal Cross Section of the Brain

atherosclerosis progressively destroys the competence of the arteries. The final events preceding tissue death are less well defined, however. The current view, known as the *thromboembolic theory*, holds that the final chain of events begins with ulceration of the atherosclerotic plaque and clot formation on its surface. Plaque and/or clot fragments then embolize to lodge in more distal arteries (Figure 1-2).

Small emboli may give rise to reversible neurological symptoms termed transient ischemic attacks (TIA). A larger embolus which lodges in an end artery will cause an infarct with tissue death in its distribution. The importance of the theory is that it suggests some practical possibilities for prophylaxis. As the presence of the reversible episodes may herald the eventuality of an infarct, they are considered an indication for workup. Depending on the location of the offending thrombus, surgery or conservative management may be indicated.

PARESIS: ITS DISTRIBUTION AND CLINICAL COURSE

The distribution of weakness tends to follow a "typical" pattern of severity in hemiplegia. The leg generally retains more strength than the arm. The leg extensors, which straighten the leg, return earlier and remain stronger than the flexors. This is fortunate, as these are the muscles of primary concern in standing and walking.

By contrast, in the upper extremity the flexors dominate.[1] Functional use of the upper extremity requires fine coordination of the shoulder to enable hand placement in addition to a prehensile hand. It is instructive to note that a functional upper extremity is seldom regained if volitional movement is not present by the third week following onset.[2] It is all too common an experience to find a massive therapeutic investment in the paretic hand which was destined to be futile, while the critical skills for the "well" arm have been ignored.

SPONTANEOUS NEUROLOGICAL RETURN AND FUNCTIONAL RETRAINING

Following the initial episode, the patient generally enjoys varying degrees of improvement of symptoms. This is generally rapid in the first days and weeks. During that period, the improvement is attributed to reduction of swelling and "neuronal shock" surrounding the zone of injury. Following the early phase of neurological return, there is a continued slower phase of return which continues as long as the patient lives. Causes of this long-term return are controversial but important—since rehabilitation seeks to enhance the return. There are undoubtedly a number of contributing mechanisms. We consider the following among the most important:[8]

1. retraining portions of the brain to new functions
2. retraining in the use of ipsilateral (nondecussating) tracts

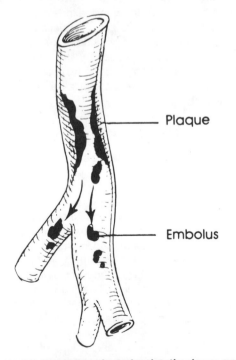

Figure 1-2 Fragments of arteriosclerotic plaque may embolize and lodge in smaller arteries.

3. disinhibition of brain functions previously inhibited because they subserved damaged portions of the brain

All three mechanisms may be enhanced by careful pertinent retraining and functional skills. The "functional retraining" approach was developed empirically by putting together techniques which proved effective. The above is the theoretical underpinning for further development.

SPASTICITY

The contraction of a "spastic" muscle is set off by the same reflexes that jerk a knee when the tendon is tapped with a percussion hammer. In the patient with spasticity, these reflexes are exaggerated because of the loss of their control by neurons in the brain. The reflexes are set off by sensors ("muscle spindles") in the muscle which respond to acceleration of stretch.[6] This is why you can often stretch a muscle slowly without it "fighting" you, but an attempt to do it faster is futile (see Chapter 12). Spasticity can promote deformity and contractures, interfere with functional volition, preclude adequate bracing, and, when very severe, obstruct good hygiene. It is not painful, however, and does not demand treatment unless it produces some of the above effects. Dantrolene, baclofen, and diazepam are three drugs which have proved effective in controlling spasticity, but each has serious side effects against which benefit must be weighed. The same considerations apply for nerve blocks and surgical procedures such as tendon procedures and neurolysis. Over the years we have found ourselves treating spasticity in hemiplegia less rather than more.

SENSORY LOSS

Loss of sensation can vary widely in the hemiplegic patient. Occasionally it can be so severe in the upper extremity that the patient can mangle his hand in the wheelchair spokes without being aware of it. In the leg, the loss most likely to produce difficulty is loss of position sense. Severe loss of this modality in the knee can produce instability when standing on it despite adequate strength. Retraining is very effective in regaining function despite persistent sensory deficit.

HEMI-INATTENTION

A common phenomenon occurring in patients who have recently suffered a severe stroke is that the patient's head and eyes are rotated toward the normal side and the patient *ignores* the hemiplegic side of the body as well as objects, persons, or sounds on the hemiplegic side of the environment. This phenomenon is also referred to as *neglect* or *hemi-somato-inattention*.

The best suggestion advanced as to the cause of this phenomenon is that it occurs because the balance between the cerebral hemispheres is disturbed when one hemisphere is damaged. According to this view, each hemisphere directs attention toward its own visual field. When a hemisphere is damaged, the intact half of the brain appears to overdirect attention to its visual field, producing the neglect of the impaired side. The head and eye rotation will commonly resolve spontaneously and return to the midline within days or weeks. The inattention, however, will frequently remain. When it does, it can be a source of severe perceptual disability.

Inattention tends to persist when associated with right hemispheric lesions (left hemiparesis). We have suggested that the patient with a left hemisphere lesion learns to compensate for the phenomenon by scanning to find the unseen portions of spatial configurations. The associated loss of spatial ability in a patient with a right hemisphere lesion denies that patient that compensating mechanism.

It may be apparent how the loss of spatial ability could severely limit a patient's ability to compensate for hemi-inattention. Such patients will not be able to use their ability to synthesize space to cue themselves as to where the "missing" half of the world is in space. We believe that this loss of spatial ability accounts for the observation that left hemiplegic patients have a much more difficult time with hemi-inattention than patients with right hemiplegia.[8]

Hemi-inattention is different from hemianopia, but the two phenomena may be difficult to differentiate clinically when both are present.

HOMONYMOUS HEMIANOPIA

Homonymous hemianopia is the loss of half of the visual field on the same side of each eye. It commonly appears with hemiplegia and results in blindness on the same side of the hemiplegia. This can occur because only one-half of the optic fibers decussate. Figure 1-3 is a schematic of how the tracts from each side of the brain go to the retina on the same side of each eye.

This type of blindness is a much more serious problem than is generally realized. It is much more disabling than one-eye blindness. You may suppose that all a person with left homonymous hemianopia need do when reading a sign, for example, would be to look slightly to the left, thus encompassing the whole of the sign within the remaining right visual field. In practice, however, mechanisms in the brain "lock in" the eyes so that

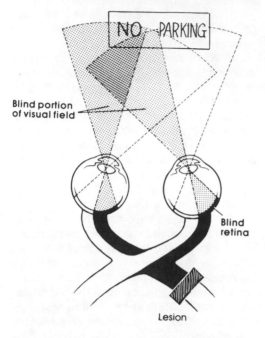

Figure 1-3 **Sight loss on the side of the hemiplegia shifts as the center of attention shifts.**

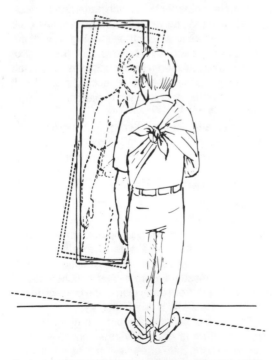

Figure 1-4 **The world is seen rotated to the side of the hemiplegia.**

the point of attention is at the center of the visual fields. The patient therefore only sees half of whatever he looks at (see Figure 1-3). The disability is compounded when combined with inattention. Much more than half of normal vision is affected.

When severe, the disability can be considerable. A "No Parking" sign could be read as "Parking." The patient might eat from only one side of his plate, write on only one side of the page, and clothe only the intact side of his body. Training to compensate for this loss is difficult, but it is possible and very important (see Chapter 13).

VERTICALITY DYSFUNCTION

Often a hemiparetic patient can be observed sitting with a lean to the hemiparetic side. A suggestion to sit straight will sometimes produce a position even further from the vertical. If you physically attempt to place the patient in the vertical position, he may simply slump back into the original position or actively resist your attempt. An attempt to stand puts the patient in danger of falling to that side. Often this is the major barrier to transfers and ambulation. Studies have demonstrated that this is a perceptual deficit that can be measured by asking the patient to report the verticality of a luminous rod in a darkened room.[3] The patient "sees" the world on a slant (Figure 1-4). The balance training described in Chapter 12 is directed at compensating for the effects of this damaging phenomenon and is often a prerequisite for ambulation.

SPECIALIZED FUNCTIONS

There are a number of functions that are considered "higher" (more complex) brain functions which have been shown to be *lateralized*—that is, to reside in one hemisphere more than the other. That hemisphere is then said to have developed those abilities because it *specialized* in them. It is important for us to recognize what these functions are so that we are aware of what losses might occur in our patients. Table 1-1 is an attempt to summarize the functions residing in each hemisphere and how they would be affected in the event of a cerebrovascular accident. It may seem intimidating but deserves some study. We will now discuss some specialized functions.

Left Hemispheric Specialized Functions

Symbolic Processing. (See Chapter 15 for discussion of aphasia.) The left hemisphere is the

TABLE 1-1 Hemispheric Specialization

The right side of the brain has (the right hemiplegic retains; the left hemiplegic has lost)	The left side of the brain has (the left hemiplegic retains; the right hemiplegic has lost)
motor control of the left side of the body.	motor control of the right side of the body.
sensation from the left side of the body.	sensation from the right side of the body.
sight from the left visual fields.	language faculties (symbol use):
timbre (musical).	use and understanding of speech and writing and reading.
ideation which is visual–spatial, gestalt-synthetic, and has a tendency for creativity.	arithmetical ability.
emotionality.	ideation which is analytical-propositional-logical, and linear in time (sequential).

seat of the processing of symbols. Thus the impairment of this function produces dysfunction of processing auditory symbols (speech), both spoken and heard; graphic symbols (reading, writing, and math); and visual symbols such as gestures and the symbolic content of objects. The inability to trade symbols—or even gestures—with another person is disastrous for effective communication. The inability to recognize the symbolic content of objects (asymbolia) leads to sometimes bizarre misuse of objects. The patient may eat lipstick, drink from a toilet bowl, or attempt to eat soup with a fork. Recognition of the underlying mechanisms of these dysfunctions will lead to more rational therapy.[8]

Analytical Ideation. It is thought that the left hemisphere specializes in problem solving that is sequential and linear in time.[2] This is the type of problem solving we utilize when we "reason through" a problem by listing points and taking them in order. This type of problem is also seen to be tied to language.

Right Hemispheric Specialized Functions

Spatial Ability. Spatial ability is the ability to nonverbally orient oneself and other objects in space. It is commonly evaluated in normal persons by such tests as mazes and road maps. It is distributed through the population rather unevenly, like musical ability. This ability is lateralized to the right hemisphere. Probably the most dramatic demonstration that this ability is lateralized is seen in patients who have had the connecting fibers (the corpus callosum) between the hemispheres transected. These patients cannot copy simple geometric figures with their right hands. This disconnection keeps the right hemi-

sphere from directing the right hand in performing the spatial tasks. This occurs despite the ability of the hand to function perfectly well in other tasks, such as writing.

A patient who has lost spatial ability may have difficulty finding the way to his room. The patient may also have difficulty with simple tasks which require spatial ability, such as donning a shirt.

Gestalt-Synthetic Ideation. The right hemisphere is thought to solve problems with its ability to freely associate and synthesize images. This ability requires spatial ability. In the right hemiplegic, it manifests itself as nonlinguistic "horse sense"; it is frequently observed that right hemiplegics retain "judgment" that may be lacking in the more coherent, seemingly reasonable left hemiplegic. This accounts for the right hemiplegic's observed ability to perform activities of daily living better than the left hemiplegic.

Emotion. Patients with right hemisphere lesions fail to appreciate emotion in the faces of others and show a paucity of emotion in their own faces and voices. Though they may be emotionally labile, they tend to show less emotional depth than patients with left hemisphere lesions. The right hemisphere seems to be the more emotionally active.

Become familiar with the hemiplegic syndromes so that you may anticipate the stroke patient's strengths as well as losses. As you will see when you begin to treat the patient using our "lateralized stroke program," you must be able to recognize the losses, but it is the patient's residual capacities you must lean on heavily to help him function independently.

We have just touched on some of the remarkable differences between the functions of the two hemispheres, but it should be enough to convince you that the hemiplegic stroke syndrome is quite different depending on which side is involved. With this background you can go on to the lateralized stroke program, which addresses the differences so that you can treat your patient in a manner appropriate to the side of the lesion. You will find that program in Chapter 13 ("Self Care Training"). The program, however, is valuable in any training that you may perform involving the hemiplegic patient.

CHAPTER REVIEW TEST

Let's see how much you have learned. Select the correct answer to complete the following statements.

1. In utilizing rehabilitation techniques,
    a. you should begin with the most challenging activity.
    b. you should assure the patient that with a little work he will be normal.
    c. you should not begin until the diagnosis has been established.
    d. you may proceed with disability-specific therapy even if the diagnosis is not known.
2. The brain
    a. works like a marvelous, perfectly efficient computer.
    b. is organized so each piece of knowledge is stored in a particular place.
    c. is organized so that each hemisphere has different but overlapping functions.
    d. uses very little energy.
3. Hemiplegia (weakness on one side of the body)
    a. is the same as a cerebrovascular accident.
    b. is produced only by a lesion in the internal capsule.
    c. usually is present in concert with other disabilities.
    d. All the above.
4. Cerebral infarction
    a. is the death of cerebral tissue secondary to insufficient blood flow.
    b. occurs when cerebral arteries are blocked by thrombi.
    c. occurs when cerebral arteries are blocked by emboli.
    d. All the above.
5. A patient with right hemiplegia
    a. has a lesion on the right side of the brain.
    b. has a right visual field defect.
    c. has serious impairment of visuospatial perception.
    d. None of the above.
6. A patient who sits leaning to the hemiplegic side
    a. will walk just as easily as one who sits upright.
    b. only needs to be reminded to sit up straight.
    c. probably does so because of weak trunk muscles.
    d. can benefit from balance training.
    e. All the above.
7. The visual field defect of hemiplegia
    a. is called a homonymous hemianopia.
    b. can be very disabling.
    c. is on the side of the hemiplegia.
    d. All the above.
8. Right and left hemiplegic disability syndromes
    a. are simply mirror images of each other.
    b. are differentiated mainly by the right hemiplegic's aphasia.
    c. are differentiated mainly by the left hemiplegic's retention of the dominant hand.
    d. are differentiated by a large number of higher brain functions.
9. The left hemisphere
    a. is intact in the right hemiplegic.
    b. solves problems in a linear fashion.
    c. enables us to draw hexagons.
    d. is larger and visibly more complex than the right hemisphere.

10. Spasticity
   a. produces massive jerks which may throw the hemiplegic to the floor.
   b. is relieved by any good "muscle relaxer."
   c. is produced by uninhibited stretch reflexes.
   d. is painful.
11. The hemiplegic secondary to a cerebrovascular accident typically
   a. has a "fixed" lesion: The patient neither improves nor gets worse.
   b. can expect some neurologic improvement with or without treatment.
   c. can expect some neurologic improvement with vasodilators.
   d. can expect some neurologic improvement with vitamin B_{12}.
   e. can expect some neurologic improvement with physical therapy.

The correct answers are as follows:

1. d	*7. d*
2. c	*8. d*
3. c	*9. b*
4. d	*10. c*
5. b	*11. b*
6. d	

If you missed any of the questions, you should review the appropriate section of this chapter.

REFERENCES AND SUGGESTED READINGS

1. Bard, G., and G. Hirschberg. "Recovery of Voluntary Motion in Upper Extremity following Hemiplegia." *Arch Phys Med & Rehabil* 46 (August 1965): 567–75.

2. Bogen, J.E., and G.M. Bogen. "The Other Side of the Brain III: The Corpus Collosium and Creativity." *Los Angeles Neurological Societies Bulletin* 37 (1972): 49–61.

3. Bruell, J.H. "Disturbance of Perception of Verticality in Patients with Hemiplegia." *Arch Phys Med & Rehabil* 38 (December 1957): 776–80.

4. De Censio, D. "Vertical Perception and Ambulation in Hemi-plegia." *Arch Phys Med & Rehabil* 51 (February 1970): 105–10.

5. Field, W. "Clinical Symposia." CIBA 26 (1974): 3–31.

6. Herman, R., "Myotatic Reflex: Clinico-Physiological Aspects of Spasticity and Contracture." *Brain* 93 (1970): 273–312.

7. Kinsbourne, M. *Asymmetrical Function of the Brain.* Cambridge: Cambridge University Press, 1978.

8. Sine, R., A. Souffi, and M. Shah. "Collosal Syndrome: Implications for Understanding the Neuropsychology of Stroke." *Arch Phys Med & Rehabil* 65 (1984): 606–10.

9. Twitchell, T.E. "The Restoration of Motor Function in Hemiplegia." *Neurologia* 4 (December 1954): 919–28.

2 Disability Syndrome of Spinal Cord Injury

Stanley K. Yarnell, M.D.

INTRODUCTION AND OBJECTIVES

Treatment of spinal cord injury is one of the most complex challenges rehabilitation has to offer. Though rehabilitation seldom changes the degree of impairment, patients with spinal cord injury are often the most inspirational as they overcome their impairment to become functional individuals. It is at once among the most draining and most rewarding types of rehabilitation to practice. This chapter will help prepare you to be part of this impressive process. After studying it, you should be able to

1. discuss the relationship between the level of injury and the type of impairment
2. discuss the Frankel classification system
3. discuss the etiologies of spinal cord injury

NATURE OF THE DISABILITY

The patient with spinal cord injury demands our attention as much because of functions he is spared as because of functions he has lost. Paraplegics can compensate for loss of normal ambulation by pushing a wheelchair. Quadriplegics will use whatever remaining function they have in the upper extremities to drive an electric wheelchair, whether it is controlled by a joy stick or a chin control. Above all, the spinal cord injured patient retains a clear mind and can direct his care even if he is unable to assist in its implementation.

Trauma accounts for most spinal cord injuries. The leading causes in the United States include motor vehicle accidents, diving accidents, gunshot wounds, and falls around the home. Traumatic spinal cord injury involves two frequently confused problems: One is the bony and ligamentous injury and the other the neurological injury.

One may occur in the absence of the other. It is important to remember that the orthopedic injury (e.g., fracture dislocation) is a repairable process whether by surgical or nonsurgical means. However, there is no medication or surgical cure currently available to allow repair of spinal neural damage.

Historically, spinal cord injured patients have been divided into two neurological categories: *complete* and *incomplete*. A complete lesion is one which stops all neural transmission at the level of the lesion. Incomplete lesions are smaller, permitting some transmission of motor or sensory information to occur. To allow better communication concerning the degrees of completeness, the Frankel classification system was devised. *Frankel Class A* indicates that the extent of injury is severe and that neurologically the patient has no motor or sensory function below the level of the injury. *Frankel Class B* indicates that the patient has some sensation below the level of the injury, though no motor control. *Frankel Class C* indicates that the patient has sensation below the level of the injury as well as motor useless function. For example, a C_6 quadriplegic, Frankel Class C, might have sensation and be capable of wiggling the right great toe, but it is of no functional usefulness to the patient. *Frankel Class D* indicates the patient has sensation and motor useful function below the level of injury. For example, the patient who had a C_6 quadriplegia, Frankel Class D, might be capable of standing and doing limited walking with an assistive device or walker. The patient might also have some volitional control of bowel or bladder. Finally, *Frankel Class E* indicates recovery. Most incomplete spinal cord patients do not remain static but may improve or may even deteriorate regardless of medical or surgical intervention.

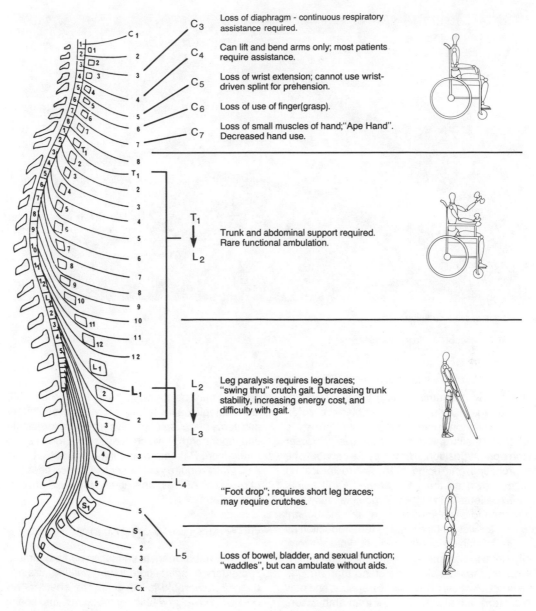

Figure 2-1 at the crucial levels:

- **C₃** — Loss of diaphragm - continuous respiratory assistance required.
- **C₄** — Can lift and bend arms only; most patients require assistance.
- **C₅** — Loss of wrist extension; cannot use wrist-driven splint for prehension.
- **C₆** — Loss of use of finger(grasp).
- **C₇** — Loss of small muscles of hand;"Ape Hand". Decreased hand use.
- **T₁ → L₂** — Trunk and abdominal support required. Rare functional ambulation.
- **L₂ → L₃** — Leg paralysis requires leg braces; "swing thru" crutch gait. Decreasing trunk stability, increasing energy cost, and difficulty with gait.
- **L₄** — "Foot drop"; requires short leg braces; may require crutches.
- **L₅** — Loss of bowel, bladder, and sexual function; "waddles", but can ambulate without aids.

Figure 2-1 Lateral View of the Adult Vertebral Column with Spinal Cord Exposed Showing the Relationship of Spinal Nerve Level to Vertebral Level.

Source: Adapted from *Clinically Oriented Anatomy* by K.L. Moore, p. 648, with permission of Williams & Wilkins Company, © 1980.

Figure 2-1 is an attempt to show the impairment incurred at crucial levels of injury. Study it carefully and refer to it when you have patients with such injuries. Remember that at each level the patient suffers all the disabilities that occur at the lower (caudal) level as well as those at that particular level. Thus, all complete (Frankel Class A) lesions will have loss of control of the bowel, bladder, and sexual organs. A C₅ quadriplegic, Frankel Class A, will have those disabilities listed and in addition all those listed below them.

ASSISTIVE DEVICES

Note that while an athletic and determined patient may manage a form of ambulation at higher levels, most spinal cord patients with a diagnosis higher than L₄ find ambulation exceed-

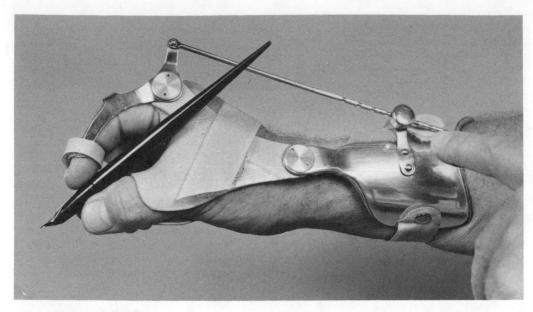

Figure 2-2 Flexor Hinge Splint.

Source: Courtesy of T.J. Engen, Orthotist.

ingly energy consuming using a swing through type gait (see Chapter 12). Paraplegic children are an exception, since their center of gravity is higher and their trunk stability is inherently greater in the upright position. They may be capable of a reciprocating gait using a special reciprocating brace known as the *LSU brace.* Adult spinal injured patients with higher paraplegias may also be braced to enable them to get into the upright position for weight bearing and tone reduction as well as stretching out the hip and knee flexors, which tend to become tight from sitting constantly. However, they usually understand that ambulation is not practical but rather therapeutic and may be content with standing rather than ambulation. In the future, computer-generated functional electrical stimulation in conjunction with braces may enable some paraplegics to do more than therapeutic standing and walking.

In scrutinizing Figure 2-1, you will also note the significant deterioration of upper extremity function with each lost cervical segment. The lost prehension and residual wrist extension peculiar to a C_6 quadriplegic allows use of an assistive device designed to harness wrist extension to move the fingers for prehension or lateral pinch (see Figure 2-2). Surgical procedures may also enhance hand function in C_6 and C_7 quadriplegic patients. Many of the more general assistive

devices may be found to have a place as well. Quadriplegic patients frequently have respiratory problems because of paralysis of the intercostals and abdominals, which makes for poor cough production. Patients who survive injuries as high as C_3 may require ventilatory assistance because of paralysis of the diaphragm in the case of complete injuries.

SECONDARY PROBLEMS

Due to impairment of sensation and movement secondary to spinal cord injury, patients are frequently vulnerable to decubiti. The chapters on decubiti, bowel and bladder problems, and social services will be of interest if you are attending a patient with spinal cord injury at any level.

Sexual function is an important part of the comprehensive rehabilitation of the spinal cord injured patient. A variety of written information is available for discussion with spinal cord patients regarding the effect of their injury on sexual function. All suggest communication and experimentation. Sensation may be lost but erection is frequently possible in upper motor neuron males, and fertility is also possible. Women have similar problems with sexual function but remain fertile and have no difficulty with their periods. Birth control remains an issue.

CHAPTER REVIEW TEST

See if you can answer the following questions.

1. A C_6 quadriplegic, Frankel Class C,
   a. has useful motor control of legs and will learn to walk.
   b. has a clear mind and no cognitive loss.
   c. retains normal sexual function.
   d. retains normal bowel function.
   e. retains trunk stability.
2. The Frankel classification system
   a. is based on the spinal cord level of injury.
   b. does not predict recovery.
   c. does not predict function.
   d. describes the degree of completeness of injury.
3. Spinal cord injured patients may suffer
   a. loss of bladder function.
   b. paralysis.
   c. loss of sensation.
   d. loss of bowel control.
   e. respiratory distress.
   f. all of the above.
   g. none of the above.
4. Levels of injury (with the same Frankel Class) predict function
   a. precisely.
   b. very poorly.
   c. quite well, with some allowances for children and athletic individuals.
   d. within wide ranges.

The correct answers are as follows:
1. b
2. d
3. f
4. c

3

Head Injury Rehabilitation

Zvi Kalisky, M.D.
Daniel Morrison, M.D.
Patrick M. Plenger, Ph.D.

INTRODUCTION AND OBJECTIVES

A formal consistent approach to the rehabilitation of head injured patients is only now evolving. The head injured were thought to either improve spontaneously or not at all. Consequently their rehabilitation generated little enthusiasm in medical circles. This new chapter is one result of the growing recognition that rehabilitation can alter the outcome for these patients. After reading this chapter, you should be able to

1. discuss the mechanisms of head injury
2. identify common medical and physical problems associated with head injury
3. identify common cognitive problems associated with head injury
4. discuss the approach to treatment of head injury
5. discuss the involvement of the family in head injury

HEAD INJURY DISABILITIES

The management of the head injured patient requires an approach different from those used in the treatment of other disabilities. Successful rehabilitation of such patients requires the recognition that the majority of these individuals have been newly involved in the process of adopting adult roles. They have recently entered a life stage in which achieving social, economic, and vocational independence is of tantamount importance. The catastrophic impact of the injury affects the patient not only physically but also cognitively, behaviorally, and socially, thus requiring a radical adjustment by the patient and his or her family.

Most traumatic brain injuries are related to blunt trauma; in industrialized countries, 50 percent are caused by motor vehicle accidents. The primary mechanism of injury is the rotational force that occurs during impact. The resulting shearing strain causes a tearing of nerve fibers in the white matter of the hemispheres and brain stem. Other factors, such as intracranial hematoma, cerebral edema, cerebral blood flow, and anoxia, play a role in the pathophysiology. The most important factors in determining outcome are the severity and extent of the brain injury.

The measurement of outcome factors is best accomplished by assessing the length and depth of coma. The Glasgow Coma Scale (GCS) (see Table 3-1) is a reliable instrument which can be used for this purpose. It scores best responses to appropriate stimuli in three areas: (1) eye opening, (2) motor response, and (3) verbal performance. Scores range from 3 to 15 points. A GCS score of 8 or less is equivalent to a clinical diagnosis of coma.

Another measure of outcome is the duration of posttraumatic amnesia (PTA). This condition is defined as the time between the emergence from coma and the recovery of continuous memory. PTA greater than seven days and coma longer than 24 hours indicate a very severe brain injury with a guarded prognosis. Other factors which alter the outcome are the age of the patient, brain stem involvement, complications, and associated injuries.

Patients with brain injury can have cognitive and physical deficits varying from mild to severe; thus, some may require long-term rehabilitation. The problems encountered in these patients may be grouped into five major categories: (1) medical, (2) physical, (3) cognitive, (4) psychological/ behavioral, and (5) social.

Some of the more common medical problems seen in the rehabilitation unit are seizures, het-

TABLE 3-1 Glasgow Coma Scale

Examiner's Test		Patient's Response	Assigned Score
Eye Opening	Spontaneous	Opens eyes on own	4
	Speech	Opens eyes when asked to in a loud voice	3
	Pain	Opens eyes when pinched	2
	Pain	Does not open eyes	1
Best Motor Response	Commands	Follows simple commands	6
	Pain	Pulls examiner's hand away when pinched	5
	Pain	Pulls a part of body away when examiner pinches patient	4
	Pain	Flexes body inappropriately to pain (decorticate posturing)	3
	Pain	Body becomes rigid in an extended position when examiner pinches victim (decerebrate posturing)	2
	Pain	Has no motor response to pinch	1
Verbal Response (Talking)	Speech	Carries on a conversation correctly and tells examiner where he is, who he is, and the month and year	5
	Speech	Seems confused or disoriented	4
	Speech	Talks so examiner can understand victim but makes no sense	3
	Speech	Makes sounds that examiner can't understand	2
	Speech	Makes no noise	1

Source: Adapted from "Assessment of Coma and Impaired Consciousness" by G. Teasdale and B. Jennett in *Lancet,* Vol. 2, p. 81, with permission of The Lancet, © 1974.

erotopic new bone formation, diabetes insipitis, aspiration, and liver dysfunction. Spastic paralysis, peripheral nerve injury, joint contractures, swallowing disorders, dysarthria, and visual and hearing impairments are only a few of the physical deficits encountered. Common cognitive problems include disorientation, short attention span, memory deficits, decreased learning capacity, aphasia, poor judgment, and visual or perceptual deficits. Frequently seen behavioral disorders are agitation, impulsivity, obtunded affect, social withdrawal, denial of deficits, depression, and personality changes.

In taking the history, one should inquire about the nature of the injury (closed, open, depressed skull fracture, etc.), the length of coma and PTA, associated injuries, the patient's premorbid personality, and the family support system. A complete mental status examination, which includes a speech and language evaluation, is a necessary complement to the assessment of the cranial nerves, gait, balance, coordination, muscle strength and tone, and joint stiffness and pain which constitutes an important part of the physical examination. Laboratory tests should be performed to rule out liver dysfunction, infections, endocrine problems, or anticonvulsant intoxication. A CT scan and an EEG may be required to rule out complications such as hydrocephalus, chronic subdural hygroma or hematoma, and seizure disorders.

TREATMENT

The hallmark of rehabilitation of the head injured patient is the integrated approach utilized by the rehabilitation team. This team effort differs from traditional rehabilitation in that deficits discovered through assessment by members of individual disciplines are reviewed daily by the entire team. The process includes carefully evaluating the patient, establishing short- and long-term goals for the patient, and monitoring the patient's progress towards those goals.

Medical problems must be addressed on admission. Early recognition and treatment of infections, intracranial complications, and metabolic and endocrine disorders will prevent complications which retard rehabilitative progress. Prophylactic use of anticonvulsant drugs is recommended for high-risk patients. This patient group includes those with prolonged coma, penetrating wounds, a depressed skull fracture, intracranial hematoma, or an early seizure.

Joint contractures can be due either to spasticity and muscle imbalance or to heterotopic bone formation. In the former case, the use of manual stretching, progressive casting, and splinting is recommended. Medication to reduce muscle tone may also be beneficial. Occasionally surgical releases or other invasive procedures are needed. In heterotopic ossification, the early use of etidronate disodium will prevent joint ankylosis. Eating disorders include excessive eating, total loss of appetite, and swallowing difficulties. Videofluoroscopy will often demonstrate evidence of aspiration before it can be seen clinically. Those patients with prolonged and persistent aspiration frequently require gastrostomy tube feeding.

Extensive neuropsychological evaluation should be done when the patient is out of PTA. PTA is monitored by frequent administration of the Galveston Orientation and Amnesia Test (GOAT), which assesses the patient's orientation and memory for events preceding and following the injury. Specific deficits are identified, such as an impairment of the ability to learn and/or remember, a decrease in the speed of information processing, slowness of reaction time, language and perceptual problems, and other intellectual impairments.

One technique for dealing with these problems is cognitive remediation. This method utilizes reality orientation, memory aids, individual and group therapy, and a structured program based on the patient's relative cognitive strengths in order to reach functional and meaningful goals. The overriding objective is reintegration of the patient into the family unit and the wider societal sphere. Goal attainment is achieved through the involvement of the entire team in designing the functional therapeutic tasks. Physical therapy, occupational therapy, medical, behavioral, and cognitive goals are jointly formulated by team members.

Behavioral disorders (e.g., inappropriate emotional control and impulsivity) frequently prevent patients from achieving their expected potential. This is especially true of patients with frontal lobe injury. Psychotropic medications, however, should be avoided where possible, since they affect cognition. Techniques such as individualized therapy, behavior modification, environmental structuring, and family education will facilitate the patient's progress. In extreme cases, the patient may require drug therapy or psychiatric consultation.

The impact of the head injury on the family system is frequently catastrophic and requires early intervention. It should begin while the patient is in the ICU. The information provided must be timely, supportive, and realistic. While it is imperative to give realistic information concerning the patient's progress, it is equally important to prevent the complete loss of hope by the family. As a consequence, it is a difficult time for medical personnel as well as family members. After the injured patient is transferred to the head injury unit, the family should be involved in the rehabilitation process through discussion of all aspects of the patient's care, frequent therapeutic observations, and team conferences. Home visits by the patient are an integral part of the program. Family involvement is critical for several reasons. First, it allows the family to feel less helpless by becoming an active participant in the treatment program. Second, it provides the family with an opportunity to learn about their significant other's recovery, progress, and persisting deficits, thus preparing them for reintegration of the patient into the family unit. Finally and most importantly, family participation allows the therapy team to learn more about the patient than can be gained through conventional assessment techniques.

After discharge from the hospital, outpatient and re-entry programs may be necessary. The rehabilitative process often requires many years of highly individualized therapy for maximization of potential. While the sequelae to head injury present significant challenges to the patient, family, and medical staff, a concerted effort by all, as well as new developments in an expanding field, will contribute to a more positive outcome than was previously thought possible.

CHAPTER REVIEW TEST

Answer *true* or *false* to the following statements.

_____ 1. The primary mechanism of injury is a rotational force occurring at the time of impact.

_____ 2. Length and depth of coma are not reliable indications of prognosis.

_____ 3. Posttraumatic amnesia is defined as length of time from onset of injury to return of continuous memory.

_____ 4. High risk for seizures include prolonged coma, penetrating wounds, depressed skull fractures, and intracranial hematomas.

_____ 5. There is no treatment for heterotropic new bone formation.

_____ 6. Information about premorbid personality is important, since it may affect the prognosis.

_____ 7. There need be no concern about hydrocephalus and subdural collections during the rehabilitation phase, since these problems are usually resolved during the acute phase.

_____ 8. The physicians, nurses, and therapist are only concerned about the medical and physical aspects of the patient's condition.
_____ 9. Difficult families who confront and criticize the team should be avoided, since their actions are counterproductive and may interfere with the patient's recovery.
_____10. Once head injured patients are discharged from the hospital, in most cases they can resume their previous jobs or go back to school.

The correct answers are as follows:

1. *True.*
2. *False.*
3. *True.*
4. *True.*
5. *False.*

6. *True.*
7. *False.*
8. *False.*
9. *False.*
10. *False.*

BIBLIOGRAPHY

Cartlidge, N.G.F., and D.A. Shaw. "Head Injury." *Major Problem Neurology* 10 (1980): 1–203.

Jenette, B., and G. Teasdale. *Management of Head Injuries.* Philadelphia: F.A. Davis, 1981.

Kalisky, Z., D.P. Morrison, C.A. Meyers, and A. Von Lanfen. "Medical Problems Encountered during Rehabilitation of Patients with Head Injury." *Arch Phys & Med Rehabil* 66 (1985): 25–29.

Levin, M.S., A.L. Benton, and R.G. Grossman. *Neurobehavioral Consequences of Closed Head Injury.* New York: Oxford University Press, 1982.

Rosenthal, M., E.R. Griffith, M.R. Bond, and J.D. Miller. *Rehabilitation of the Head Injured Adult.* Philadelphia: F.A. Davis, 1983.

4

Disability Syndrome of Arthritis

Robert D. Sine, M.D.

INTRODUCTION AND OBJECTIVES

Disease of the joints is so widespread it is easy to forget that the "pain and stiffness of arthritis" can constitute a serious disability. There are numerous diseases which may affect the joints, but by far the most important are osteoarthritis and rheumatoid arthritis. When you have read this chapter you should be able to

1. describe the pathophysiology of rheumatoid arthritis
2. describe the features of osteoarthritis
3. discuss the differences between rheumatoid arthritis and osteoarthritis
4. discuss some elements of treatments for the two major types of arthritis

RHEUMATOID ARTHRITIS

Rheumatoid arthritis starts in the lining of the joint (the synovium). It tends to be very destructive and may attack the underlying cartilage and bone as well. An acutely involved joint is warm, swollen, and red. Deformity of the joint is accelerated by the swelling, which loosens the ligaments that hold the bones forming the joint in position. The laxity at the joint produced by the swelling allows the bones to slip out of their normal position (subluxate). This usually occurs in the direction of strongest use. In the hand, this mechanism may produce subluxation at the wrist and metacarpophalangeal joints (Figure 4-1). You can see how in this stage (when joints are swollen), use of the hand could promote deformity.

With time, the structures surrounding the joint become tight and the deformities become fixed. When attempting to correct these deformities by stretching the joint, linear pull should be exerted (Figure 4-1). An episode would follow this sequence:

1. appearance of warm, swollen, painful joint
2. joint subluxation (slippage)
3. periarticular structures tighten, "fixing" the deformity in its new, deformed position

Management

Commonly, the patient with arthritis is told "rest and exercise" are needed. This sounds contradictory, but it is not—at every stage, both rest and exercise *are* necessary. The proper balance is determined by the degree of inflammatory response: The more inflammation, the more rest and less exercise, and vice versa. In the acute stage, movement of the joint is painful and, in addition, aggravates the inflammation. The episode is shortened if both the joint and the patient are rested as much as possible. In this stage, the "rest" half of the rest and exercise prescription is more important. Splints are occasionally used to ensure resting the joint. Exercise is reduced to only a few movements carefully done through the range of motion to the joint of pain. This is to ensure retention of mobility. Suspension of the joint in warm water or the use of hot paraffin could make these maneuvers less painful and more complete.

You will know the inflammation is decreasing as the joint swelling and warmth subsides and the pain lessens. Then range of motion exercises can be somewhat more vigorous, or at least encouraged in the face of discomfort. Vigorous use of the joint should be resumed only after active inflammation is judged to be absent.

At this point, the patient may also engage in the full spectrum of activities of a normal life. In this

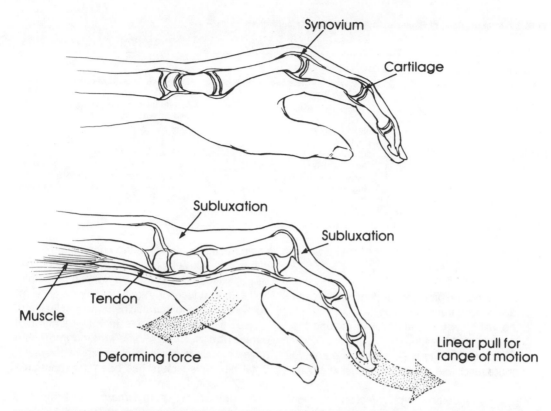

Figure 4-1 Joint swelling stretches the connective tissue structures that bind the joints. This allows the dynamic forces applied by the tendons during use of the hand to produce deformities.

disease, however, there should be no pressure to engage in exercise for its own sake and no impression given that exercise will "cure" the disease. Most patients are subject to episodes of recurrence. With these cautions in mind, chapters in this book on the mobilization program and the activities of daily living may be applied. Exercise should have increased function as its goal, and energy conservation techniques and assistive devices should be utilized if they are found helpful.

Aspirin is still the mainstay of drug therapy. Unfortunately the public holds this familiar drug in ill-deserved contempt. This is probably because they are familiar only with its analgesic properties. One of the most valuable services nursing personnel can perform is educating the patient about the value of aspirin for its anti-inflammatory effect and about the need to adhere to prescribed dosage schedules (on the order of twelve tablets per day) to obtain that effect. Nonsteroidal anti-inflammatory drugs, gold salts (now available as an oral drug), antimalarials, and oral corticosteroids all have their place in drug therapy for rheumatoid arthritis. In each case, however, the beneficial effects must be carefully weighed

against side effects. Intra-articular corticosteroids are very helpful in aborting an acute attack or remobilizing one or two joints, but they cannot be used with multiple joint involvement.

OSTEOARTHRITIS

Osteoarthritis starts with degeneration of the cartilage. Replacement of the degenerated cartilage by bone and subsequent overgrowth of the bone produce the deformity of bony enlargement of the joints. The joints affected are largely weight-bearing joints such as the knees, hips, and joints of the spine. The exceptions to this rule are the small joints of the fingers. The condition progresses slowly, and despite being very prevalent in the population, it seldom causes disability before the fifth decade. By the age of 70, however, few individuals are entirely free of it; and significant numbers of disabled individuals— mostly from hip involvement—are seen at 60 years old and older.

The first lines of defense for hip involvement are proper use of a cane and range of motion exercises (see Chapter 12). Use of the cane can

TABLE 4-1 Comparison of Rheumatoid Arthritis and Osteoarthritis

Factor	Rheumatoid Arthritis	Osteoarthritis
Primary tissue involvement	Synovium	Cartilage
Type of disease	"Systemic"—connective tissue through-out body involved	Degenerative local "wear and tear"
Joints (location)	Any synovial joint	Weight-bearing joints (hips, knees, spine) and fingers
Joints (appearance)	Spindle-shaped, soft swelling, symmetrical	"Knobby" enlarged joints
Blood	Positive latex fixation test; increased sedimentation rate	No blood changes
Course	Acute severe episodes of synovial swelling and warmth; can produce joint destruction and deformity	Slow boney enlargement produces large, boney joints and limitation of range of motion

unweight the hip 80 percent. You must emphasize to the cane user that

1. he will not become "dependent" on the cane and muscles will not atrophy
2. he will slow the disease and prolong the useful life of the hip
3. he will be able to walk farther, see and do more, and lead a fuller life by using a cane

Intra-articular corticosteroid injection has been helpful to gain range of motion in the hip and control acute episodes in the knee. Involvement of the fingers is seldom disabling (except for specific activities such as typing) but can be painful and can produce unattractive deformity. Heat applied by water or paraffin helps relieve the pain.

Aspirin is also valuable in management of osteoarthritis. Butazolidine and indomethecin have been used particularly for hip involvement. Total hip replacement has been the most successful surgical approach.

A comparison of rheumatoid arthritis and osteoarthritis is summarized in Table 4-1.

CHAPTER REVIEW TEST

Select the correct answers to complete the following statements.

1. The primary site of involvement in the joint of rheumatoid arthritis is
   a. the cartilage.
   b. the bone.
   c. the endothelium.
   d. the synovium.
2. Osteoarthritis
   a. is a disease of the ends of the bones.
   b. produces red, hot, swollen joints.
   c. is very prevalent in the geriatric population.
   d. has a rapid downhill course and disablement in two years.
3. Intra-articular corticosteroids
   a. can be helpful in managing osteoarthritis.
   b. can be helpful in managing rheumatoid arthritis.
   c. can be helpful in joint remobilization.
   d. All the above.
   e. (b) and (c) only.
4. "Rest and exercise" in managing rheumatoid arthritis means
   a. there should be a period of rest after each exercise period.
   b. different types and amounts of each depending on the extent of inflammatory activity.
   c. as much exercise as possible and then a rest period.
   d. "rest" is for the joint—not the patient.
   e. "rest" is for the patient—not the joint.

The correct answers are as follows:
1. d
2. c
3. d
4. b

If you missed any of the questions, please review the appropriate section of this chapter.

5 Disability Syndrome of Parkinsonism

Robert D. Sine, M.D.

INTRODUCTION AND OBJECTIVES

The impairments of parkinsonism are so widespread and yet so little recognized that we often think of them as just part of getting old. Young actors who play old people assume an expressionless face, speak with a strained monotonal voice, and affect a hand tremor and shuffling gait. They are unaware that they are not portraying age but symptoms of a disease. When an old man (or woman) is quite free of parkinsonism symptomatology, we say he is "spry," suggesting he is atypical rather than simply free of disease.

This chapter should aid in your understanding of parkinsonism. After studying it, you should be able to

1. discuss the pathophysiology of the disability of parkinsonism
2. discuss the impairments of parkinsonism
3. discuss the treatment of parkinsonism

SYMPTOMS

The onset of symptoms is very slow and insidious. Though they are not disabling in their early stages, they do cut down the patient's mobility and safety. It is likely many a broken hip is a complication of early parkinsonism. One may argue whether it is the insidious onset or our deplorable disinterest in the elderly which produces the general complacency surrounding this syndrome. It is a fact, however, that the symptoms are frequently untreated.

This seems particularly true of patients who lack the characteristic "pill-rolling" tremor of the hands. These patients may still have the syndrome's most disabling symptoms. These result from a slowness in initiating movement. A patient may have great difficulty arising from a chair. His muscles may be strong but he has difficulty initiating the movement. Once standing, the patient could have difficulty initiating corrective movements if he starts to fall. You can test such a patient by giving him a gentle push on the chest backward. He will tend to fall like a piece of timber, so place a hand at his back to catch him. You might also note on observing the patient's gait that he has difficulty starting, stopping, and turning. There is nothing wrong with his muscles of degultition, but if the patient does not swallow spontaneously, saliva collects in his mouth and he will drool. The patient might also seem dull: the face is expressionless and his verbal responses are often delayed. It is all too natural to forget that the patient's mind is quite clear and to talk around or through him.

Another phenomenon—rigidity—may be present. Rigidity is never so severe that the muscles cannot be stretched and the joint cannot be put through range of motion. Rigidity plus the paucity of movement, however, may lead to contractures. The severely involved patient with multiple contractures requiring total bed care but with a clear mind is at the other end of the parkinsonism spectrum. Unfortunately this patient often goes untreated, as does the early patient, for he is assumed to be beyond help. The assumption becomes a self-fulfilling prophesy.

A pathology in parkinsonism is becoming more precisely assigned to the dopamine-producing cells of the substantia nigra within the basal ganglia.

TREATMENT

Medications which alleviate the symptomatology most effectively are those which increase the availability of L-dopa. The most common is L-dopa itself. It is usually used in combination with cardiodopa (Sinemet). The cardiodopa presents breakdown of the drug peripherally, thereby decreasing side effects. Other drugs which increase the availability of dopamine and find use are bromocriptine and amantadine. It is as important to know the drugs which decrease the availability of dopamine. These include haloperidol, chlorpromazine, reserpine, vitamin B_6, and apomorphine—drugs very commonly found among those taken by geriatric patients.

Drugs which decrease availability of acetylcholine have also found use for parkinsonism. However, since geriatric patients tend to be "acetylcholine-shy," there tends to be more side effects in these patients—the most devastating being cognitive, especially memory, impairment.

The nurse is often in the best position to discover whether antagonistic drugs are being taken and to evaluate the side effects.

Much of the material in later chapters will deal with motor activities. When dealing with parkinsonism patients, it will be well to recall the peculiar features of slowness in initiating a change in movement patterns. In practical terms this means (1) you must allow for a long "reaction time" while giving instructions, (2) the patient must develop "start up" techniques, (3) the early patient could have selective difficulty with specific activities (turning, getting up from a chair), and (4) the severely involved patient could have more potential than is evident from superficial observation.

Techniques described in the following chapters can make significant differences in the quality of life of patients with parkinsonism. Although it is true that the wide prevalence of this disease makes it seem an overwhelming problem, that is hardly an excuse for neglecting the individual. Rewards can still be gratifying, dealing as we must with one patient at a time.

CHAPTER REVIEW TEST

Select the correct answer.

1. Symptoms of Parkinsonism do not include
    a. rigidity
    b. shuffling gait.
    c. spasticity.
    d. hand tremor.
2. Drugs of value in treating parkinsonism are
    a. L-dopa.
    b. valium.
    c. vitamin B_6.
    d. dantrium.
3. The lesion producing parkinsonism is in the
    a. internal capsule.
    b. cerebral cortex.
    c. substantia nigra.
    d. muscles.

The correct answers are as follows:
1. c
2. a
3. c

Check your answers. If you missed any, you should review the appropriate section of this chapter.

Common Medical Problems Associated with Rehabilitation

6

Management of Chronic Pain

David C. Bradshaw, M.D.
Gerald P. Keane, M.D.

INTRODUCTION AND OBJECTIVES

The goal of this chapter is to provide the reader with an overview of the nature of chronic pain and its associated disability and to provide an understanding of the basic techniques involved in working with individuals who suffer from chronic pain. The use of a multidisciplinary team approach will be emphasized.

After completing this chapter, you should be able to

1. understand the difference between acute and chronic pain in terms of its cause, medical treatment, and psychology
2. understand that chronic pain causes significant disability and that multidisciplinary treatment in a structured environment by a rehabilitation team is the best current treatment
3. understand the overall goal of the treatment program and what it does not promise to do
4. understand the criteria for patient admission and the goals of each stage of the treatment program
5. understand that tight, coordinated teamwork is necessary and that frequent team conferences are needed for effective communication
6. understand the need for frequent and objective recording of patient progress (activity, medication, behavior)
7. understand that medication is a major issue
8. understand how to use a pain cocktail, how to use psychological adjuncts in detoxification and pain control, and how to avoid using p.r.n. medication
9. understand the basics of behavior modification, "pain games," patient education, and family involvement
10. understand the need for long-term "management" of chronic pain rather than emphasizing cures

TREATMENT

Treatment of chronic pain patients can be among the most challenging areas of medicine—not only are they frequently quite disabled by their pain but they are often very resistant to the treatments required to allow them to move toward recovery.

There is no doubt that chronic pain patients can be quite disabled. They often function at a level well below many other people with more clearly identifiable impairments, for example, the well-adapted paraplegic. Their functional levels are often quite low in terms of mobility, activities of daily living, vocation, and social interaction. They often spend much of the day in bed and are generally quite deconditioned physically. Sexual activities, social outlets, vocational pursuits, and family dynamics are usually significantly disrupted. Financial resources are often a major additional stress, and chronic pain patients often see themselves as trapped in the role of a helpless victim. Depression is common.

Clearly, this type of multifactorial problem often requires a team approach and long-term support to maximize chances for a successful resolution.

The Road to Chronic Pain

Unlike most other disabilities requiring major rehabilitation efforts, the onset of chronic pain often coincides with an anatomic insult that appears relatively minor. Frequently, however, difficulties related to curing or relieving the pain set off a downhill spiral that results in a disability far out of proportion to the original insult. The patient eventually becomes trapped in a physical, psychological, and social system in which failure and frustration are the usual outcomes. The patient is then at the mercy of doctors, family, friends (those who remain), drugs, and frequently a medicolegal system designed to actually encourage continued disability.

The physical, psychological, and social system mentioned above is characterized by the "six Ds" of chronic pain:

1. Drug misuse: Despite claims that the constant and severe pain is not relieved by high doses of narcotic analgesics, the patient will request ever increasing doses. In contrast to acute pain patients, whose psychological parameters become more normal after the administration of narcotics, the chronic pain patient may demonstrate behavioral and psychological functioning which deteriorates after their administration.
2. Disuse and deconditioning: As the patient becomes less active in vocational, social, and leisure activities, there is progressive decline in muscular function and endurance. Increased amounts of time in bed or at rest lead to a situation where even if the pain were to be alleviated, tasks done previously have become too difficult to carry out.
3. Depression: This is one of the most important associated factors that must be addressed, as must the associated sense of helplessness and frustration (see the section below entitled "Key Concepts in Chronic Pain").
4. Disability and litigation: From one standpoint, the patient receives something for nothing. The behavioral consequence of being paid for not working is definitely not a desire to return to work. Yet this is a double-edged sword, since disability payments are often not on a par with the patient's prior income. Such payments thus provide both positive and negative reinforcement for return to work.
5. Dependence and passivity: The chronic pain patient often feels that he is unable to do anything for himself and, in a behavioral way, begins to enjoy having other people do things for him. His pain becomes a universally accepted excuse for avoiding unpleasant activities and, in particular, for not taking positive steps toward making himself better. Dependence and passivity are manifested, especially toward the family but also toward the medical system. If the patient is given a treatment program that requires exercises and follow-through on his part, then he will seldom do it at home. Passive treatments, such as heat and massage, are readily accepted, because they require no effort. The concept of self-control of pain or of responsibility for a positive program tends to be rejected. A chronic pain patient will seek out magic cures and solutions that have the promise of total relief with little effort on his part.
6. Doctors and the health care system: The chronic pain patient often overuses the medical system, both in treatment of exacerbations of pain (which can often be handled at home and have no identifiable causes) and in seeking new diagnoses and treatment for an existing pain syndrome. He is able to apply all of the first five Ds of chronic pain when he reaches the doctor's office. He often elicits the doctor's sympathy and he is provided with drugs, prescriptions for passive treatment, and told to rest in bed; meanwhile he builds an ever thickening medical file that documents his suffering for later use at legal proceedings.

You should note that the six Ds of chronic pain are secondary complications of the primary process, whose exact nature is often vague or unsatisfactory as an explanation for the chronic pain and disability.

Pain is a subjective, personal experience, and there is no simple correlation between organic pathology and the amount of suffering experienced by the individual. However, patients' behavioral manifestations and expressions of pain can be premorbid and learned through reinforcement, and these can be affected without actually changing the source of pain itself. All of the six problems listed above can be alleviated by a well-designed treatment program. The expectation should be not to alter a patient's source of pain, but to improve the patient's means of coping with and adapting to the pain. Those areas that *are* reversible should be addressed and any plans must be clearly explained to the patient in advance. Many patients in the chronic pain spiral are unable to see past their current dilemma and their previous organically based outlook. If goals are not clearly stated in advance (usually in writing), then the chances of a successful outcome are often markedly reduced.

Goals of the Chronic Pain Program

1. The patient should become involved in the recovery program and should also accept responsibility for his progress and develop some insight into the ways he perpetuates his own disability.
2. The patient should undergo detoxification from narcotics and sedatives, hypnotic medications that promote depression and dependency and only continue the downhill spiral.
3. The patient should acknowledge associated psychological factors—particularly depression and anxiety—and become actively involved in the recovery program. Appropriate medication, psychotherapy, behavioral modification, group support, and other techniques may be used.
4. The patient must be shown ways to increase function, initially through the use of a regular, appropriate exercise program, which should be monitored and made progressively more demanding. Activities of daily living must be gradually made more strenuous. The progression demanded should be time-contingent and not pain-contingent.
5. Planning for future vocational and social reintegration must be initiated, even if long ignored. Here the medicolegal system will often work against the patient's real needs.
6. Education must be provided in basic methods of back care, proper medication use, and the limitations of the medical model regarding the cure of chronic pain. Once it is clear that adequate medical tests have been performed and opinions obtained (often far too many), further doctor shopping and cure seeking should be discouraged.

Key Concepts in Chronic Pain

One of the challenges in working with the pain patient is the subjective nature of the pain experience. Pain is a symptom, not a diagnosis, and is affected by a variety of physical, psychological, cultural, and social factors. Pain behavior is one way in which the pain experience is communicated to others.

Acute pain is pain resulting from a direct injury that can be clearly diagnosed and treated. The treatment is clearly defined, relief is quick and reassuring, and recovery is predictable and controlled. The relevant psychological response to acute pain is anxiety. The anxiety leads to the search for relief. In acute pain, relief, either by pharmacological means or by direct treatment of the cause, yields a prompt reversal of the psychological effects. The person with acute pain may at first rest the affected part and then, as relief begins, systematically start to use the part again, even though some pain may still be experienced. The person feels in control of the injury and actively takes steps to return it toward its normal function, realizing that restoration of an injured part necessitates some effort and discomfort.

Chronic pain may have a sudden or gradual onset and may or may not be related to an actual physical injury. The key feature is that, despite treatment, the pain persists. The origin of the pain might not be clearly diagnosable, the treatment might not be adequately controlled, and the individual's life style might be seriously disrupted. If the pain is of uncertain or uncorrectable etiology, all medical treatments have failed, and it has gone on more than six months, then it is termed *chronic pain*. As pain passes from acute to chronic, the patient's psychology changes from anxiety, through various stages, into depression. Frequently, psychological testing will reveal elevation of scales indicative of hypochondria, depression, and hysteria.

Pain behavior evolves because pain cannot be objectively measured and must be communicated by the patient in order for anyone else to know he is in pain. This communication is achieved through "behavior." The pain communication (behavior) may be verbal, emotional, physical, or in the form of activities not done. The patient may verbally tell others that he hurts, adding various, often dramatic, descriptions of how much. He may communicate that he hurts through facial expressions of anxiety or depression. He may exhibit pain behavior, such as holding the area that hurts, crying, moaning, groaning, lying down, getting angry, or asking for help with things that he would ordinarily do himself. The use of canes, braces, and other appliances is a clear visual statement that a patient has pain. The patient may also avoid activities that he used to enjoy, including hobbies, sports, and other recreational activities. For the patient the pain behavior becomes a habit and provides a sense of identity, thus tending to be self-perpetuating. As he communicates to others that he hurts more and more, he perceives increased pain himself. Decreased pain behavior equals decreased pain. If a patient's perception of the pain is to be changed, family members must be made aware of their own involvement in perpetuating pain behavior and encouraging disability.

Pain games come about when the patient, in the course of being passive, depressed, and frustrated, becomes angry with the medical profession for its inability to help him. As the patient settles into a painful invalidism, he will have subconscious fears about giving up the stability of dependency and passivity for the more questionable goal of improvement, for nothing has produced improvement before. Physicians with a strong ego, who feel that they can help the chronic pain patient, often find themselves in the middle of a game where the patient actually resists treatment rather than cooperating with it. Confrontations over relevant issues (whether the pain is real, whether medications are excessive, whether to return to work) often produce increased verbal and physical pain behavior as the patient attempts to prove to the physicians that the pain is real and severe. Commonly a patient's only means of exerting control (and only pleasure) is to frustrate the treatment plan. Many variations of the pain game are played whenever the family or society begins to pressure the patient with respect to any of the six Ds.

Behavior modification works in the following manner. Pain behavior exists because the patient derives more benefit from having pain behavior than from having healthy behavior. Any behavior that is reinforced (rewarded) increases. Behaviors that meet with poor results or are criticized often do not disappear, however; they only produce other behaviors designed to avoid the unpleasant response. The best way to "extinguish" an unwanted behavior is to ignore it completely. Healthy behavior should be recognized by the staff and reinforced. Healthy behavior, if it is to continue after the period of artificial reinforcement from the staff, must ultimately get the patient more of something than the painful behavior did. The family and treatment team must identify the "something" for which the patient is willing to work and they make the awarding of this contingent on healthy behavior and not pain behavior. Whatever sustains a behavior is called a *reinforcer*. (The words *reward* and *reinforcer* are synonymous.) The goal in working to change the pain behavior is to interrupt the downhill cycle and encourage increased adaptation to the disability in a "healthy" way.

Test on Treatment of Chronic Pain

Please answer the following questions.

1. What are the six Ds of chronic pain?
   a. _____
   b. _____
   c. _____
   d. _____
   e. _____
   f. _____

2. How does the patient attempt to communicate pain that is not directly measurable?
   _____
   _____
   _____

3. Psychological factors are important, but they ought to be considered separately from the treatment of pain itself. True or false?

4. What are the six major treatment goals of the chronic pain program? (Remember the six Ds.)
   a. _____
   b. _____
   c. _____
   d. _____
   e. _____
   f. _____

5. What is the basic psychological response to acute pain? To chronic pain? What is the difference in the psychological response of acute and chronic pain patients to narcotic analgesics?

_____

_____

_____

_____

6. What is the basic principle of behavior modification? Give an example of how pain behavior may be made to occur more frequently.

_____

_____

_____

_____

Compare your answers with the following:
1. *(a) drug misuse, (b) disuse and deconditioning, (c) depression, (d) disability and litigation, (e) dependence and passivity, and (f) doctors and the health care system.*
2. *Through pain behavior.*
3. *False.*
4. *The general goal of pain treatment programs is to return patients to society at their maximum functional level and with the ability to cope with any residual discomfort in a realistic and appropriate manner. Specific treatment goals with regard to the six Ds include*
   a. *achieving drug detoxification and instituting appropriate medication at reasonable levels*
   b. *increasing the patient activity level and the overall level of general body conditioning*
   c. *educating the patient in psychological issues and treating the patient by psychological methods for underlying depression*
   d. *educating and counseling the patient concerning the establishment of appropriate vocational goals*
   e. *teaching the patient that he or she may have an active role in the treatment and that the prognosis depends more on the patient's enthusiasm and willingness to work than on the ability of others to "do something" for the patient*
   f. *teaching the patient self-reliance and not to depend so heavily on doctors and the medical system*
5. *The basic psychological response to acute pain is anxiety. Chronic pain produces depression. Narcotics decrease the anxiety of acute pain, but they increase the depression and pain behavior of chronic pain.*
6. *Any behavior that is reinforced increases. Pain behavior will occur more frequently if pain medication is given upon demand.*

ORGANIZATION OF THE TREATMENT PROGRAM

The material in the first part of the chapter was designed to introduce some of the basic concepts for working with chronic pain patients and to introduce some of the issues that arise. The next section is intended to outline a treatment program in more detail.

The Team Approach

The team approach to chronic pain utilizes all the members of the standard rehabilitation team, with a heavy emphasis on psychological support and guidance. The team typically includes a coordinating physician, psychologist, physical therapist, occupational therapist, social worker, and, for inpatients, nurses. Access to recreational therapy, dietary, and other health professionals is also essential.

The key to successful management of the chronic pain patient is effective communication among team members. During the early portion of the program, typically the first three to four weeks, a regular weekly team conference is invaluable. Personnel who will be involved in the aftercare of the patient—particularly vocational rehabilitation counselors or nurses—ought to be invited. One team member should act as coordinator for each patient, and feedback from the meeting should be presented to each patient. The rationale for such a system is that it presents a unified message or "party line" to the patient. Manipulative patients are common, and the use of "team rounds" may be necessary to demonstrate to such patients that they cannot successfully play one team member off against another. Team members working with inpatients must be able to answer questions and communicate regularly about a variety of areas and also be informed about the type of treatment and approaches of other team members. Those individuals responsible for monitoring patients during the 14–16 hours of the day that are not formally scheduled must also be kept informed about treatment plans and goals. Pain patients may typically attempt to manipulate team members during the hours outside formal treatment. Pain behavior and other nonacceptable coping mechanisms must be addressed continually, and all team members need to be well versed in how to deal with such problematic behavior. Regular access of team members to the psychologist for counseling in appropriate techniques can be particularly helpful.

Inpatient Treatment

One of the central elements of working successfully with chronic pain patients is detoxification from narcotic and sedative-hypnotic medications. The inpatient ward allows a great deal of control over the very difficult process of detoxification.

The use of so-called pain cocktails—medication combinations that appear more neutral (generally a colored or flavored liquid) and that have gradually tapering doses of the narcotic/sedative components—is the usual means of accomplishing this. The medication is given on a time-contingent basis, generally every four to six hours, and in a constant liquid volume. This avoids the usual p.r.n. method, where expression of pain behavior is only reinforced, for the patient must first demonstrate pain to the staff and then increase the anxiety level while awaiting arrival of the medication. The nursing staff, as primary caregivers on the pain ward, are the key to a successful drug withdrawal process. Presentation of medications as planned, without allowing the patient to draw the nurse into pain behavior games, allows the patient to focus on the "well" rather than the "sick" role.

During this time, the nursing staff must note the patient's daily activity level, the time spent in bed, the amount of social interaction, the motivation

level, the level of pain behavior, etc. This allows the team members to assess the progress of the patient and make modifications as needed. The initial days of the program are spent assessing the patient's level of activity and medication use and providing a very open introduction to the goals of treatment. As it progresses, the program is made more challenging and daily goals are set to encourage a feeling of success. Goals are revised regularly and all team members must be involved.

Physical and occupational therapy are the keys to daily assessing the physical and functional capability of the patient. Endurance level, strength, cardiovascular conditioning, body mechanics, posture, etc., are all evaluated. A functional approach is emphasized, including sitting tolerance, lifting and carrying capability, household activities, prevocational plans, and other issues.

Social services is often the essential link to the family during the treatment program, and it is often family involvement that is most important for continued success after the patient leaves the very structured environment of the inpatient ward. Additionally, family stress issues, financial concerns, vocational history, employment opportunities, resources for retraining, etc., are all within the area of expertise of the social worker. Information about these issues and provision of counseling and assistance to the patient and family are indispensable for a successful long-term outcome.

The role of the psychologist is to provide support directly to the patient and to assist team members in dealing with a variety of issues concerning patient management. Evaluating the patient for issues of secondary gain, identifying reinforcers of the disabled life style, dealing with the family environment, and developing an approach to be uniformly adopted by team members are primary responsibilities. Psychometric testing; monitoring for evidence of depression, anxiety, and other commonly associated issues; and direct work with the patient on behavioral approaches to the chronic pain life style are also included in the psychologist's role.

Goals of the Treatment Program

The central concept in treatment of the chronic pain patient is the *management* of pain rather than its *cure*. The approach is in some ways similar to popular approaches in drug and alcohol rehabilitation, with the emphasis on day-to-day coping skills.

Education is probably the primary treatment modality. As the patient becomes more aware of the six Ds of chronic pain, his ability to cope with the pain itself can be enhanced. Ignorance only exacerbates anxiety, fear, depression, dependence on medication, and maladaptive pain behavior. Through a better understanding of anatomy, the basic physiology of pain, and the psychological issues involved, the patient can develop insight about his problems and improve coping skills.

The patient must also be taught less dependent and harmful means of coping with and managing the pain itself. The proper use of rest, alternating with activity, must be emphasized. The goal is to provide means by which the patient can manage his own treatment during times of increased pain and thereby avoid a dependent or "sick" role. Such means include biofeedback, ice, heat, self-hypnosis, stretching, proper exercise, relaxation tapes, and other techniques the patient can use independently. Visiting health professionals for chronic problems on a pain-dependent rather than time-contingent basis is to be discouraged.

Patients must be directed away from short-term fixes (pain medication, "feel good" modalities, and therapy bed rest) and toward well behavior (increased vocational, family, and social interaction).

The team must expect the chronic pain patient to "test" the treatment program. Anger, hostility, attempts to divide staff members, complaints of increased pain, low tolerance for activity, and other ploys used in the "pain game" must be anticipated. The team must then work to communicate with each other and develop a uniform and consistent response to these tests. Inability to adapt effectively to the patient's demands will allow the patient to control his own participation and treatment and the result will be long-term failure.

Outcome

The latter part of the program should emphasize long-term planning, including continued progression of physical activity, vocational issues, ongoing psychological support, and family involvement.

Emphasis must be placed on objective measurements of success and improvement. If team members allow a patient to set the emphasis on subjective feelings, then management of the patient will soon be "going in circles." Comparison of objective gains, first weekly and then monthly, should be the method by which progress and recovery is measured. Hours out of bed, lifting capability, days of work missed, and other measurements can be devised and utilized to follow recovery.

Unfortunately, many patients, in spite of a carefully managed program, will not recover successfully. The program may be too difficult, destabilize far deeper emotional and psychological factors, or simply be premature (the patient may not be ready to face his status realistically). Such patients should be identified, discharged as soon as possible from the program, and given an honest assessment of their situation, including what types of treatment, particularly medications, the team is willing to continue to provide, if any.

Test on the Treatment Program

Please answer the following questions.

1. Why is close coordination of the team more important with chronic pain patients than with physical disability patients? Please answer from the point of view of the patient and of the team.

_____

_____

2. The social worker should obtain a work history from the patient. True or false?
3. Since all pain patients demonstrate marked psychological disturbances, a prior history of psychological derangement is unimportant. True or false?
4. Medications given on a p.r.n. basis require the patient to communicate pain to you through pain behavior and thus the medication reinforces (rewards) overt and obvious pain behavior. True or false?
5. After talking with the patient, you feel that the program definitely exceeds his capabilities and you feel guilty for not providing pain-relieving medications. What should you do?

_____

_____

_____

6. All chronic pain patients can benefit from a behavioral modification and activity program. True or false?
   Explain: _____
   _____
   _____

7. Subjective pain complaints must be monitored closely in order to achieve successful pain treatment. True or false?

8. Family involvement serves only to allow the patient to be diverted from the central issues of pain treatment and should be discouraged. True or false?

Compare your answers with the following:

1. *The team must be closely coordinated so that the patient does not receive conflicting or ambiguous messages from different team members, which will raise doubts about their competence and provide excuses for noncompliance. It must also be closely coordinated so that when the patient gives ambiguous and double behaviors to different staff members, these can immediately be detected and dealt with directly and behaviorally.*

2. *True. However, a work history should also be obtained through direct contact with the employer.*

3. *False. Although all pain patients develop depression and various maladaptive behaviors secondary to their pain, the fundamental assumption is that they were basically normal before the pain started. A history of significant psychological dysfunction prior to the onset of pain is a poor prognostic factor.*

4. *True. P.r.n. medications reward pain behavior. All pain medications should be given on a time schedule without regard for expressions of need that are highly dramatic.*

5. *You should not feel guilty. The patient has just played the pain game that he has played so long and so well, has evoked the desired recognition of suffering, and perhaps will obtain a reward (pain medication) for his skill at the game. You should be firm but gentle with him. You should ignore his pain behavior. Narcotics are ineffective and have no role in the treatment of chronic pain.*

6. *False. Some pain patients cannot benefit from a behaviorally oriented rehabilitation program. Hopefully, most of these are rejected after the evaluation phase. Many make it into the treatment phase and are easily recognized by their lack of progress with respect to the objective parameters.*

7. *False. Monitoring subjective complaints closely only encourages pain behavior and keeps the patient in the "sick role"; it is to be avoided.*

8. *False. Many times family members act as "enablers" who unknowingly encourage the patient to remain in the sick role, in particular, the chronic pain role.*

SUGGESTED READINGS

Aronoff, G.M., ed. *Evaluation and Treatment of Chronic Pain*. Baltimore-Munich: Urban and Schwarzenberg, 1985. A comprehensive textbook.

Aronoff, G.M., and W.O. Evans. "Evaluation and Treatment of Chronic Pain at the Boston Pain Center." *J. Clin. Psychiatry* 43 (August 1982): 4–9. An excellent general article.

Behavioral Methods for Chronic Pain and Illness. St. Louis: Mosby, 1986. A complete text on behavioral modification.

Fordyce, W.E., R. Fowler, J. Lehmann, B. DeLateur, P. Sand, and R. Treischmann. "An Operant Conditioning in the Treatment of Chronic Pain." *Arch. of Phys. Med. and Rehab.* 54 (September 1973): 399–408.

Gottlieb, H., S. LaBan, R. Koller, A. Madorsky, V. Hockersmith, M. Kleeman, and J. Wagner. "Comprehensive Rehabilitation of Patients Having Chronic Low Back Pain." *Arch. of Phys. Med. and Rehab.* 58 (March 1977): 101–8. Emphasizes self-regulation of pain.

Sternbach, R.A. *Pain Patients' Traits and Treatment*. New York: Academic Press, 1974. A good text on "pain games."

Wall, P.D. and R. Melzack. *Textbook of Pain*. Edinburgh: Churchill Livingstone, 1984.

White, Arthur, ed. "Failed Back Surgery Syndrome: Evaluation and Treatment." *State of the Art Reviews* 1 (September 1986). General textbook on low back pain aspects.

7 Special Problems in Rehabilitation Management of the Elderly

Franz U. Steinberg, M.D.

INTRODUCTION AND OBJECTIVES

Pediatrics has generally benefited from the recognition that children are not simply "little people"; geriatrics has benefited from the recognition that aging involves more than simply the passing of years. The differences in anatomy and physiology of the aged in almost all systems produce differences in exercise tolerance, tolerance to medications, susceptibility to disease, and other phenomena which produce "special problems in rehabilitation." This chapter addresses these special problems and should help you to

1. identify the present and growing need of the aging population for rehabilitation
2. identify the obstacles to successful rehabilitation in old age
3. understand cardiovascular problems and cardiac monitoring
4. identify common neurological and mental problems
5. identify common musculoskeletal problems
6. adjust rehabilitation goals to take into account the special problems of the aged

IMPORTANCE OF REHABILITATION

Why is rehabilitation an important component of the care of the elderly? This question is asked quite often, and it needs to be answered before the problems of geriatric rehabilitation are described in detail.

The aging population is growing steadily, both in absolute numbers and in proportion to the total population. In 1900, individuals above the age of 65 constituted 4 percent of the total U.S. population; today they constitute 11 percent of the total. In 1940, there were 9 million persons over the age of 65 in the U.S.; by 1980, the number had grown to 25 million. The population above the age of 75 is growing even faster proportionately.

Aging is often accompanied by a deterioration of health. Elderly persons may suffer from several diseases at the same time, such as cardiovascular disease, diabetes, and arthritis. These disease processes interact and aggravate each other. Progress in medicine and surgery has made it possible for elderly, chronically ill patients to survive for much longer periods of time than in the past. But all too often the price of survival is a physical disability: an amputation, paralyzed limbs, or increasing stiffness of joints.

It is the task of rehabilitation medicine either to remedy the disability or, if this is not possible, to develop means of compensating for it, for example, by a brace, by an artificial limb, or by an exercise program to strengthen weak muscles or build up muscles to make up for those that can no longer function adequately.

Severely disabled elderly patients who can no longer take care of most of their personal needs will wind up in a nursing home. However, all too often nursing home confinement is premature and can be avoided or at least delayed by rehabilitative care. It is the mission of rehabilitation to minimize loss of function and to keep the disability from becoming the cause of a social decline. Old people fear nothing more than the prospect of losing their independence and of having to rely on others for their daily care. Rehabilitation will help the elderly to maintain their independence for as long as possible.

OBSTACLES TO SUCCESSFUL REHABILITATION IN OLD AGE

As mentioned before, elderly persons all too often suffer from one or several chronic diseases that deplete their energy and reduce their endurance. Rehabilitation is a learning process, and the exercises and other activities that are part of rehabilitation require energy expenditure and mental concentration. The chronically ill and disabled patient may not have the stamina to successfully participate in a rehabilitation program. Even among the well elderly, effort tolerance is diminished. The aging organism gradually loses its reserve powers. An elderly individual may do well with usual activities yet may be unable to draw on reserves whenever an extra effort is needed. This problem will be discussed in reference to various body systems.

Cardiovascular Problems

The heart responds to effort by increasing the heart rate and the stroke volume (i.e., the amount of blood that the ventricles eject with each contraction). This response to effort has an upper limit. The maximum heart rate that can be achieved with maximal exertion is roughly calculated as 220 minus age. Therefore, the older the person, the less the heart can accommodate an increase of effort. The amount of oxygen that an individual can expend with exertion also has an upper limit, and this limit likewise diminishes with age. The decline can be slowed by exercising during the middle years of life and into old age, but it cannot be halted completely. The patient admitted to a rehabilitation program may not have been physically active for some time and his level of fitness may have declined considerably. In the

EXHIBIT 7-1 Exercise Guidelines

Before exercise:
1. Obtain heart rate
2. Obtain blood pressure

During exercise, stop if:
1. Heart rate exceeds 65% of estimated maximal rate
2. Diastolic blood pressure exceeds resting level more than 20 mm Hg
3. Systolic blood pressure falls
4. There is an increase of irregular heart beats
5. There is shortness of breath, chest pain, dizziness, pallor, diaphoresis, cold and clammy skin

---

physical therapy department, he may be called upon to exert himself well above his usual activity level and his tolerance. The elderly patient, therefore, may become rapidly exhausted with moderate or even minimal exertion and develop signs of cardiovascular failure. His participation in the rehabilitation program will quickly reach a limit.

The elderly patient should have a physician's evaluation of his cardiovascular status before engaging in a rehabilitation program. This should include an electrocardiogram and a chest x-ray. In addition, the physical therapist should monitor heart action while the patient is exercising. (See Exhibit 7-1). The following procedure is recommended:

- Count the pulse before the beginning of the exercise. Observe for irregularities.
- Take the blood pressure before the beginning of the exercise.
- Check the pulse and blood pressure repeatedly during the activity. The heart rate will increase with exercise but should not exceed 65 percent of the estimated maximal rate for the individual. Both systolic and diastolic blood pressure will rise. The diastolic pressure should not exceed the resting level by more than 20 mm Hg. Note that a fall of the systolic pressure during exercise means that the heart muscle is stressed beyond tolerance. The activity must then be stopped.
- An increase of irregular heartbeats may be an ominous sign. The exercise should be stopped until after evaluation by a physician.
- Shortness of breath, chest pain, a sensation of dizziness or faintness, excessive sweating, cold and clammy skin, and pallor are indications for stopping the activity.

When the therapist has become familiar with the patient's effort tolerance, the monitoring can become less frequent. Yet vigilance will always be in order. Many elderly patients have suffered myocardial infarctions or catastrophic arrhythmias during exercising or gait training after strokes or amputations. In general, physical therapy activities should be carried out more slowly, for shorter periods, and with adequate opportunities for rest.

Orthostatic hypotension (i.e., a significant drop in blood pressure when assuming an upright position) may be a serious problem when rehabilitating an elderly patient to standing or walking. It is usually due to rigidity of the internal carotid arteries and their branches. The patient may become very dizzy or even faint when arising from

Internal abdominal lesions, such as a penetrating duodenal ulcer or a perforating diverticulum of the colon, may cause little pain. Another common acute problem is dehydration due to poor fluid intake in the presence of excessive sweating or diarrhea; it can materially reduce an elderly person's performance level. The same goes for overhydration with dilution of serum electrolytes, usually caused by the excessive administration of intravenous fluids. A search for organic causes is indicated whenever a sudden loss of endurance, inability to concentrate, and deterioration of function become apparent.

REHABILITATION GOALS FOR THE GERIATRIC DISABLED

Not all elderly disabled patients are suitable candidates for rehabilitation. Their potential for successful rehabilitation must be carefully assessed before such patients are accepted into the program. At the same time, specific goals must be set in cooperation with the patient and his family.

For any patient, the setting of goals requires the acquisition of facts about the patient's status before the present illness and about the patient's present condition. The rehabilitation team needs to know about the patient's physical and mental health before the illness, the previous degree of mobility and the patient's self-care ability, and the extent of the patient's involvement in family life and in the community. The current status is assessed by a thorough physical examination, including pertinent laboratory data. The emphasis should be on cardiopulmonary functions and on the neurologic status, including vision, hearing, speech, and language. There needs to be an evaluation of mental functions such as attention span, short- and long-term memory, and general alertness. Musculoskeletal function must be assessed, as must the patient's current ability to take care of personal needs. The diagnosis of the prevailing disease will help to establish a prognosis. If the patient suffers from a disease that will materially shorten life expectancy, then the rehabilitation goals should obviously be more modest.

Goal setting also requires a good social history. What is the family composition and who will be potential caregivers if the patient needs assistance? What are the financial resources? If a patient is expected to return home, the rehabilitation team needs to know something about the physical structure of the home, such as the accessibility of the kitchen, bedroom, bathrooms, etc., for a patient who may have difficulty climbing stairs or is in a wheelchair. The goals as perceived by the patient and family need to be taken into consideration. A family that is willing and obviously capable of assuming the responsibility of caring for the elderly disabled patient at home should be given all the assistance and preparation needed to make this possible. Even if the patient is to go to a nursing home, every effort should be made to make him as independent as possible before leaving the rehabilitation department. Patients fare better in nursing homes and the quality of life is much improved if they are not totally dependent on nursing home staff for every aspect of their care.

Goals should be reviewed periodically and revised as needed. For this purpose, staff conferences should be conducted at least every two weeks. There physicians, nurses, therapists, and social workers should report on progress that may have been made and reiterate the goals of their activities. Discharge plans need to be initiated when it becomes apparent that the progress is slow and that no additional achievements can be anticipated.

CONCLUSION

Rehabilitation of the physically disabled elderly patient is an essential ingredient of overall geriatric care. However, it may be difficult, since often several medical problems are present that need to be taken into consideration. Goals and objectives need to be set clearly and be pursued vigorously. The overall goal for all patients is improvement of function and self-care ability. Time and effort should not be wasted on minor objectives that may be of no functional value to the patient.

CHAPTER REVIEW TEST

Mark the correct answer (there is only one correct answer for each question).

1. A rehabilitation program for an elderly patient is most likely to fail if
   a. the patient shows little interest and the motivation is poor.
   b. the patient's leg muscles are weak.

c. the patient cannot recall instructions from one day to the next.
d. the patient has had a myocardial infarction within the last year.

2. Pseudodementia
   a. is a condition in which patients fake confusion in order to have family members care for most of their personal needs.
   b. may be caused by adverse reactions to sedatives.
   c. may be caused by systolic hypertension.
   d. is associated with dehydration due to excessive use of laxatives.

3. Sedatives may become toxic in elderly patients
   a. only if given in a larger than customary dosage.
   b. if given at a dosage usually well tolerated by younger adults.
   c. in the presence of a low potassium level.
   d. if combined with diuretics.

4. An exercise will be considered too strenuous and should be stopped if
   a. the systolic blood pressure drops below the pre-exercise level.
   b. the heart rate rises to 110/minute.
   c. systolic and diastolic blood pressure rise above the pre-exercise level.
   d. the patient complains of leg pain.

5. During the last 40 years (from the 1940 census to the 1980 census) the population above the age of 65
   a. doubled.
   b. quadrupled.
   c. grew by 20 percent.
   d. increased two and a half times.

6. Loss of joint range of motion is caused by
   a. muscle weakness.
   b. osteoporosis.
   c. contractures of ligaments or tendons.
   d. joint pain.

The correct answers are as follows:

1. c	*4. a*
2. b	*5. d*
3. b	*6. c*

If you missed any of the answers, review the appropriate sections of the chapter.

SUGGESTED READINGS

Cape, R.D.T., ed. *Fundamentals of Geriatric Medicine*. New York: Raven, 1983.

Libow, L.S., and F.T. Sherman. *The Core of Geriatric Medicine: A Guide for Students and Practitioners*. St. Louis: Mosby, 1981.

Rock, R.C. "Monitoring Therapeutic Drug Levels." *Geriatrics* 40 (1985): 75.

Steinberg, F.U., ed. *The Care of the Geriatric Patient in the Tradition of Cowdry*. 6th ed. St. Louis: Mosby, 1983.

Identification and Management of Bladder Problems

Shelly E. Liss, M.D.

INTRODUCTION AND OBJECTIVES

The goal of bladder training is to make filling and emptying the bladder as normal as possible for the individual patient. Mrs. Smith will be our patient for this lesson. We will begin by reviewing her physiological problem, why she has a problem, and what her incontinence implies.

Upon completion of this chapter, you should be able to

1. identify the normal physiology and anatomy of the urinary tract
2. identify four types of incontinence
3. describe proper catheter care
4. identify complications of incontinence
5. identify pertinent questions and information to be gathered from the patient and family before devising a care plan
6. identify factors involved in bladder control and training
7. formulate a bladder training program and care plan using knowledge gained in this chapter

Figure 8-1 provides diagrams of the male and female urinary systems. Please study this figure to refresh your memory of this portion of human anatomy.

VOIDING

Urine enters the bladder, producing tension in the bladder wall to threshold level and causing the detrusor muscle fibers to stretch. Sensory impulses resulting from bladder pressure go to the central nervous system, and motor impulses return to the bladder. These return impulses produce detrusor muscle contraction waves; the sphincter muscles relax and voiding occurs.

(Cerebral control can cause voluntary inhibition of the reflex as well as voluntary initiation.)

TYPES OF INCONTINENCE

1. *Stress Incontinence.* This is most commonly seen in females with relaxation of pelvis musculature secondary to childbirth. The patient loses urine when coughing, sneezing, or straining. The patient does not feel the need to void but the urethral pressure is incapable of holding back the urine.
2. *Urge Incontinence.* This is the most common type of incontinence in the elderly. This can be secondary to bladder irritation from infection or caused by the patient's inability to inhibit the urge to void because of brain damage, as in senility or a stroke. Such patients feel the urge to void. Proper antibiotics are required to treat the infection. Bladder training should be tried in dementia.
3. *Incontinence of High Spinal Cord Dysfunction.* This is seen in "high" paraplegics and quadriplegics. The bladder empties without the patient feeling the urge to void or being able to inhibit voiding. The bladder is working through the spinal reflex, which has been disconnected from the brain, but the sphincter contracts as well, preventing voiding (dysynergia). These patients may learn to initiate the reflex by stroking their abdomen or by some other trigger mechanism if the urethral sphincter is not so spastic that it prevents voiding.
4. *Incontinence of Low Spinal Cord Dysfunction.* This is seen in "low" paraplegics and spina bifida patients. The bladder has been disconnected from the spinal cord, and the patient is unable to feel fullness or initiate

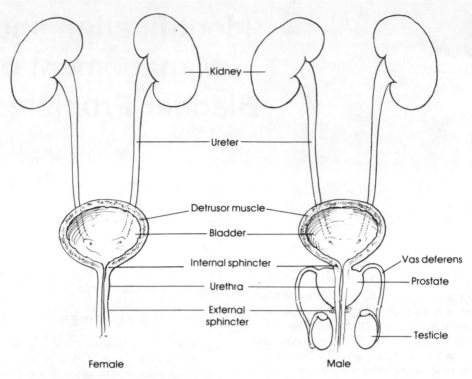

Kidney

Ureter

Detrusor muscle

Bladder

Internal sphincter

Urethra

External sphincter

Vas deferens

Prostate

Testicle

Female   Male

Figure 8-1 Anatomy of the Female and Male Urinary Systems

voiding. These patients can be rendered catheter free if there is no other mechanical impediment.

5. *Incontinence of Mechanical Urethral Obstruction.* This type of incontinence is due to enlarged prostate, urethral stricture, etc.

The last three types of incontinence are signals of possibly life-threatening situations. This is because the distension and/or high pressures that can accompany these types of incontinence can create a reverse flow (reflux) of urine back toward the kidneys. Reverse urine flow produces pyelonephritis and hydronephrosis. These diseases can destroy kidney tissue and are the leading causes of death in spinal cord patients. The treatment is catheter drainage, which prevents high pressures or distension. Removal of the catheter, however desirable, should be undertaken only after careful study and with follow-up that includes periodic intravenous pyelograms.

Test on Types of Incontinence

Assess your comprehension of the previous material by answering the following questions.

1. What is the goal of bladder training?

_____

_____

2. What normally happens physiologically as urine accumulates in the bladder?

_____

_____

_____

3. Name four types of incontinence.
   a. _____
   b. _____
   c. _____
   d. _____

4. According to the material on reverse flow incontinence, what is the reason for caution in removing a catheter?

_____

_____

_____

_____

The correct answers are as follows:
1. *The goal of bladder training is for the patient to fill and empty the bladder as normally as possible.*
2. *Once in the bladder, urine initiates the following chain of events:*
   - *The bladder wall tension increases to threshold level.*
   - *The detrusor muscle fibers stretch.*
   - *Sensory impulses go to the brain.*
   - *Motor impulses return to the bladder.*
   - *The detrusor muscle begins contraction waves, increasing bladder pressure.*
   - *The external sphincter relaxes.*
   - *The bladder is allowed to empty.*
3. a. *Stress incontinence*
   b. *Urge incontinence*
   c. *Incontinence of high spinal cord dysfunction*
   d. *Incontinence of low spinal cord dysfunction*
   e. *Incontinence of mechanical urethral obstruction*
4. *Patients diagnosed as having reverse incontinence are of clinical concern because of reflux (i.e., urine backing up the ureters), resulting in kidney infection and eventual destruction.*

If you missed any of the answers, review the material.

INFORMATION GATHERING

We must evaluate Mrs. Smith's existing condition of incontinence in order to formulate her care plan for bladder training.

On the basis of your education and experience, identify six pertinent questions you might ask when gathering information regarding the patient's voiding habits:

1. _____
2. _____
3. _____
4. _____
5. _____
6. _____

Compare your list of questions with the following:

1. *How frequently does she void?*
2. *When is she incontinent?*
3. *What is her reaction to this incontinence?*
4. *Is she ever aware of the need to void? If so, how has she indicated this?*
5. *How much does she void?*
6. *Is there ever any dribbling involved?*
7. *Does she ever have urgency in voiding? If so, does she actually void then or later?*
8. *Does she ever have difficulty initiating voiding?*
9. *Is her stream of force relatively normal?*
10. *What methods have proven effective in the past to assist her in voiding?*
11. *What is the character of her urine (e.g., are there signs of an existing infection from poor emptying)?*
12. *Does she or her family have any additional helpful information or suggestions?*

If you put down any six of the above questions, we are in agreement. If you could not identify six appropriate questions, look over and think about the listed questions before you proceed.

BLADDER TRAINING AND CONTROL

Bladder training can be initiated when the patient is (1) alert enough to cooperate, (2) mobile enough to participate, and (3) catheter-free.

Frequently, geriatric patients will have a catheter prior to entering a rehabilitation program to avoid overfilling of the bladder or incontinence. If possible, the catheter should eventually be removed, as its presence *always* causes a bladder infection and can cause other complications such as pyelonephritis, bacteremia, and epididymitis. If Mrs. Smith is unable to void effectively after her catheter is removed, it must be replaced after a reasonable period of time to prevent discomfort, bladder overdistension, bacteremia, and reflux. If it is necessary to replace the catheter, an accurate measurement of bladder residual after voiding should be made to assist the physician in evaluating the problem.

Some physicians use intermittent clamping of the catheter. We do not recommend this technique, because it does not increase the bladder's ability to contract, nor does it increase the bladder's capacity. It can also lead to complications.

Do not expect immediate control. It can take several days before real progress occurs, and occasional incontinence can persist much longer, even permanently. If incontinence occurs at night, try having a scheduled time to offer a bedpan, a urinal, or assistance to the bedside commode (the latter is preferred). Try to determine whether incontinence occurs at a specific time of the night; if so, offer help just prior to that time. Withholding or limiting fluids after the evening meal might help. When Mrs. Smith calls for a bedpan, it should be provided immediately if bladder training is to be effective. The physician could order a culture and sensitivity study and a colony count of the urine for the purpose of ordering antibiotic therapy if incontinence is secondary to infection.

Be aware of Mrs. Smith's bladder capacity. If it was never more than 200 cc, it will not change simply because she is being bladder trained. If frequent assistance in voiding is required, be sure such assistance is available, offered, given, and understood by nursing personnel.

Be sure to note the patient's awareness of the need to void. If it is diminished, she could need help and reminders, such as easy access to the commode, a nurse, or an alarm clock. Or she might only need to have a watch or clock in easy view.

Initial attempts at voiding should be made hourly. Thereafter, time intervals should be gradually increased to four hours and progressively increased even more as the bladder tolerates such increases. The usual nursing intervention techniques to initiate voiding should be used.

Remember that in order to void, urine must first be produced; therefore, fluid intake should be encouraged approximately one-half to one hour before an attempt to void. Mrs. Smith could, at first, have residual that might go unnoticed if her voiding appears to be "quantity sufficient." Intake-output records facilitate giving accurate accounts of what the patient is doing.

Test on Bladder Training and Control

Answer the following questions.

1. If nocturnal incontinence is prevalent, what might you do to help Mrs. Smith?
   a. _____
   _____
   _____
   b. _____
   _____
   _____
   c. _____
   _____

2. Identify two major factors that will affect Mrs. Smith's program.
   a. _____
   b. _____

The correct answers are as follows:
1. a. Withhold or limit fluids after dinner.
*   b. Note the usual time of occurrence, if any, and offer help just prior to it.*
*   c. Offer a bedpan, a urinal, or commode assistance at routine times.*
2. a. Bladder capacity
*   b. Awareness of the need to void*

If you missed any answers, please review the appropriate section before proceeding.

INTERMITTENT CATHETERIZATION

Intermittent catheterization is a useful alternative to permanent indwelling catheters. There are three reasons for using this technique: (1) intermittent catheterization with aseptic or even clean technique may lower the incidence of infection; (2) when a Foley catheter is used, recovery of bladder function may not be discovered; and (3) the presence of a permanent indwelling catheter may be repugnant to patients concerned about intimacy. Intermittent catheterization should be the technique of choice when there is expectation of bladder recovery, particularly when the patient is alert and sufficiently dextrous to learn self-catheterization.

Intermittent catheterization is performed three to five times per day, utilizing soft rubber catheters in a clean technique (sterile technique is not always required). It may be performed by nurses, technicians, relatives, or the patients themselves. It should be performed enough times to maintain bladder urine at 500 cc's or less. Fluid restrictions may be employed to aid in achieving this goal.

CATHETER CARE

Correct care of indwelling catheters is of the utmost importance. It is very common for a urinary tract infection to occur secondary to bacteria ascending either through the catheter lumen or by way of the outer wall of the catheter. Therefore, it is imperative that perineal care be executed regularly. In the case of males, it is recommended that the external urethral meatus should be cleansed with soap and water three times a day. In the case of females, the labia should be spread and washed with a mild soap and water detergent, and then the area around the urethral meatus should also be cleansed.

We do not recommend the use of continuous irrigation or routine irrigation of the Foley urethral catheter for several reasons. It is felt that a closed system is probably the safest system in inhibiting the development of urinary tract infections. The presence of a catheter causes a localized urinary tract infection; an open system for routine irrigation will introduce additional bacteria. Continuous irrigation with antibiotic irrigant is not routinely performed either. As soon as the irrigation is discontinued, the bladder is once again rapidly reinfected because of the presence of a foreign body (i.e., the Foley urethral catheter). If the catheter is not draining well or the patient is voiding around the catheter, the catheter should be irrigated under aseptic conditions with either a Toomey syringe or a bulb-type catheter syringe. The solution used to irrigate can be either normal saline or sterile water.

If possible, the catheter used should be one of the silastic types. They are inert and less apt to cause formation of encrustation and bladder calculi as rapidly as the usual latex Foley catheter. In the male, the catheter should be taped to the abdomen to prevent pressure at the penile scrotal junction and prevent development of urethrocutaneous fistula.

The catheter should be changed every four to six weeks, depending on how it drains. When changing a catheter in the male, it is of utmost importance to be as atraumatic as possible to prevent injury to the prostatic urethra. "Coudé" catheters, which have a curved tip, may be preferred for male patients over age 50. The catheter should be well lubricated, and the penis should be held in a stretch position and on a slight angle, pointing toward the abdomen. The catheter balloon should never be blown up unless there is a return of urine from the lumen of the Foley catheter. If this is in question, one should irrigate the catheter prior to inflating the balloon.

Another important aspect is the urinary drainage bag. The bag should not be allowed to overfill, thus preventing drainage and causing all the complications of an obstructed bladder.

MEDICATIONS

The treating physician may treat the patient with certain medications. Medications which are frequently used to maximize bladder function include the following:

- *Bethanechol Chloride (Urecholine).* Bethanechol chloride is used for treatment of urinary retention and underactive bladder tone. This medication stimulates parasympathetic activity. This activity increases the tone of the detrusor muscle, producing a contraction which may initiate voiding and thereby empty the bladder.
- *Oxybutynin Chloride (Ditropan).* Oxybutynin chloride has an antispasmodic effect on smooth muscle inhibiting the parasympathetic outflow of the autonomic nervous system, thereby minimizing incontinence in some patients.

When all else fails, diapers or adult protective briefs can be used to absorb urine, protect the skin, and prevent soiling the furniture.

CARE PLAN

You are now ready to formulate your own bladder training program care plan for Mrs. Smith.

Study the sample in Exhibit 8-1 and use it as a guide in designing your plan.

When you have finished, take the review test.

Exhibit 8-1 Sample Record of Urinary Bladder Training for One Week

DATE	Sunday		Monday		Tuesday		Wednesday		Thursday		Friday		Saturday	
TIME	In-take	Out-put	In-take	Out-put	In-take	Out-put	In-take	Out-put	In-take	Out-put	In-take	Out-put	In-take	Out-put
6 a.m.	240cc													
7 a.m.		360cc												
8 a.m.	480cc													
9 a.m.		300cc												
10 a.m.	480cc													
11 a.m.		330cc												
12 noon	480cc	I												
1 p.m.		120cc												
2 p.m.	480cc													
3 p.m.		300cc												
4 p.m.	240cc													
5 p.m.		210cc												
6 p.m.	240cc													
7 p.m.		180cc												
8 p.m.														
9 p.m.-6 a.m.														
Total ounces in 24 hours	2640cc	1800cc												

Under "Intake" record (in cc) all fluids taken by mouth.
Under "Output" record (in cc) all urine passed, Record "I" for incontinence or accidental urinating.

Source: Reprinted with permission of author from *Nurses Can Give and Teach Rehabilitation,* 2nd ed., by M.J. Allgire, Springer Publishing Company, © 1968.

CHAPTER REVIEW TEST

Please answer the following questions.

1. Indicate whether the following statements are true or false by placing "T" or "F" in the blank by each statement.
___a. Bladder training is always effective.
___b. Bladder training refers to the achievement of filling and emptying.
___c. Incontinence occurs when reflex emptying is uninhibited.
___d. Bladder training can begin any time and has little or no relation to the patient's medical condition.
___e. Cerebral control causes not only voluntary inhibition of voiding but voluntary initiation as well.

___f. Questioning the patient and family to determine the voiding history is not helpful in the bladder training program.

___g. Even though a bladder training program has been successful, occasional incontinence might occur.

2. Given a patient with a full bladder, indicate the sequence of events by numbering the statements in order of occurrence.

___a. Sensory impulses are sent to the brain.

___b. Motor impulses return to the bladder.

___c. Detrusor muscle fibers stretch, causing bladder wall tension.

___d. The detrusor muscle contracts.

___e. The bladder empties.

3. Circle the statements that apply to bladder training.

   a. The patient's bladder capacity must be determined.

   b. Nocturnal incontinence is almost inevitable and can rarely be corrected or diminished.

   c. Scheduling times for voiding is useless; one must be ready for each voiding as it happens.

   d. The patient's awareness of the need to void must be determined and appropriate aids devised and used.

   e. Hourly attempts at voiding are a good starting point, and progression from that is determined by bladder tolerance.

   f. Withholding or limiting evening fluids can decrease incontinence at night.

   g. Accurate intake-output records help to determine if large residual persists, which could cause infection from stagnation.

The correct answers are as follows:

1. *a. False.*
    b. True.
    c. True.
    d. False.
    e. True.
    f. False.
    g. True.
2. *a (2), b (3), c (1), d (4), e (5).*
3. *a, d, e, f.*

If you missed any of the answers, you should review the appropriate section of the chapter.

9 Pressure Sores: Development, Pathogenesis, Prevention, and Treatment

Robert D. Sine, M.D.

INTRODUCTION AND OBJECTIVES

Pressure sores can be a major problem for patients with various disabilities; therefore, the pathogenesis, prevention, and treatment of pressure sores are important components of the rehabilitation process. This chapter will help you to

1. understand the pathogenesis of pressure sores
2. recognize which patients are vulnerable to the development of pressure sores
3. recognize some basic techniques and devices that can be used in the prevention of pressure sore development
4. identify acceptable methods for treating pressure sores

PATHOGENESIS OF DECUBITI

There should be no mystery surrounding pressure sores. The mechanism of their formation is well known. Patients who get decubiti have normal skin. They sustain no more than normal pressures. The reason they get sores is that they do not move and the pressures are sustained for an abnormal length of time. The rest of us avoid sores because tissues starved of their blood supply become painful and we move off them (even in our sleep), allowing return of full blood supply. Patients who do not move sustain pressures greater than capillary pressures past a critical period of time beyond which the tissues die from lack of nutrients delivered by the blood. This death of tissues from lack of blood (infarction) will occur to tissues squeezed between weight-bearing bone and the underlying surface.

When infarction does occur, it takes place at all levels from skin to bone. We may not be aware of the damage that has been done until the skin ulcerates and the dead tissue sloughs. This may take days. The redness we see under points of pressure is a normal phenomenon known as hyperemia. The redness tells us that this is an area to be observed. However, it may disappear when the pressure is removed, even when the tissue is doomed to necrosis. We cannot take comfort, therefore, when an area returns to normal appearance.

The first defense against sores, then, is to restore movement, thus relieving areas from pressure before the critical time period has elapsed. The second defense is to attempt to minimize the pressure in vulnerable areas.

Check to be sure we are off to a good start. Answer the following statements True or False and then check your answers with those provided below.

____ *1. Despite medical advances, the mechanism of decubitus formation is shrouded in mystery.*
____ *2. The contour of bony prominences protects against decubitus formation.*
____ *3. The redness under a pressure point heralds impending ulceration.*
____ *4. Friction is a major cause of ulcer formation.*

All the above are false.
 1. The mechanisms are well known.
 2. Ulcer formation occurs under bony prominences.
 3. The redness only signals a vulnerable area.
 4. Friction does not play a role.

An ounce of decubitus prevention is worth many pounds of cure. Let's examine some preventive techniques.

IDENTIFYING THE PATIENT AT RISK

Remember that patients who get decubiti have normal skin and sustain normal pressures. The only abnormal variable is the length of time these pressures are applied. Such abnormal duration of pressure occurs when a patient cannot or will not move. The identification of such patients allows you to initiate preventive techniques.

Vulnerable populations include

1. patients with loss of sensation and mobility (paraplegia, multiple sclerosis)

2. patients with loss of sensation only (peripheral neuropathies)
3. patients with loss of mobility only (parkinsonism, Guillain-Barré, ALS)
4. patients with loss of consciousness (comatose, heavy sedation)
5. patients unwilling to move (postop, arthritis, psychosis)

The common denominator the patients share is the immobility which results in prolonged duration of pressure. *Be alert to immobile patients.* They are vulnerable to decubiti which may be prevented by your intervention (see Figure 9-1).

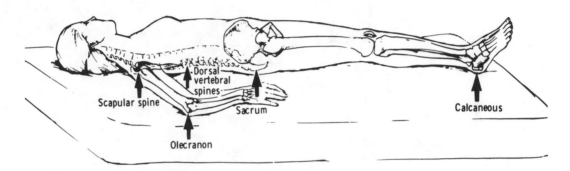

Supine Position

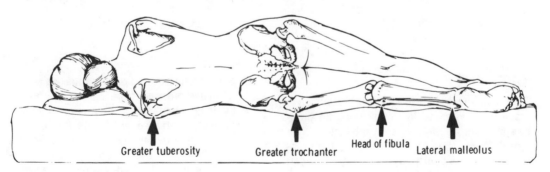

Sidelying

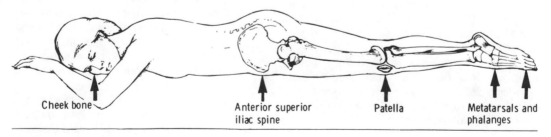

Prone Position

continues

Figure 9-1 These illustrations depict the areas under bony prominences vulnerable to break down. Study them so you can anticipate "trouble" spots.

Figure 9-1 continued

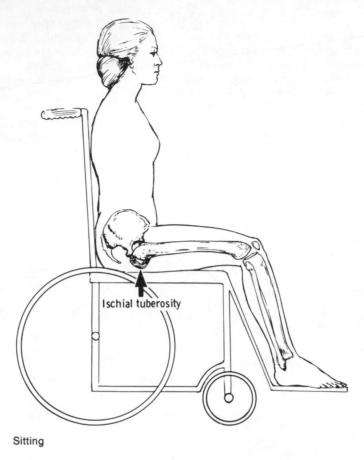

Ischial tuberosity

Sitting

MOVEMENT

The key concept in pressure sore prevention is to *restore movement*! We must live with pressures that are capable of sore production. The major defense, therefore, is to relieve the pressure before the critical time has elapsed. This can only be done by the patient moving off the area. You should encourage as high a degree of mobility as is feasible in an effort to keep durations of pressure as short as possible. Unfortunately, due to their physical condition, many patients move only with difficulty.

You must help patients weave continual movement back into their lives. When planning and expediting patient care activities to prevent prolonged pressure on any one area, you should keep these points in mind:

1. An ambulatory patient should stay out of bed and move around as much as his condition permits.

2. A wheelchair-bound patient must be taught to relieve pressure from ischial tuberosities by doing wheelchair push-ups and by shifting weight in bed, even at night. It is better to lose a little sleep than to develop a pressure sore. You may even wish to teach the patient to inspect hard-to-see pressure areas by using a mirror. The three illustrations in Figure 9-2 are examples of techniques for relieving pressure over ischial tuberosities.

3. To teach the patient to turn himself is your responsibility, but it is not enough. You must see that he does it. Therefore, you should plan individual positioning schedules for bed patients (such as the schedule in Table 9-1). *Remember:* (a) the overall goal is self-care—the patient should learn to do this himself; (b) this is only a sample schedule and can be varied.

4. When a reddened area is noticed and the patient must be repositioned, the reddened

area should be bridged. *Never* add more padding directly over the spot.

5. Setting the alarm clock at night is a good way to remind an alert patient to reposition himself. An alarm wristwatch is a good investment, since it can be readily used during the day as well.

6. If a patient is to be discharged whom you do not feel has learned to care for himself adequately and there is no visiting nurse service available, you should ask the physician to defer discharge until after this has been accomplished.

We know it must be up to individuals and treatment centers as to what methodology to use in handling patient care activities, but we hope these suggestions are helpful.

B. Shifting weight—relieves pressure in patients who can't do wheelchair push-ups

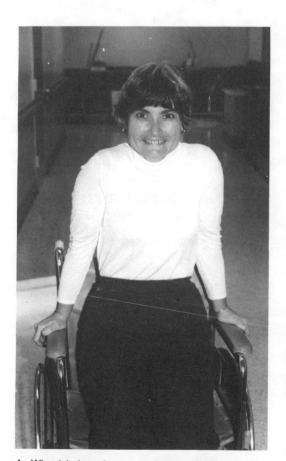

A. Wheelchair push-ups—maintain as long as possible

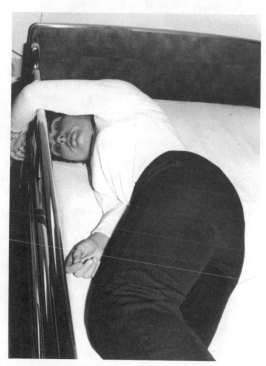

C. Using side rails

Figure 9-2 Techniques for Relieving Pressure over Ischial Tuberosities

TABLE 9-1 Sample Positioning Schedule for Patients on Complete Bed Rest

TURNING SCHEDULE

6:00 a.m.– 8:00 a.m.	left side lying	breakfast—feeds self; bowel program every other day
8:00 a.m.–10:00 a.m.	supine	bed bath, including range of motion
10:00 a.m.–11:00 a.m.	prone	back care; work up tolerance, now tolerates 40 min. (turn to right)
11:00 a.m.– 1:00 p.m.	right side lying	lunch—feeds self
1:00 p.m.– 3:00 p.m.	left side lying	visiting
3:00 p.m.– 4:00 p.m.	prone	back; range of motion; tolerates 40 min., try increase (turn to supine)
6:00 p.m.– 8:00 p.m.	right side lying	dinner—feeds self visiting
8:00 p.m.–11:00 p.m.	left side lying	evening care
11:00 p.m.– 3:00 a.m.	supine	sleeping
3:00 a.m.– 6:00 a.m.	right side lying	sleeping

Positions that can be used:
Supine
Left and right side lying
Prone (build up tolerance)

SURFACE MODIFICATIONS

Another less important technique for the prevention of pressure sores is to attempt to reduce pressure on vulnerable areas by modifying the surfaces in contact with these areas. This includes efforts to distribute pressure more evenly and efforts to redistribute pressure. See the illustrations in Figure 9-3.

Three important principles should be remembered when surface modifications are used:

1. They "buy time" in that they might delay the onset of tissue breakdown. Movement is still the key, however; if the patient does not move, breakdown will still occur, as there is still pressure. Do not be lulled into a false sense of security.
2. Sheets and dressings between the skin and the modification should be loose and soft or they could eliminate the effectiveness of the device (especially true in the case of alternating air mattresses). It might look messy, but do not yield to the impulse to pull that sheet tight and smooth!
3. Do not add padding or other material under a bony prominence to raise it up. No matter how soft the material is, it will increase the pressure!

There are a large number of devices available commercially that, when applied intelligently to address a patient's particular needs, can be helpful. None is a cure-all, and none will take the place of fundamental nursing care, which ensures movement.

TREATABLE CONDITIONS PREDISPOSING TO DECUBITI

Any condition that reduces delivery of nutrients to the cell predisposes to decubiti development by reducing the time during which a given pressure can result in necrosis. Such conditions include the following:

1. *Edema.* It is not usually appreciated how seriously edema interferes with the delivery of all nutrients. The presence of interstitial fluid increases the distance from capillary to cell. The rate of diffusion of nutrients is reduced by the square root of that distance. Thus, local edema which doubles the capillary-to-cell distance decreases the supply of nutrients to one-quarter of what it would otherwise be. Even a minor amount of local edema can be a very important negative factor. (See Figure 9-4.) "Dependent

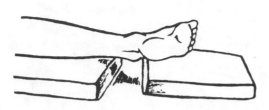

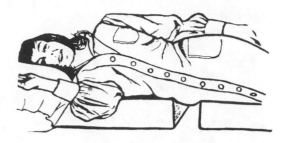

A. Foam padding bridging an ankle. Foam padding has many uses, including bridging (as shown here) and as seat cushions or back supports.

B. Foam padding bridging of greater tuberosity. Another way to use foam padding for bridging.

C. Pillows are a must. (Note: Any pillow under the head should be small and support only the head.)

D. Doughnuts and rings. *Never* use doughnuts for bridging, as they could increase edema.

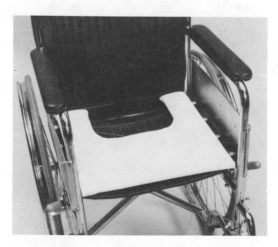

E. Seat boards. These can be added to wheelchairs and are removable, making such wheelchairs easier to handle than those with a solid seat.

F. Water beds. Inexpensive water beds can be made by filling an air mattress one-third full of water. Water beds are good up to a point. Some patients get disoriented and some get motion sickness; others tolerate them well. They do tend to limit a patient's overall mobility by making bed mobility and transfers more difficult. Avoid the use of pins and sharp objects—keep dry!

continues

Figure 9-3 Devices for Reducing Pressure

Figure 9-3 continued

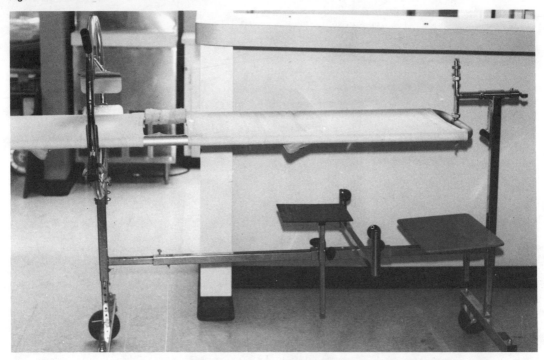

G. Turning frames. These are very valuable in special cases (e.g., with comatose patients). They should be discarded as early as possible, however, in favor of remobilization.

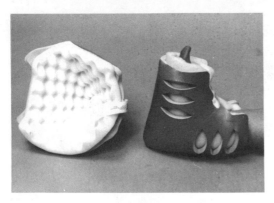

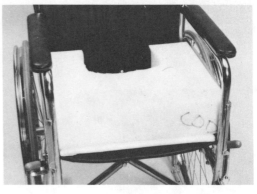

H. Spenko Stryker boot. The Spenko Stryker boot is the best boot we know for preventing pressure on heels and lateral maleoli. It will also help keep foot aligned at a 90° angle.

I. Horseshoe-shaped cushions. These are most effective when used over a seat board for reducing ischial tuberosity pressures.

◄ J. Air cushion. This air cushion by ROHO appears to distribute pressure well, though at first it seems "wobbly" to the patient.

edema" is commonly seen in immobile patients as collections of edema in the very areas most susceptible to decubiti (e.g., the sacral area). In such cases, systemic treatment for edema can be attempted and localized treatment can be used even should they require intermittent increases in pressure (massage, pneumatic massage boot, sitting).

2. *Negative Nitrogen Balance*. This can occur with sepsis, surgery, cancer, or simple inattention to nutrition. A high protein diet is often helpful, particularly in the early stages of paraplegia.

3. *Anemia*. This condition decreases oxygen delivery. It is easily diagnosed and usually responsive to treatment.

HEALING

Healing is a natural process which occurs without any treatment and will close large wounds given time and absence of complications. Your task is to have patience and avoid complications. No treatment accelerates the process. Overzealous treatment can slow it, however. There are myriad treatments that are hotly defended because they "work." It is the body that "works." Any treatment should simply provide it with a suitable environment.

Decubiti, once established, are no different from any other wounds. Wound healing follows the same sequences regardless of what produced them. Healing is a complex process. Cells called fibroblasts migrate into the area. Simultaneously a chain of about 15 catalyzed chemical reactions change an exudate from ground substance into collagen. Eventually this produces a highly vascular tissue commonly seen at the bottom of wounds known as granulation tissue. This tissue eventually differentiates into layers of normal tissue while the skin epithelializes to cover the wound. Such an involved and delicate process is vulnerable to disruption by chemical and physical agents. These may include infection or treatments such as strong disinfectants, debriding agents, mechanical cleansings and debridements, and coverings that might increase internal pressures. The least treatment which maintains a clean wound is the best. My favorite is sucrose sprinkled into the wound until super-saturated (some remains undissolved). The highly osmotic solution keeps down bacterial growth and poses little threat to the healing process. One or two gauze pad dressings will protect the wound and soak up sloughed tissues and exudate.

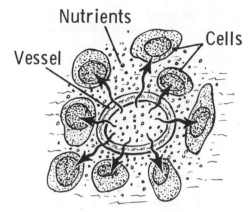

Normal

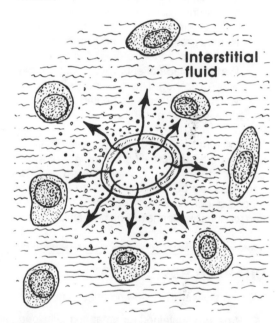

Edematous Tissue: Perfusion of nutrients decreased by the square of the increase in distance from capillary to cell.

Figure 9-4 Comparison of Normal and Edematous Tissue

Here are some dos and don'ts:

1. Attend to the above sections on movement and surface modifications. They still apply during the healing phase.
2. Treat "treatable conditions."
3. Measure weekly—either by a tracing or volumetric measurement. It will reward you by showing progress and give you confidence and much-needed patience.
4. Watch for purulence (yellow or green—not white; white is simply necrotic tissue), edema, undermining, etc.

5. Cleanse gently as needed. Light, usually blunt, debridement may be needed on occasion.
6. Do not introduce any treatment which might irritate tissues and disrupt healing.
7. Do not treat with dressings which will increase pressures; offenders are packings, wads of wet dressings, and foam directly over the wound, which compresses. We have some of the same concern regarding occlusive dressings, which may have a place when "shear" forces need to be addressed but not in the case of most decubiti.
8. Do not interfere with the mobilization program. This may mean the patient may sit on the wound—so long as the precautions in the section on movement are observed. Normal pressures for normal durations may actually be beneficial in reducing edema. We have had patients who would not heal when restricted to prone positions but whose boggy wounds healed dramatically once they were mobilized.

Occasionally the skin heals faster than the underlying tissue, creating the danger of a sore being "roofed over." An apparently small decubitus will be found to be quite large when probed under the skin. An opening for drainage and reasonable cleansing can be maintained with loose packing using narrow iodoform gauze stripping. The underlying tissue will then fill in.

Another problem encountered is an underlying osteomyelitis. Osteomyelitis is not uncommon, as necrosis usually dissects to the bone. It should be suspected whenever a decubitus refuses to heal. It can be diagnosed easily by x-ray, and when treated, the decubiti will begin to heal over it. Osteomyelitis must be thought of, however, as there is often no other outward sign.

Surgery and/or grafting is most firmly indicated if the area seems in such poor condition that, without a procedure, future ulcerations are inevitable. Procedures might also be considered if they promise a shorter healing period without interfering with mobilization.

Decubiti theoretically should not appear if the care is good, but will occasionally appear even with the best of intentions and care. They should be the object of concern, but not despair. They will heal if not interfered with by improper treatment or not neglected. The tissues will fill in and re-epithelialize in all but very large ulcers. A high protein diet will aid this process. We doubt that any of the numerous remedies that are topically applied affect the healing process, despite the claims of their proponents.

Remember that the job is not done until the patient can take care of himself. Only then can he be assured of freedom from sores after discharge.

CHAPTER REVIEW TEST

Try to answer the following questions.

1. Pressure sustained for an abnormally long duration is the factor leading to pressure sore development. True or false?
2. A decubitus ulcer—being of different origin than a wound of similar appearance—must be handled in a unique fashion. True or false?
3. Pressure sores do not necessarily form in bed. True or false?
4. Patients most prone to the development of pressure sores are those who do not perceive pain and those who cannot move when pain is perceived. True or false?
5. The less the degree of pressure, the longer tissue can withstand it without infarction. True or false?
6. The precautions applying to decubitus prevention also are applicable to healing. True or false?
7. Any condition that slows or decreases the delivery of nutrients to the tissue predisposes toward formation and interferes with healing of decubiti. True or false?
8. The prevention of pressure sores is an easy task. True or false?
9. To cure a pressure sore is more difficult than to prevent one. True or false?
10. Relief of pressure by movement soon enough to prevent the development of pressure sores is the best way we know to prevent them. True or false?
11. It is dangerous to develop a sense of security through the use of surface modification. True or false?
12. Pressure sore prevention must be the concern of all who work with chronically ill patients, and especially the alert patient himself. True or false?

13. Decubiti are skin ulcers, and good skin care will prevent them. True or false?
14. Antibiotics and debridement are required for decubiti healing. True or false?
15. The seriousness of decubiti requires that they take priority over other rehabilitation efforts, which should be stopped. True or false?
16. Decubiti are not likely to heal without intensive treatment—the more intensive, the faster the healing. True or false?

The answers are as follows:

1. True	9. True
2. False	10. True
3. True	11. True
4. True	12. True
5. True	13. False
6. True	14. False
7. True	15. False
8. False	16. False

Results: If you got 100%, the race is won. A score above 80 percent is very good; 0–80 percent indicates you should review the chapter.

SUGGESTED READINGS

Colorado Public Health Service. *Elementary Rehabilitation Nursing Care*. Public Health Service Publication no. 1436. Washington, D.C.: GPO, 1966.

Downey, John A. and Robert C. Darling. *Physiological Basis of Rehabilitation Medicine*. Philadelphia: Saunders, 1971.

Kosiak, M. "Etiology and Pathology of Ischemic Ulcers." *Arch Phys Med & Rehabil* 42 (1969).

Krusen, Frank H., Frederick J. Kottke, and Paul M. Ellwood.

Handbook of Physical Medicine and Rehabilitation. 2d ed. Philadelphia: Saunders, 1971.

Ma, Dong-Myung, D.S. Chu, and S. Davis. "Pressure Relief Under The Ischial Tuberosities." *Arch Phys Med & Rehabil* (July 1976).

Rossman, Isadore. *Clinical Geriatrics*. Philadelphia: Lippincott, 1972.

Stryker, Ruth. *Rehabilitative Aspects of Acute and Chronic Nursing Care*. Philadelphia: Saunders, 1972.

10 Identification and Management of Bowel Problems

Robert D. Sine, M.D.

INTRODUCTION AND OBJECTIVES

The identification and management of bowel problems are very important aspects of the management of rehabilitation patients. Here we attempt to give insight into the nature of the problem and its alleviation and to offer helpful suggestions pertaining to the establishment of bowel control. Once you have completed this chapter you should be able to

1. differentiate between normal and abnormal bowel habits
2. identify causes for the interruption of normal bowel habits
3. recognize proper management procedures to handle specific bowel problems pertaining to constipation, diarrhea, and the neurogenic bowel
4. recognize the role that diet, fluids, physical activity, and timing play in habit training for bowel control
5. identify a procedure that could be followed when planning a particular patient's bowel training program

PATHOPHYSIOLOGY

The two conditions that confront us most commonly are diarrhea and constipation. Both are produced by stool spending an abnormal duration in the colon. The ability of the colon to extract water from the stool accounts for the change from the watery stool entering it to the well-formed stool found in the rectum.

Diarrhea occurs when an irritable bowel with increased peristalsis hurries the stool, shortening the time available for water resorption. The result-

ing stools are frequent and watery. Any irritating agent can initiate the process. Most commonly that agent is infectious, but toxic agents, especially drug side effects, are prevalent in hospital populations.

Decreasing peristalsis has the opposite effect, prolonging the duration of the stool within the colon and causing excess water extraction. Infrequent, hard stools (constipation) result. The process tends to perpetuate itself: The stool is hard to pass and slows the passage of that behind it, which in turn hardens. Stool continues to harden and accumulate until the condition is relieved.

PROPHYLAXIS

Among the many causes of constipation, probably the most prevalent in a hospital population is inactivity, especially among bed rest patients. Inadequate dietary bulk and/or water intake are other very common offenders in the general population. Prophylaxis requires particular attention to these three factors. In patients who cannot be taken off bed rest or given adequate dietary bulk, stool softeners and bulk producers (Metamucil) can be given prophylactically.

EVALUATION

Constipation is a condition that progresses in severity and may vary in form. It becomes important to be able to recognize the actual condition of the bowel, as your treatment will be based on this assessment.

The history will always include infrequent stools. This is not a symptom of pathology by itself, however, and alone it may not require treatment. If, however, stool is accumulating, additional symptoms will appear. The patient will report fullness, distension, cramps aggravated by eating, anorexia, and malaise. Palpation of the abdomen will show tenderness in the left lower quadrant in early cases. As the condition progresses, the tenderness becomes more diffuse over the lower abdomen. The finger pressed forcefully into the abdomen encounters an unmistakable "doughy" feeling. It may leave an impression, which can feel as if it were made in clay. In severe cases, the temperature and white count may be elevated.

If the elevated temperature and white count are not connected with the distension, a search for "more important" pathology may ensue. The constipation can be overlooked, with the result that the situation deteriorates. The most frequent cause of confusion in making an early, correct diagnosis, particularly in the geriatric group, is when watery stools leak around an impaction, creating a condition which simulates diarrhea. This calls for disimpaction and treatment of the constipation. Treating for diarrhea can, of course, aggravate the condition a great deal. You can also be led astray by an evacuation that discharges only a small portion of a large accumulation of feces.

None of these errors will occur if you properly evaluate. Include palpation of the abdomen and digital examination in your assessment.

TREATMENT

We feel that the "laxative of choice" usually turns out to be whatever "worked" last and that this is a hit or miss method of treating a very troublesome and potentially chronic problem. Any therapy should begin with an evaluation of the severity of the condition, and constipation is no exception. Overtreatment is worse yet, as incontinence or diarrhea can result, which is then itself overtreated. The patient can be chronically whipsawed between constipation and diarrhea.

Evaluation for treatment can be made by estimating the degree of accumulation of colonic contents (see Figure 10-1). The top three boxes represent stages of progressive accumulation. You begin by determining within which group your patient falls, using the findings mentioned. The next tier of boxes suggests treatments appropriate for the conditions. Many of the common laxatives work by drawing large amounts of water into the colon, which increases the volume within it and causes reflex peristalsis (Metamucil, MOM). They can be used on a sluggish, nondistended colon. Obviously this is not a reasonable approach (although it might work) in the case of an already distended colon. Drugs that act primarily on the colon's neural plexus without causing irritation of the wall—senna (Senacott) and bisocodyl (Dulcolax)—are indicated. If the primary therapy is not effective, you should not hesitate to move to re-evaluation (the third tier of boxes) and further therapy. Again, the choice of enema, if indicated, should be appropriate to the findings on evaluation.

No drug, oral or rectal, should be repeated without digital examination. If impaction is present, the use of laxative forces the colon to attempt to move feces with nowhere to go. Cramps result. The longer the exam is avoided, the harder the impaction and the larger the accumulation. Once disimpaction is accomplished, enemas can be used freely and are effective. Oil is helpful when stool is hard, and high enemas might be required when accumulations are large.

Finally, each episode should call attention to the importance of prophylaxis.

NEUROGENIC BOWEL

The neurogenic bowel is a special case in bowel management. Peristalsis, which is retained in the spinal cord patient, is under autonomic nervous system control. It is generally sluggish, however, so the patient is vulnerable to constipation. Additionally, he does not feel the rectum fill and cannot "answer the call" by using the commode at the appropriate time, exerting control of his anal sphincters, or using his abdominal muscles to "bear down." Incontinence might be a problem as well. This symptom alone can be enough of a social nemesis to produce a shut-in.

While bowel management is often called "bowel training," it is well to remember the common clinical warning, "You don't train the bowel—it trains you." In practical terms, this means any "routine" must be the bowel's routine—not yours. If you are flexible, you can bend it enough to fit into a daily schedule, but attempts to overregulate could result in the spinal cord patient's dread—incontinence at work or play.

The remarks in the previous section about constipation prophylaxis should be reviewed and are even more important in the face of a neurogenic bowel. We routinely add stool softeners, but these should be discontinued if stools become watery.

Attempts to initiate evacuation should follow a hot meal with tea or coffee by about one-half hour. The patient should be comfortably seated on a commode. A large glycerin suppository can be used to initiate reflex evacuation. If this is not successful, digital massage and distension of the

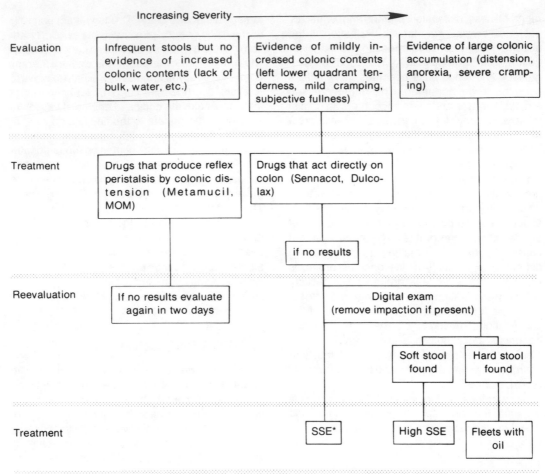

Increasing Severity ───────────────►

Evaluation	Infrequent stools but no evidence of increased colonic contents (lack of bulk, water, etc.)	Evidence of mildly increased colonic contents (left lower quadrant tenderness, mild cramping, subjective fullness)	Evidence of large colonic accumulation (distension, anorexia, severe cramping)
Treatment	Drugs that produce reflex peristalsis by colonic distension (Metamucil, MOM)	Drugs that act directly on colon (Sennacot, Dulcolax)	
		if no results	
Reevaluation	If no results evaluate again in two days	Digital exam (remove impaction if present)	
			Soft stool found / Hard stool found
Treatment		SSE*	High SSE / Fleets with oil

Prophylaxis: Maintain bulk and water intake. Initiate stool softener until texture satisfactory. Mobilize if possible—use commode. Establish routine for defecation—avoid bed pan.

* Soap suds enema

Figure 10-1 Management of Constipation

anal sphincter can be attempted—by the patient, if at all possible. If there is still no evacuation, attempts should be dropped until the following day. Medication, chosen according to the criteria in the preceding section, can be used eight hours before the next attempt. The second day, the procedure is repeated. A Dulcolax suppository can be added.

Enemas are to be avoided if at all possible!

Impactions are common, and huge accumulations of stool can occur painlessly. Digital exam should follow any suspicion of a problem. Keeping a good record can be crucial.

SUMMARY

To initiate an evacuation, provide or do the following:

1. a hot meal with tea or coffee
2. one-half hour later, comfortable seating on commode
3. if no evacuation, large glycerin suppository
4. if no evacuation, massage of anal sphincter
5. if no evacuation, medication eight hours prior to next attempt
6. repetition of steps 1 through 4
7. if no results, Dulcolax suppository

Maintenance activities include the following:

1. maintaining a soft stool (adequate bulk, water, and stool softeners)
2. checking frequently for impaction
3. checking abdomen frequently for stool accumulation
4. avoiding enemas
5. avoiding overtreating—a state of mild con-

stipation is preferable to episodes of incontinence

A spinal cord patient will not die of an unmanaged bowel. The complications of constipation and incontinence, however, can result in episodic illness and paralyzing social fears. Social and vocational horizons can constrict to within the tight radius of the commode, all for want of personnel with some skill and lots of patience.

CHAPTER REVIEW TEST

Now let's see how much you have learned. Please try to answer the following questions.

1. A hyperactive colon
   a. can lead to constipation.
   b. prolongs the duration stool spends within the colon.
   c. results in hard, dry stools.
   d. may be a drug side effect.
   e. All the above.
2. Prophylaxis in bowel management does not include
   a. maintaining physical activity.
   b. maintaining water intake.
   c. daily use of a gentle laxative.
   d. maintaining dietary bulk.
3. Symptoms of constipation do not include
   a. myalgia.
   b. cramps.
   c. anorexia.
   d. elevated temperature and white count.
   e. distension.
4. In a patient with constipation, cramping, and tenderness, senna has not resulted in evacuation. The next step is
   a. a high soap suds enema.
   b. Metamucil.
   c. a digital exam.
   d. a Fleet enema with oil.
5. The patient with neurogenic bowel retains
   a. anal sphincter control.
   b. peristalsis.
   c. the sensation of rectal filling.
   d. the ability to "bear down."
6. In managing the neurogenic bowel, there is no need to
   a. observe frequently for distension.
   b. produce an evacuation every second day by enema.
   c. check digitally if there is suspicion of impaction.
   d. maintain a soft stool, using stool softener if necessary.
   e. avoid incontinence, allowing mild constipation if necessary.

The answers are as follows:
1. d
2. c
3. a
4. c
5. b
6. b

If you missed any of the answers, you should review the appropriate sections of this chapter.

Rehabilitation Management

11 Rehabilitation: A Nurse's Viewpoint

Susan Ellison Dominguez, R.N.

INTRODUCTION AND OBJECTIVES

The purpose of this chapter is to help the reader answer these questions:

1. What is rehabilitation nursing?
2. What makes it different from traditional or bedside nursing?
3. How does one function as a rehabilitation nurse?

To begin with, rehabilitation (or rehab) nursing is characterized by a different attitude than that of traditional nursing. This attitude must permeate every task—even opening a milk carton on a breakfast tray—and is reflected in these two questions:

1. What can I do for my patients?
2. What can I help my patients learn to do for themselves?

The overall goal of this chapter is to help each nurse understand the fundamental difference between the two questions above and to respond as a rehab nurse should respond to the functions implicit in the second question.

The specific objectives of this chapter are to

1. share with you my impressions, thoughts, and ideas of rehab nursing
2. explain the attitude necessary for rehab nursing
3. define the role of the rehab nurse as coordinator, planner, patient ally, coach, and teacher
4. explain the relationships of atmosphere and staff attitude to rehab nursing
5. convince you and your doctors of the value of rehab nursing and encourage you to use the basic rehabilitation techniques presented in this book

Do you need a specialized rehab unit to make rehab nursing techniques available to your patients? While the experiences I have had on an actual rehab unit permeate my comments here, my answer is no. If a rehab nurse is present, all aspects of rehab nursing can be made available on general nursing units, in nursing homes, and in patients' homes. Rehab nurses utilize all the resources at their disposal.

Many of the concepts presented in this book can be utilized by you to prevent the deterioration of routine surgical or medical patients. You may even be able to decrease the length of their stay by preventing the development of overdependence and inactivity.

IMPRESSIONS

When I first made the switch from medical-surgical nursing to rehab nursing, I was not sure that I was emotionally ready to handle the devastation left by stroke and brain injury. Here in my care were crippled bodies, some without voices to call for help, some whose voices repeated the same words over and over. Only weeks before, many of these people were walking, talking, contributing members of their families and occupations. Now many of them could not control their bowels or bladders, could not feed themselves, and were totally dependent on those who would care for them. As a nurse, death had often seemed to me a merciful end to the suffering of many of my patients. Now, here on rehab, death was not threatening, but life with disability was a stark reality.

The philosophy of rehab nursing is based upon possibilities and achievement, not upon limitations and inabilities. Rehab nursing involves building positive goals from the deficit of negative physical impairments. It is helping the patient develop a mental attitude of "I will try" and "I can" rather than "I can't." It is helping patients learn to do for themselves. It is one of the most positive and rewarding fields of nursing.

ROLES AND ATTRIBUTES

All nurses are taught early to speak softly and wipe each fevered brow. A rehab nurse speaks more like a football coach and has the patient wipe his own brow. Let me add, however, that sincere, wholehearted praise is given to patients as they try to do what you tell them. Each improvement is celebrated and each newly learned skill is a source of pride. When a stroke patient urinates on the commode after several days of unsuccessful bladder training, our joy and pride in that accomplishment is easily communicated. I would challenge each of you to experience this pride in your patients as they gain independence and begin to function for themselves.

Rehab nurses are very special people. They must develop attributes and skills beyond those required in traditional bedside nursing.

A good rehab nurse

1. has a strong basic nursing knowledge
2. is compassionate and patient
3. is fearless
4. thinks positively
5. plans well
6. is a good coordinator
7. is an effective teacher
8. is the patient's ally

Knowledge

The rehab nurse needs a strong basic nursing knowledge of varied disease processes and their treatment and must also master the techniques of rehabilitation, many of which are foreign to bedside nursing care. All of these techniques can be found in the chapters of this book.

Patience

The rehab nurse must have unlimited compassion and patience. If you visibly lose control for even a moment, your effectiveness can be lost and the patient's progress hampered.

Fearlessness

Mobilization is one of the first goals in rehab nursing. It should become one of your primary goals as soon as your patient is medically stable or has the doctor's approval to get out of bed.

One of the hindrances to mobilizing a stroke patient, a postoperative hip fracture patient, or a craniotomy patient is your own fear. You are afraid that the patient will fall or suddenly become much worse. You may also have become accustomed to having an orderly lift these patients out of bed and are afraid you cannot handle it. These are valid fears. They show that you have your patient's best interests at heart. Those of us who work in rehabilitation experience the same fears; however, by utilizing the techniques of progressive mobilization and transfer, we are able to safely and effectively begin getting our patients out of bed on the first day.

You can do the same thing and know the thrill of success as your patient advances from being out of bed for 10 minutes, three times a day, to staying out 2 to 3 hours at a time. You'll also experience a feeling of pride when the same patient, who previously needed the assistance of two nurses, is able to transfer to a wheelchair with little assistance.

If you have access to physical therapists where you work, get to know them. They are professionals with knowledge that can help you attain many of the goals you have set for your patients. They can help with ideas about transfers and positioning of patients and can help lessen your fears by their special training.

Positive Thinker

The rehab nurse must be an eternal optimist. When you receive a patient who has an n/g tube and Foley catheter, who is incontinent of stool, and who can only speak incoherently, you must be able to honestly see the possibilities of rehabilitation. When the staff members throw up their hands because the patient is incontinent several times a day, you must believe in the efficacy of bladder training and communicate your optimism to the staff.

Planner

Hand in hand with this optimism must go the ability to assess the patient's primary and long-term needs and to begin a plan of care from your first contact with the patient.

A thorough nursing history upon admission will provide a good basis for an effective nursing care plan. The nurse must know how severely affected the patient is. Is the patient able to use the call bell, incontinent, able to turn in bed, able to tolerate being out of bed in the chair, etc.? All this information will form the basis for planning the patient's program of care. Probably more so in rehabilitation than other fields, nurses must set goals for their patients in the first days. For example, if on admission the patient is incontinent of urine, bladder training must be instituted as soon as possible. Each subsequent shift will follow this plan, and hopefully bladder control will be one of the patient's first accomplishments.

Discharge planning must be a consideration from the first day as well. If the patient was living in a nursing home, he may not need exactly the same training as one who lives alone. All factors of the patient's life need to be considered.

Coordinator

Rehabilitation is a team approach to patients' needs. The rehab nurse must work closely with all therapy departments to effect a schedule suitable for the individual patient's activity tolerance level, bowel and bladder needs, and any special medical care needs. The most important basic ingredient for this teamwork is genuine respect for the knowledge and abilities of the other team members—the occupational therapist, physical therapist, doctor, speech therapist, and social worker.

Communication between therapy departments and nursing is very important. Often a quick morning meeting with a representative from each department will prevent misunderstandings and allow all those involved to get up-to-date on each patient's condition. The rehab nurse must never allow personal differences to interfere with the team effort and must develop an attitude of understanding and flexibility. The rehab nurse is constantly reinforcing the work of all the other team members and the quality of that reinforcement will greatly influence the length of the patient's stay.

Teacher

Rehab nurses must also develop effective teaching skills, for they are often the primary instructors of other nursing team members, as well as patients and their families. Skills that are second nature to the rehab nurse must be taught over and over until they become second nature to the staff. Also, techniques that patients are first exposed to in therapy settings (such as correct transfers and self-feeding) must be understood by the nurse and reinforced to the patient on the unit. If the patient is fed a meal after the occupational therapist has taught self-feeding skills, then much hard work is neutralized and discouragement and bad feelings may develop on the therapist's part. The rehab nurse, by reinforcement, can decrease the length of the patient's stay simply because of carry-over from therapy class to daily living activities.

Patient-Family Ally

In a rehabilitation unit, patients interact with various allied health professionals, all working together toward a common goal. The nurse must be the patient's ally. Communicating to the patient by conversation or by warm and gentle touching that he will be protected and encouraged and helped to meet physical and emotional needs is imperative.

The nurse must be the family's ally as well. Often family members are confused and afraid for their loved one, who has recently been in a life-threatening condition. They need to be reassured again and again that the loved one is being well cared for, that the medical condition is being closely supervised, and that stress will be within tolerable limits. Families not having easy access to the physician place their confidence in the nurse. They must feel the rehab team can be trusted. Here it may be advisable to mention that each family complaint should be given careful consideration and treated respectfully, regardless of the validity. In this way, families may learn that even though our methods may surprise them, our goals and our concern for the patient are the same as theirs.

ATMOSPHERE

In order for rehab nurses to function effectively, they must appreciate the fact that the atmosphere created by the staff's attitude has an effect on patients, their families, and other members of the rehab team. A positive atmosphere engendered by the *esprit de corps* evident on a good rehab unit facilitates important socialization activities among patients.

You might utilize the principles of rehab nursing on an acute care floor, in a nursing home, or in a visiting nurse's role; however, if you were to visit a rehab unit, you would find immediately that the atmosphere is different. Very few patients are in bed during the day. Most of them are rolling about the halls in wheelchairs. The mood is generally cheerful and warm, almost like a family. This atmosphere is present on admission.

When patients first come to a rehab unit, they are greeted by a nurse who assesses their disability—bowel and bladder incontinence, loss of movement of an arm or leg, or inability to turn over in bed. In doing this assessment, a blueprint of care and teaching can be formulated. Optimism and hope are communicated that the patient will soon be learning to overcome or compensate for all of these problems.

You can set the same atmosphere as you learn the techniques in this book and decide to use them with your patients.

ATTITUDE

The next difference you would note on a rehab unit is the attitude of both the staff and the patients. A patient was recently overheard telling a visitor who offered to push his wheelchair up the hall, "No thank you. I'm supposed to do this myself. It's strengthening my arms."

The attitude of rehabilitation is very positive and optimistic, while confronting realistically a patient's limitations. The patient must learn to think "I can" and "I will try" rather than "I can't."

This may seem to be a trivial point, but in fact a patient's mental attitude can determine his success or failure. You can do much to mold this attitude, but your encouragement must be consistent with your optimism based upon reality.

SOCIALIZATION

This is an area which we take for granted on a rehabilitation unit. Our patients eat all of their meals in a main dining room. They are dressed daily in street clothes. They sit in the halls together in wheelchairs, some chatting, some reading newspapers, and all hearing soft radio music in the background. They have a beauty parlor available to them twice a week. More than once I've assisted in taking an incontinent and confused patient into the beauty shop for a wash and set; the stimulation of normal daily activities contributes to the cure.

You will frequently see elderly patients, who were alert patients preoperatively, become confused and disoriented after surgery. The "drugs" we use to bring them around are socialization and mobilization.

You may be able to use some of our approaches on a limited basis: dressing patients for therapy, grouping their meals together in one room, and even having small groups of patients gathered in the hall to chat or just to listen.

Socialization activities are an important adjunct to recovery from stroke or spinal cord injury, because these patients usually tend to have lowered self-esteem. Also, isolation from others only prolongs and encourages negative feelings.

CONCLUSION

Once you have become convinced of the validity of rehabilitation concepts, don't keep it to yourself. The doctors of many of your patients will be grateful for a suggestion that will accelerate their patient's recovery.

If you see that your hospital does not have the facilities for maximum rehabilitation of a patient who has had a stroke or other brain injury, don't drop the ball. Inquire about rehab units in your area and give this information to your patient's doctor and family. There are many patients in nursing homes today who could have gone back to their homes and families if they had spent time in a comprehensive rehabilitation program.

Along with learning the information in this book goes a responsibility to use it every day on your unit. The return for your efforts will be the pride you see in your patients' faces as they are able to feed themselves, get in and out of bed, and control their bladders.

All of the foregoing is only one rehab nurse's viewpoint, but I believe the ideas espoused in this chapter are good ones. They work where I work; they can work where you work.

12 Progressive Mobilization

Georgianna Burbidge Wilson, M.Ed., P.T.

INTRODUCTION AND OBJECTIVES

You may be wondering what *Progressive Mobilization* is. In completing this chapter, you will learn techniques for the gradual, step-by-step development of a patient's ability to move around. The activities discussed start with the patient lying in bed and end with the patient up and walking.

Due to the amount of material in this chapter, we have divided it into four sections. These sections are interrelated and arranged sequentially. You may use any one section independently, but to make effective use of the Progressive Mobilization Program, you must understand the relationships among the sections. The importance of these relationships is demonstrated through the use of a "staircase" model for Progressive Mobilization. You will learn that if you decide to use the techniques in the last section with a patient, the steps in the preceding sections must have been completed. You will also note that these "steps" are small ones. Techniques of basic rehabilitation depend on the tasks being presented in small increments of increased difficulty so that adequate performance in the preceding task insures success in the new one.[1] Thus the staircase model—one successful step leads to the next.

The intent in writing and selecting the material for this chapter is to provide information necessary to rehabilitate your patient. It does not mean that other methods cannot be used along with the techniques recorded here. Note also that some information, e.g., normal gait, only brings out points pertinent to the activities and are not intended to be comprehensive discussions of the subject. The material is basic material and will produce the desired effect if followed carefully.

We expect that you will study this chapter and refer to it as you treat patients. Following this method, you should be able to

1. recognize the "Independent Staircase"
2. observe and monitor for cardiac symptoms (also see Chapter 7 for information about geriatric patients)
3. progress the patient through a sitting tolerance program
4. protect yourself while helping the patient use good body mechanics
5. identify the major functional limitations usually seen in common disability syndromes
6. perform proper bed positioning
7. perform range of motion exercises
8. move a patient through the staircase activities of moving up, sideways, and rolling over in bed
9. help a patient through pregait training, sitting activities, and transfers
10. perform stand-ups exercises
11. perform step-ups exercises on stairs
12. perform gait training
13. analyze the need for assistive devices for gait and choose ones that are appropriate

WHAT IS PROGRESSIVE MOBILIZATION?

Have you ever been in bed with the flu for a few days or a week? Have you ever climbed four flights of stairs after a considerable period of inactivity?

What did you feel like when you got out of bed? What did you feel like after climbing the stairs?

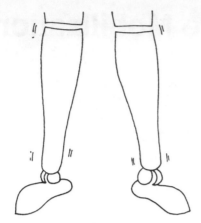

Legs weak and wobbly?

Head dizzy?

Feeling of great fatigue after just a little exercise?

If you answered yes to the first three questions, you have experienced some of the undesirable effects of bed rest or inactivity.

Note that weakness, dizziness, and fatigue are among the many negative effects of bed rest. Others include contractures, pneumonia, thrombophlebitis, and pressure sores.

How can you prevent these effects from occurring? Try using the tools of Progressive Mobilization.

Progressive Mobilization is a program composed of specific activities to mobilize patients and to help them gain independence. Each activity is geared to fit the individual needs and abilities of the patient. During these activities the patients are taught to move around on their own, with as little assistance from you as possible. The activities are designed to build on one another, forming a staircase. Each step is necessary for the next step to be accomplished. For example, if a patient does not have the mobility or strength to roll over in bed alone, he will not have the mobility or strength to sit up alone. If he cannot sit up alone, he will not be able to stand up alone. At the top of this staircase complete or partial independence occurs. Review the Independent Staircase shown below, and note carefully each step. Each of these steps will be taught to you in detail in the remainder of this chapter.

As the steps in Progressive Mobilization build on one another to form a staircase, so does bed rest and/or inactivity. The difference in the two staircases is that the inactivity staircase is a downward one, which leads to dependence rather than independence. The longer the patient stays in bed or remains inactive, the less muscle strength he has, and the less he can perform activities alone. The trick to Progressive Mobilization is to get the patient out of bed and keep him out of bed. Review the Dependent Staircase shown below. Note each step. This staircase is the one that needs to be avoided.

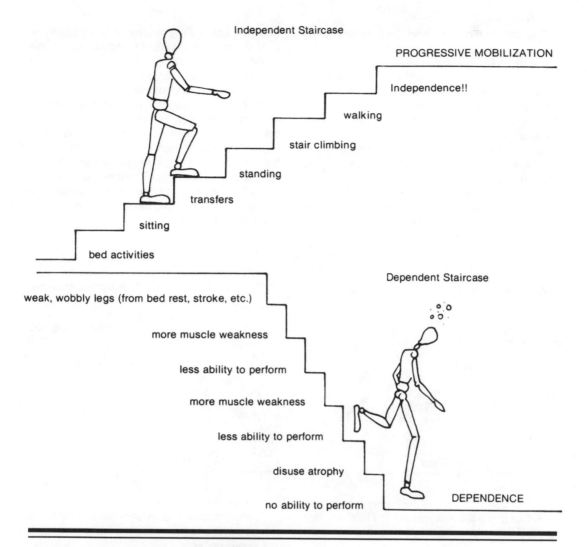

Independent Staircase

PROGRESSIVE MOBILIZATION

Independence!!

walking

stair climbing

standing

transfers

sitting

bed activities

Dependent Staircase

weak, wobbly legs (from bed rest, stroke, etc.)

more muscle weakness

less ability to perform

more muscle weakness

less ability to perform

disuse atrophy

no ability to perform

DEPENDENCE

Test on Progressive Mobilization

Please answer the following questions.

1. What should be the end result of Progressive Mobilization?

   _____

2. You want the patient to have as quick a recovery to independence as possible. Name three things which must be done to allow this:
   a. _____
   b. _____
   c. _____

Answers:
1. Patient independence.
2. a. Encourage the patient to do activities without assistance as much as possible.
   b. Get the patient out of bed and active quickly.
   c. Keep the patient out of bed.

Question 2 concerns the most important points for the success of the Progressive Mobilization Program. If you answered correctly, go on. If not, please review before proceeding.

If people without physical disabilities experience the negative effects of bed rest or inactivity, you can certainly imagine what a patient with a disability, e.g., stroke, hip fracture, or parkinsonism, would experience. Dr. Gerald Hirschberg, in *Rehabilitation: A Manual For the Care of the Disabled and Elderly*, states that the uncomplicated stroke patient can be out of bed within one to three days after the incident. In most cases, a hip fracture patient could and should be up a few days after surgery to prevent thrombophlebitis and other negative effects of bed rest.

Please remember that it is the physician's responsibility to decide the who, what, when, and where of using Progressive Mobilization. However, you must be aware of the benefits and value of Progressive Mobilization and work with the physician to help your patient toward independence as quickly as possible.

We have discovered that the dependent staircase, unfortunately, is the steeper staircase. It takes far less time for a patient to become dependent than to become independent or gain back the strength lost during an excursion down the dependent staircase. The less you allow your patient to descend the dependent staircase, the easier and faster it will be to help him become independent again.

Before going on, ask yourself the following two questions:

1. Who should order a program of Progressive Mobilization?
2. Now that you know the benefits of Progressive Mobilization, would you remind your physician of the importance of rapid institution of Progressive Mobilization?

If you answered "The physician" and "Yes," we are pleased.

By using the methods that will be presented in the remainder of this chapter, we have found that the adverse effects encountered by inactivity or bed rest greatly outweigh the risk of early mobilization of the patient. Thus, Progressive Mobilization is the answer!

Remember:

1. The undesirable effects of bed rest are progressive weakness and fatigue, which can lead to a state of dependence.
2. Progressive Mobilization is a program of activities to help produce independence in your patients.
3. The sooner the program is instituted, the less loss there is in the patient's ability to perform.
4. The patient must perform each activity alone or with minimal assistance.
5. You must work with the physician.
6. Strength is lost faster than it can be built up.

The purpose of this chapter is to instruct you in specific techniques that will enhance your patients' independence. In the next section we shall discuss some safety factors that should definitely play a part in your nursing care.

TOOLS TO PROMOTE PATIENT SAFETY DURING TREATMENT

Ignoring these factors might prove hazardous to your health and the health of your patients. So pay close attention!

We have selected three tools which should be used as guides to prevent problems during mobilization activities. They are as follows:

1. observing for cardiac symptoms
2. monitoring the pulse
3. using proper body mechanics

In applying rehabilitation concepts to general nursing care, these three tools are of utmost importance. The reasons are as follows:

1. Progressive Mobilization activities often prove to be very strenuous for your patients.
2. It takes more energy for patients to move around on their own than to be moved by you.
3. Patients often need a great deal of assistance as they start Progressive Mobilization activities.

Tool 1: Observing for Cardiac Symptoms

Even a short stay in bed for disabled patients, whether young or old, makes it difficult to perform some of the Progressive Mobilization activities without stress. Therefore, keep in mind the following rule:

Always observe for cardiac symptoms in your patients.

Easily observed cardiac symptoms include

- shortness of breath
- substernal chest pain—left arm pain
- skin temperature—cold sweat
- nausea
- skin color—pale or flushed
- dizziness—syncope (fainting)
- diaphoresis (sweating)

Observe your patient for these signs first at rest and then during each mobilization activity. If any occur, allow the patient to stop the activity and rest. The signs should reverse themselves readily. If they do, make note of them and continue the activity at a lower level, more slowly and, perhaps, with more assistance, so the activity is not as strenuous.

If any of the signs occur and do not reverse themselves readily at rest, the activity should be stopped and the physician notified. The physician should determine if the activity should be continued or its pace changed.

Test on Tool 1

Please answer the questions below.

1. Name two cardiac symptoms. a. _____
   b. _____

2. What should you do if cardiac symptoms occur during Progressive Mobilization activities?
   a. _____
   b. _____
   c. _____
   d. _____

3. When do you first check for cardiac symptoms?
   _____

4. Would you start a Progressive Mobilization activity if cardiac symptoms were present at rest?
   _____

You were correct if you answered the questions as follows:
1. *(Any two of the following): shortness of breath, chest pain, skin temperature, nausea, skin color, dizziness (syncope), sweating (diaphoresis).*
2. *Allow the patient to rest, slow down the activity, lower the level of activity, or give more assistance.*
3. *At rest.*
4. *No.*

Tool 2: Monitoring the Pulse

A change in the patient's pulse rate is an important cardiac symptom. We deliberately left it out of the list of cardiac symptoms because we wanted to discuss it in terms of pulse monitoring. Pulse monitoring is the method of watching the pulse rate during Progressive Mobilization activities. It is an indication of the patient's tolerance for a particular activity. As with other cardiac symptoms, the pulse response would indicate whether the exercise should be continued, decreased, stopped temporarily, or permanently discontinued. The two important items to observe about the pulse at this time are

1. the speed of the pulse (pulse rate)
2. the rhythm of the pulse

The pulse rate should be taken first at rest—before any activity is begun. This will be called the *resting pulse*. After this is determined, begin the activity and take the pulse rate at the completion of each activity.

If your patient is elderly, please also read Chapter 7 for more detailed information about cardiovascular assessment and the calculation of a target pulse rate.

1. *When should the pulse rate be taken?*
   a. _____
   b. _____

Figure 12-1 Pulse at Wrist

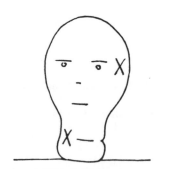

Figure 12-2 Pulse at Temple and Jaw

2. *What are the two important items to observe regarding the pulse?*
   a. _____
   b. _____

Answers:

1. a. *At rest.*   b. *After activity.*
2. a. *Rhythm.*   b. *Speed or rate.*

The discussion below on how to take a pulse rate is written primarily for nonprofessionals. If you are a nurse, O.T., P.T., or physician, you might like to review it as a teaching tool for your nonprofessional assistants. If not, proceed to the discussion of rate and rhythm of the pulse.

How to Take the Pulse Rate. Take the pulse at the thumb side of the wrist on the palm or inner side of the forearm, as shown in Figure 12-1. Place your fingers at the area marked "X"; you will feel a throb there. Do not use your thumb, because your thumb has its own pulse.

Look at the second hand on your watch and count how many beats you feel in fifteen seconds. Multiply this by four to get the pulse rate for one minute. The pulse rate is recorded per minute. If the pulse is irregular, count the pulse for sixty seconds.

If the pulse rate cannot be found at the wrist, use the temple or under the jaw at the carotid artery (Figure 12-2).

The normal resting pulse rate is 65–85 beats per minute.

Feel for your own pulse at the designated areas. Did you find it? Now figure it out for one minute. Record your pulse rate here: _____. Now find it on a friend. Everyone's pulse feels a little different. The more pulse rates you take, the easier it will be to take them.

The Rhythm of the Pulse Rate. The rhythm of the pulse should be regular. It should be an even throb: 1, 2, 3, 4. An irregular pulse can be described as one which skips beats: 1, __, 3, 4, or 1, __, __, 4. If a patient has an irregular pulse, the physician should be notified. This is often an indication that the activities are contraindicated, and continuation of the activity should be at the physician's discretion.

1. *What is the normal range of the resting pulse?*
   _____

2. *Where should the pulse rate be taken?*
   _____
   _____
   _____

3. Over what period of time is the pulse rate calculated and recorded?

_____

4. What does an irregular pulse feel like?

_____

Answers:

1. 65–85 beats per minute
2. Wrist (radial side), temple, jaw at carotid artery
3. Per minute
4. It skips or beats unevenly.

If you answered correctly, put this knowledge to work and get to the heart of the subject.

How to Relate Pulse Taking with Activity. It is important to take the pulse rate as the patient performs the activities. It should be done in the following manner:

1. Take resting pulse.
2. Do appropriate activity.
3. Take pulse immediately following the activity.
4. Rest for two minutes. Take pulse again.
5. Repeat every two minutes until the pulse is within ten counts of the resting pulse.

EXAMPLE

Pulse Rate	Normal Results
Resting	60–85
Activity	90–120+
Two-minute rest	60–95

As a general rule, most patients experience an increase in pulse rate during the course of exercise. The amount of increase and the length of time it takes to return to the resting level are the important considerations.

Complete the following exercise:

1. Take your resting pulse: _____
2. Stand up and jog in place for two minutes.
3. Take your pulse immediately after activity:

_____

4. Take your pulse after a two-minute rest:

_____

5. Take your pulse after a four-minute rest:

_____

6. Take your pulse after a six-minute rest:

_____

Did your pulse rate change?
How long did your pulse take to return to its resting rate?

First Test on Tool 2

Please answer the questions below.

1. Name five steps in taking a pulse rate in relation to activity.
   a. _____
   b. _____
   c. _____
   d. _____
   e. _____
2. What two factors are the important considerations of pulse rate with activity?
   a. _____
   b. _____

Answers:
1. a. Take a resting pulse.
   b. Do the appropriate activity.
   c. Take pulse immediately after the activity.
   d. Rest for two minutes—take pulse again.
   e. Repeat every two minutes until pulse returns to within ten counts of the rest level.
2. a. Amount of increase
   b. Length of time to return to resting level

If you missed any answers, review the information and try again. Remember, you must do pulse monitoring with all your patients during their activities. Once you answer correctly move on—there is more information about this important subject.

A pulse increase of 20 beats per minute during exercise is acceptable as normal. It should ideally return to the resting rate or within 10 beats per minute of the resting rate within two minutes after the cessation of activity. If it does not return to the resting rate after six minutes following the cessation of exercise, the physician should be notified and exercise halted until he determines if the activity should be resumed or carried out at a lower level.

The more difficult an activity is for the patient, the more it will stress his heart and the higher his pulse rate will be. During a strenuous exercise such as walking, stair climbing, or stand-ups, a rise in the pulse rate of up to 50 beats, or about 122 beats per minute, would be considered satisfactory. At a fifty-beat-per-minute increase or greater, the activity should be stopped, the patient should rest for a period of time, and later the activity should be adjusted to result in less exertion by the patient. This is done by doing the activity slower, by doing it for a shorter period of time, or by giving the patient greater assistance. If the pulse rate increases too much each time the activity is performed, regardless of the level at which the patient is exercising, then the particular activity is too difficult for the patient and should be stopped. A similar course of action should be taken if a patient develops an irregular pulse during the course of the exercise or activity.

It would be considered unsatisfactory if, during the activity of sitting in a wheelchair, the patient's pulse rate increased 50 beats to about 122 per minute. Sitting in a chair is as important as any other activity on the Independent Staircase, but the patient cannot be allowed the same pulse rise as he can during strenuous exercise. Sitting is often very stressful to the dehabilitated patient. Frequently, such a patient cannot even roll over in bed alone without a tremendous rise in pulse rate.

Nonetheless, the patient must get out of bed to gain any strength at all.

As a companion to exercise, a patient's sitting tolerance parallels his ability to progress up the steps of independence. Table 12-1 is a Sitting Tolerance Schedule, which if followed carefully, produces a rapid increase in the patient's general strength.

Continue the schedule progressively, as shown in Table 12-1, until the patient is out of bed as follows:

- out of bed five hours in morning
- nap one to one and a half hours after lunch
- out of bed five hours in the afternoon

The ultimate goal is for the patient to be out of bed from 12 to 14 hours per day.

All patients will not start at the same point on the Sitting Tolerance Schedule. To determine where to start, a number of things must be considered:

1. How much time the patient has been up previously. If the patient cannot tell you this information, the family or chart notes should be able to. If it cannot be determined, start the patient according to Day 1 on the schedule.
2. The pulse response of the patient and other cardiac symptoms.

The most important determination of the sitting tolerance of the patient is his pulse response. Patients will beg to go back to bed, but as long as their pulse is satisfactory and they have no other cardiac symptoms, they must stay up. We tell them, "You might feel tired, but your heart is not tired yet. So you can sit up longer." Often in early rehabilitation of a patient, only bed exercises and sitting can be tolerated. If the dehabilitated patient experiences syncope when first sitting on the edge of the bed (prior to the transfer to a chair),

TABLE 12-1 Sitting Tolerance Schedule

DAY	TIME OF DAY	ACTIVITY
No. 1	9:00 a.m. or 10:00 a.m.	Patient sits in chair or wheelchair for 15 minutes
	1:00 p.m. or 2:00 p.m.	Same activity for 30 minutes
	5:00 p.m. or 6:00 p.m.	Same activity for 45 minutes
No. 2	9:00 a.m. or 10:00 a.m.	Patient sits in chair or wheelchair for 1 hour
	1:00 p.m. or 2:00 p.m.	Same activity for 1 hour 15 minutes
	5:00 p.m. or 6:00 p.m.	Same activity for 1 hour 30 minutes
No. 3	9:00 a.m. or 10:00 a.m.	Patient sits in chair or wheelchair for 2 hours
	1:00 p.m. or 2:00 p.m.	Same activity for 2 hours 15 minutes
	5:00 p.m. or 6:00 p.m.	Same activity for 2 hours 30 minutes
No. 4	9:00 a.m. or 10:00 a.m.	Patient sits in chair or wheelchair for 3 hours
	1:00 p.m. or 2:00 p.m.	Same activity for 3 hours and 15 minutes
	5:00 p.m. or 6:00 p.m.	Same activity for 3 hours 30 minutes

the blood pressure should be taken. If hypotensive, support stockings should be considered. If the patient still experiences syncope while sitting upright, neurochairs or a recliner wheelchair might have to be utilized. As the patient tolerates a ninety-degree angle in the neurochair without dizziness, he can be mobilized to a regular wheelchair. (See Chapter 14 for neurochair and recliner wheelchair information.)

A patient's out-of-bed tolerance has to increase to a certain amount before he can go any further on his strengthening program. As mentioned previously, a patient's sitting tolerance and ability to strengthen correspond very closely. You will find that the patient who still continually begs to go to bed might be able to walk only a few feet while the patient who sits up all day is able to walk around the block.

Sitting time and the sitting pulse response are evaluated in the following manner:

1. If the pulse is 100 beats or less per minute and there are no other cardiac symptoms, the patient should stay up. Remember that with transferring the patient into the chair or even with lifting him, his pulse rate may increase above this level. But if within six minutes after the transfer activity his pulse is at his resting rate (100 or less), continued sitting as planned is fine.
2. If the pulse remains higher than 100 beats per minute, the patient should be returned to bed. The activity should be tried again at the next scheduled time.

To summarize:

1. Take pulse rates often.
2. Do activities for short periods of time.
3. Let your patient rest between activities—five minutes will usually be sufficient.
4. A strenuous activity after rest will not cause as much stress on the patient as it would if done immediately following another activity.
5. Do not let the patient return to bed too quickly.
6. If the pulse rate sitting is 100 or less, the patient should stay out of bed.
7. If the pulse rate sitting is over 100, try sitting the patient later.
8. Keep the patient up longer each time he is out of bed.

Second Test on Tool 2

Please answer the following five questions.

1. What should be done if the patient develops an irregular pulse or a pulse increase greater than 50 beats per minute? Name three steps:
    a. _____
    b. _____
    c. _____
2. What is the longest length of time a pulse rate could remain high (above resting level) and still be okay? _____
3. How do you adjust an activity to a lower output level without stopping the activity? Name two ways:
    a. _____
    b. _____
4. How long should the patient be able to sit up at one session by the end of Day 3? _____
5. What does this comment mean: "Your heart's not tired yet so you can stay up longer"?
    _____
    _____
    _____
    _____

The correct answers are as follows:
1. *Stop activity, rest for a period of time, adjust the activity.*
2. *Six minutes.*
3. *Make the activity periods shorter, help the patient more, or do the activity slower.*
4. *Two hours thirty minutes.*
5. *That a patient's pulse is 100 or less, strong, and steady and there are no other cardiac symptoms.*

Tool 3: Using Proper Body Mechanics

An important aspect of safety in the application of Progressive Mobilization, both for you and for your patients, is the knowledge and proper use of body mechanics. In addition to using correct body mechanics for safety, you will be teaching your patients to use their bodies in such a way that the mechanics of the body will make the activities easier for them to do.

In most activities related to patient care, the four basic principles of body mechanics are as follows:

3. Hold the object as close to you as possible.

1. Keep your back straight.

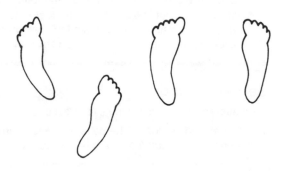

4. Keep a wide base of support by placing one foot in front of the other or sideways.

To avoid situations that are dangerous to you and your patient, follow these four principles and "look at yourself" while working.

The following dialogue might serve as a good example of what *not* to do.

NURSE: Mr. Smith, can I help you get out of bed?
MR. SMITH: Oh, yes!

2. Bend your knees, squat, and use your thigh muscles.

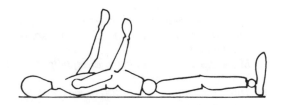

Mr. Smith reaches up with both arms.

The nurse bends over. Mr. Smith puts his arms around the neck of the nurse, whose hands are placed under his shoulders.

This is the proper procedure for getting a patient out of bed. This procedure will be explained in detail in the next section.

Two Activities to Try

1. Put a book on the floor.
   a. Stand up, put your feet close together until they touch each other, bend your knees, keep your back straight, and pick up the book. Stand up.
   b. Now get a wide base of support by spreading your feet forward or sideways. Bend your knees, keep your back straight, and pick up the book. Stand up.

You felt off balance using method 1a, didn't you? Your feet did not give you a good stable foundation in that position. Method 1b is more stable. If the book had been a person who moved suddenly, you would have certainly lost your balance.
   Now try this:

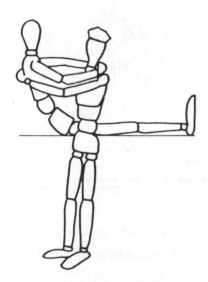

The nurse then pulls up.

Review the four principles of body mechanics and then look at the nurse. What is wrong? (Circle the appropriate answer for each item.)

1. The nurse *has* or *has not* kept the back straight.
2. The nurse *has* or *has not* held the object close.
3. The nurse *has* or *has not* bent the knees.
4. The nurse *has* or *has not* spread the feet to keep a wide base of support.

Answer: None of the principles of proper body mechanics has been followed. Review this drawing:

2. Place a book on the table.
   a. Bend your elbows and pick up the book (see Figure 12-3).
   b. Now keep your elbows straight and pick up the book (see Figure 12-4). The book felt heavier with your elbows straight, didn't it? This is explained by the physics principle that a weight is heavier at the end of a long lever arm. Keeping your arms straight created a long lever arm.
   c. When you lift a patient, be sure to bend your elbows and hold him close so that he will be lighter. When you bend over at the hips and reach down to the floor to pick an object up, a long lever arm is created. See Figures 12-5 and 12-6 for the correct and incorrect method of lifting an object off the floor.

Figure 12-3 Short Lever Arm

Figure 12-4 Long Lever Arm

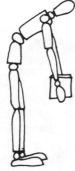

Figure 12-5 Incorrect Method of Lifting
Note: Long Lever Arm

Figure 12-6 Correct Method of Lifting
Note: Short Lever Arm

Test on Tool 3

Consider the principles of body mechanics when answering the following questions.

1. Circle the picture that shows how to correctly assist Mr. Smith from a seated position to a standing position.
2. Under each picture, list the correct or incorrect procedures the nurse is using.

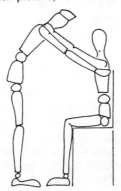

A.

_____
_____
_____
_____

B.

_____
_____
_____
_____

Remember to keep these principles in mind whenever working with a patient, making a bed, or lifting something off the floor at work or at home. They will prevent back injuries!

Nurse A. *did not* remember.

Nurse B. *did* remember.

Other safety points will be mentioned as the activities are presented. There are two precautions which apply to *all* situations:

1. If you are not sure that you can carry out an activity alone because of the weight or the condition of the patient, discontinue the activity and get help.

2. Always work in an area where you can summon help if you need it.

Continue reading to determine how to coordinate all this information.

WHERE TO BEGIN PROGRESSIVE MOBILIZATION?

Have you ever seen two patients alike?

On May 25, three stroke patients arrived at your hospital. Mr. A. is unconscious. He is unable to move at all. He is medically stable. Mrs. B. is awake, alert, talkative, and wants to get up immediately. She is accustomed to being up all day. She can move her right arm and leg easily, although the right side is not quite as strong as the left. Mr. C. is awake but confused, disoriented, completely paralyzed on his right side, and weak on the left side. His family tells us that he has sat up in a wheelchair for 30 minutes twice a day.

Now, what do you do?

You know what Progressive Mobilization is, but how do you apply this program? Remember the Independence Staircase? Remember the Sitting Tolerance Schedule? Keep them in mind and use them as a guide to evaluate your patients. Use them as an evaluation checklist when you see a patient for the first time. Check the patient out on every step of the Independence Staircase. If the patient passes step 1, good; go on to step 2, 3. If the patient falters on step 4, that is where the work begins. As you study the steps in detail, you will be able to tell quickly what your patient can do and where you need to go from there.

By testing the patient in each activity, you can determine:

1. whether the patient can do the activity
2. whether the patient needs to be taught to do the activity
3. whether the patient needs to practice several activities simultaneously

Here are some questions regarding where to begin Progressive Mobilization activities. In answering these questions, you may refer back to the drawing of the Independence Staircase, the Sitting Tolerance Schedule (Table 12-1), and the descriptions of the three patients. Please name the step in the Progressive Mobilization program at which you would start each patient.

1. *You asked Mr. A. to move in bed alone. He could not respond to your command. Step:* _____
2. *You asked Mrs. B. to move in bed. She did it easily. You asked her to sit up. She jumped up out of bed the minute the siderails went down. She stood up easily but after a few steps her right knee gave way. Step:* ____
3. *You asked Mr. C. to move in bed. He did. You asked him to sit up. He needed moderate assistance getting to a sitting position, and after he sat a few seconds he started leaning badly to the left. Step:* _____

Do you think you put your patient on the correct step? Compare your answers with these.

1. *Bed activities. Even at this point it looks as if you are going to have to do all the bed activities for Mr. A. until he starts gaining consciousness and can start helping himself. He should sit in a neurochair for 15 minutes.*
2. *Walking step. You could return to the standing step. Even though Mrs. B. did it easily, you could use the exercise to strengthen her right knee. This will be clearer after you read the discussion of the activities. The patient should sit up all day.*
3. *Sitting. Start with Day 2 of the Sitting Tolerance Schedule—sit up in wheelchair for 45 minutes and continue as scheduled. Practice sitting balance. Mr. C. does not have enough trunk control or general strength to proceed to standing yet.*

How did you do?
If you reread this section after you have learned how to do all of the activities, the decision of where to start Progressive Mobilization will be even clearer.
Now, complete the following review test for this unit.

Unit Review Test on Progressive Mobilization

Write your answers in the space provided.

1. What is a Progressive Mobilization Program? _____
2. At what rate should a patient's time sitting in a chair be increased? _____
3. Your patient has casts on both wrists. Where can you feel the pulse? _____
4. Mr. Jones has been in bed for one day. Mrs. Williams has been in bed for three weeks. If their diagnoses are the same, which patient would be rehabilitated quicker? _____
   Why? _____
5. In a Progressive Mobilization Program, when should you first take the patient's pulse rate? ____
6. Mr. Jones has a pulse rate of 132 when resting in bed. You are supposed to start Progressive Mobilization activities. What should you do? (The chart said his pulse rate averages 85.)
   a. _____   b. _____
7. You have been exercising Mr. Jones. His resting pulse rate was 80.
   a. After the activity it is 100. What would you do?
      (1) _____   (2) _____
   b. After the activity it is 130. What would you do?
      (1) _____   (2) _____
8. Mr. Jones is very heavy and he needs to get to the bathroom. What would you do? _____
9. The Independence Staircase can be used as an _____
10. State the relationship between the steps of the Independence Staircase. _____
11. If Mrs. Williams' pulse is 99 and she complains of being tired while sitting in a chair but has no other cardiac symptoms, what would you do? _____
    _____
    _____

12. You are going to lift a two-year-old child off the floor. Applying good body mechanics, how are you going to hold the child? _____

Answers:
1. *Activities to gain independence and mobility.*
2. *Each time should be fifteen minutes longer.*
3. *Feel it at the temple or at the jaw at the carotid artery.*
4. *Mr. Jones. Because he has had less time to become weak from staying in bed.*
5. *At rest.*
6. a. *Don't do the activity.*   b. *Notify the doctor.*
7. a. *(1) Let him rest.*
     (2) Continue the exercise
   b. *(1) Let him rest.*
     (2) Stop the activity; later try it again, giving the patient assistance or exercising slower.
8. *Get someone to help you with him.*
9. *Evaluation guide.*
10. *Each step is necessary for the next to be accomplished.*
11. *Reassure her that she is all right and keep her sitting up.*
12. *Hold the child close to your body.*

If you answered 11 or 12 questions correctly, excellent—go on. If you answered 8 or 9 correctly, that is satisfactory, but please review. If you answered less than 7 correctly, please repeat this unit.

You are now prepared to learn more about specific Progressive Mobilization activities. The objective of the instruction in this chapter is the following: Given details of patient history and clinical diagnosis, you should be able to promote the patient's mobility by using the proper activities and assistive devices. Specifically, once you have completed this chapter you should be able to

1. identify the steps in each of the activities
2. perform the activities yourself
3. demonstrate the activities to the patient
4. select activities appropriate to the particular patient
5. select assistive devices appropriate to the particular patient
6. teach the patient the activity

(The student should be able to perform a certain activity or group of activities for the clinical instructor, or, if a clinical instructor is not present, your patient should demonstrate the activity to you as you stand by. If the patient is able or knows how to perform the activity after you have taught him, you have fulfilled this objective.)

Each step of the Independence Staircase represents a specific activity. Each of the following activities will be discussed and carefully explained to you:

- bed activities
- sitting
- transfers
- standing
- stair climbing
- walking

To make the descriptions of the activities easier to follow, most of the activities are presented in the form of interactions between a nurse and a Mr. Jones. Mr. Jones and the nurse "climb" the steps on the Independence Staircase. The nurse "sets the scene" and then the activities are presented. The best way to begin to study these activities is to have the book in hand and act out each step yourself as if you were Mr. Jones or the nurse.

The activities are presented in a basic form. Their adaptation by you in practice depends upon the diagnosis of the patient. For example, a stroke patient and a non-weight-bearing hip fracture patient would transfer using the same basic technique, except that the fractured hip patient would keep the involved foot off the floor.

Table 12-2 lists some common diagnoses with their accompanying major functional limitations. These limitations are the ones that are important to consider carefully when adapting a particular exercise to a particular patient and when selecting activities for your patient. (See reference materials for more detailed explanations of these disabilities.) Table 12-2 contains only a few considerations, but these pertain directly to the topic of Progressive Mobilization activities.

Take a break—then join Mr. Jones and his nurse in "Bed Activities" for their climb up the Independence Staircase.

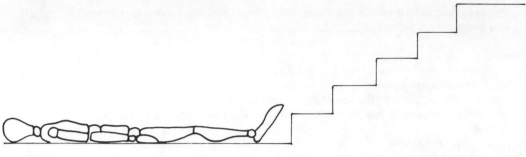

Bed Positioning

BED ACTIVITIES

The first step on the Independence Staircase consists of bed activities. These activities should be started as soon as the patient is hospitalized. Because they are actually a part of everyday nursing care, these activities are readily initiated. Before we list them, visualize this:

You have been assigned to give Mr. Jones a bath. When you enter the room, you notice that Mr. Jones has slid down too low in the bed. What should you do? You have two choices after lowering the head of the bed:

1. Pull him up in bed yourself or call a nurse to help. Both of you then pull Mr. Jones up in bed. Mr. Jones does *none* of the work.
2. Tell Mr. Jones where to hold onto the bed and how to push with his feet. Then you and Mr. Jones work together to move him up in bed.

Get the picture? One task, two different approaches. If you use approach no. 2, the next day Mr. Jones will be able to help you again—and help more because he will be stronger from having done the activity on the first day. Soon Mr. Jones might be able to move up in bed alone.

Remember the theory of Progressive Mobilization as stated in our introduction? The sooner the patient is encouraged and taught to move around on his own, the sooner his recovery comes about and the sooner he is independent again.

There are five activities that can be listed as bed activities. They are as follows:

1. bed positioning
2. range of motion (ROM)
   a. passive range of motion
   b. active range of motion
   c. functional range of motion
3. moving up and down in bed
4. moving sideways
5. rolling over in bed

Bed positioning and passive range of motion activities are preventive. They are important in preventing joint and muscle contractures. They are not done actively by the patient and therefore will not make him stronger. If the patient is out of

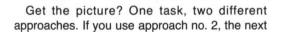

TABLE 12-2 Common Diagnoses and Accompanying Disabilities

TYPE OF DISABILITY	MAJOR FUNCTIONAL LIMITATIONS
1. Stroke	Paralyzed upper and lower extremities on one side
	Partially paralyzed upper and lower extremity on one side
	Hemianopsia—the ability to see only out of one side of each eye
	Poor balance
	Impaired ability to comprehend, follow directions, or communicate
2. Fractured hip: surgically pinned	Unable to put weight on involved leg
3. Fractured hip: closed reduction	Same as above
4. Austin-Moore prosthesis or total hip prosthesis	Able to bear weight as specified by physician; amount of hip flexion may be limited by the physician
5. Arthritis	May have limited motion in joints; may have painful joints
6. Parkinsonism	Rigidity; limited range of motion; decreased effective communication; delayed response to directions
7. Quadriplegic/quadriparesis	No muscle function or muscle weakness in all 4 extremities
8. Paraplegic/paraparesis	No muscle function or muscle weakness in both lower extremities

bed and moving about, the need for these two activities diminishes greatly. Remember:

1. Only by doing activities himself does the patient gain strength.
2. Use the Sitting Tolerance Schedule (Table 12-1) as soon as possible and while the patient is learning the different steps to independence.

Bed Positioning

Bed positioning is important if the patient cannot get out of bed yet or is in bed for long periods of time. When positioning the patient, think of him as a person who will be walking some day. Consequently, his arms, legs, and head should be positioned in such a way that deformities do not result from the way he lies in bed. This is why positioning is so important for a bedbound patient. Let us now discuss the different parts of the body, how they should or should not be positioned, and why they should be positioned in the manner described. (Refer also to the chapter on pressure sores.)

Area to Be Positioned: The Head

Correct Position

Use one flat pillow.

Incorrect Position

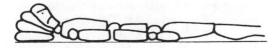

Do not use a stack of pillows.

Why?

The patient's head and neck could get stiff in a forward flexed position and his posture would be out of alignment. He would be looking down at the floor all of the time. Frequently patients beg to be propped up. This is because with age and some medical conditions, the head naturally assumes a forward flexed position. Some of this cannot be avoided. *Do not initiate the habit of propping the patient up in bed*. If the patient is comfortable lying flat, leave him flat and encourage him to stay that way.

Area to Be Positioned: The Knees

Correct Position

Keep the knees straight.

Incorrect Position

Do not put pillows under the knees that hold them flexed.

Why?

Pillows under the knees produce flexion of the knee and also flexion of the hip joints. This position held for long periods of time will produce shortening of the hamstrings and hip flexors and stiffening of the respective joints. When the patient tries to walk, he will not be able to straighten up and will probably look like this:

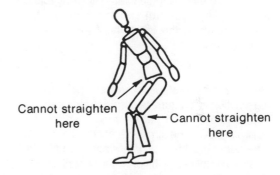

Cannot straighten here — Cannot straighten here

If his head is bent down also, he will look like this:

Could you walk this way? Do you recognize any patients you have seen? Parkinson and arthritic patients are the most hindered by these two problems.

Area to Be Positioned: The Legs

Correct Position

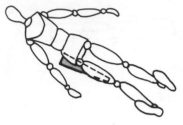

Keep the toes and knees pointed toward the ceiling. Place a rolled bath mat under hips at an angle as shown to keep the proper position.

Incorrect Position

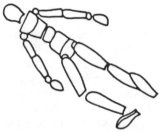

Do not let the leg remain in an externally rotated (or leg rolled outward) position. Do not place sandbags along the leg to hold the leg in the correct position.

Why?

Outward rotation of the leg in a supine or backly-ing position is a natural occurrence for a patient in bed, and one need not be concerned for most patients. But for the stroke patient or a patient with a fractured hip this is an important consideration. If the leg is not kept in the position described here, the hip will tighten in an outward position. When the patient starts walking, he will look like this:

Toes and knees cannot point straight ahead. This makes gait very difficult or impossible. External rotation of the leg is a motion of the hip joint and correction of it is most effective when made at the hip.

Area to Be Positioned: The Ankles

Correct Position

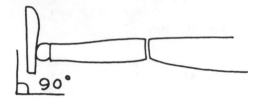

Keep ankle flexible at least to a 90° angle.

Incorrect Position

Do not let heel cord (gastrocnemius muscle) shorten.

Why?

If a patient cannot dorsiflex his feet to at least a 90° angle, he will walk on his toes all the time—this is very debilitating. Stroke, Parkinson, and arthritic patients seem to have the most difficulty with this. Instruct the patient to move his ankle up and down by himself many times during the day. Active movement of the ankle will keep the heel cord from tightening and will strengthen the ankle muscles. The nurse can also perform passive ROM on the ankle each time she is in the room. Keep covers loose over feet. Tight sheets pull the feet down into plantar flexion and prevent the patient from moving his feet by himself. Foot-boards are effective if patients do not move away from them.

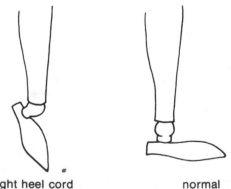

tight heel cord   normal

Area to Be Positioned: Arms and Hands

Correct Position

Keep arms abducted from the body.

Incorrect Position

Do not keep arms tightly pressed against sides. Do not allow the elbows to be kept maximally flexed.

Why?

Correct positioning of the arms is very important in order to prevent pressure sores and contractures of hand and elbow musculature. During the course of the day, the shoulder can be positioned at different points of ROM of the joint. (Positions will be discussed further in the ROM exercise section.) Elevating arms and hands reduces or prevents further swelling in hands and arms. Placing hands stretched out flat against the bed or pillow and keeping the wrist in a neutral position or placing a roll in the hand keeps the wrist and fingers flexible and in a functional position. If shoulders, elbows, wrists, and fingers have contractures, functional use of them is impaired. If limitations occur in the upper extremities, the patient may not be able to feed or dress himself and may not be able to use walking aids (i.e., crutches or walkers) if they are needed.

To reinforce the importance of proper positioning, I would like to tell you about a patient I saw years ago. She was an obese woman who had diabetes and bilateral strokes. She was alert and in obvious discomfort. She lay in the fetal position. Her arms were tightly adducted against her body and her fingers were bent into tight fists. Her knees and hips were flexed and tightly adducted. She had developed pressure sores everywhere that the surfaces of her body touched each other. We could not move her arms away from her body and she had sores under her armpits and under her breasts where her hands pressed hard against her.

The need for getting this woman moved around was very evident to me. But when we started to treat her, we found that nothing could be done to help her. A great deal could have been accomplished if Progressive Mobilization had occurred when she first became ill. Need I say more?

Bed positioning is a difficult job. It is much easier to work with a patient who is out of bed, so your goal should be to get him up and around. I hope that from this discussion you can see the need to position any newly hospitalized and bedbound patient. If you do not, you could be responsible for deformities that could possibly prevent independence.

Test on Bed Positioning

Answer the three questions below.

1. Which two joints can stiffen if you place pillows under a patient's knees when he is in bed?
   a. _____ b. _____

2. Where do you put the roll to prevent outward movement of the whole leg?
   _____

3. What are the two best ways to prevent a tight heel cord or ankle stiffness for a bedbound patient?
   a. _____
   b. _____

The following answers are correct:
1. *a. The hip.*   *b. The knee.*
2. *At the hip (remember external rotation is a hip motion).*
3. *a. Have the patient do the motion himself.*   *b. Use passive range of motion.*

We have discussed bed positioning from a backlying position. Now that you know the theory of what position is best for each joint, you should apply it appropriately when your patient is in a different position.

The trick to positioning is good alignment of the body in all positions. Changing positions often (at least every two hours) helps prevent contractures and pressure sores. (Remember also to review Chapter 9 on pressure sores.)

The Theory of Range of Motion—Passive, Active, and Functional

Range of motion (ROM) refers to the amount of movement present in a joint. This motion is present in relation to the different planes of the body. Basically, there are ten types of motion for joints:

1. flexion (bending)
2. extension (straightening)
3. abduction (motion away from the midline of the body)
4. adduction (motion toward the midline of the body)
5. circumduction (circular motion)
6. internal/external rotation
7. pronation/supination of elbow
8. plantar flexion (downward motion of the foot at the ankle joint)
9. dorsiflexion (upward motion of the foot at the ankle joint)
10. inversion/eversion of ankle

Some joints can exhibit more of these movements than other joints.

There are three ways of performing range of motion activities. They are as follows:

1. *Passive ROM.* In this activity the nurse moves the extremity in such a way that full motion occurs at the joint. For example, moving the arm produces ROM at the shoulder.
2. *Active ROM.* In this activity all movements are the same as passive ROM except that the patient uses his muscles to do the moving.
3. *Functional Activities for ROM.* The patient rolls over in bed, moves up in bed, sits up, stands, gets dressed, etc. When the patient pulls himself up in bed, he reaches over his head to the top of the bed, which produces flexion of the shoulder. Many functional activities produce full ROM of the joints.

The following is a breakdown of what each type of ROM will accomplish.

PASSIVE ROM	ACTIVE ROM	FUNCTIONAL ACTIVITIES FOR ROM
Keeps joints limber	Keeps joints limber	Keeps joints limber
Keeps muscles limber	Keeps muscles limber	Keeps muscles limber
	Strengthens	Strengthens
		Accomplishes a necessary activity

Notice that passive ROM does not strengthen. The proper use of ROM activities is very important. It is a physiological fact that muscles will become stronger only if they do work. Passive ROM makes the nurse stronger—not the patient.

Can you see why our goal is to have the patient move around by himself? When a patient is active, the need for most specific ROM activities is greatly diminished or eliminated. The importance of ROM, how it relates to strengthening and functional activities, and how to do it will now be discussed.

The Importance of Range of Motion

We discussed in the section on bed positioning the necessity of good positioning to prevent contractures. Stressed was the fact that if contrac-tures were allowed to develop, functional abilities would be greatly impaired. Movement of the joints and muscles also prevents contractures. ROM, like positioning, is a method to guarantee an absence of contractures and to promote rehabilitation. For example, if a patient's elbow becomes contracted, he may not be able to dress himself. If knee contractures develop, he may not be able to walk.

How to Use Range of Motion Activities

1. *Use range of motion as an evaluative guide.* First do passive range of motion on your patients to find areas that seem tight. Once these areas are located, use the ROM techniques to loosen them and to keep them loose. Then, again by

using ROM activities, test the patient's strength. Remember, never do range of motion "passively" when the patient can "actively" do it himself. Assist him to do the range of motion fully (active-assistive range of motion). This will eventually make the patient strong enough to do ROM activities alone (active ROM). When a patient has some active strength, he may be able to use range of motion in his daily activities, e.g., rolling over in bed. When strengthening by using functional activities, be sure to give the patient time to try to perform the activity or to utilize his muscle strength maximally. Also, proper instructions in utilizing functional activities are very important. (You will learn that later.)

2. *Do not overemphasize range of motion.* ROM can be done effectively one time per day in conjunction with the following nursing activities:

a. Bed Bath. Instead of moving the patient's arm just enough to squeeze in a wash cloth, move the arm out to the side and back over his head as far as it will go. This will accomplish two things at once—range of motion and a good bath. Also, have the patient roll over by himself. This will help to strengthen his muscles and keep his joints limber.
b. Bed Positioning. (Already discussed).
c. Mobilization. When a patient sits, his hips and knees are bent. When he lies down, his hips and knees are straight. (See Figures 12-7 and 12-8.) The patient receives range of motion on his hips and knees while sitting in a chair.

Figure 12-7 Hips and Knees Bent

Figure 12-8 Hips and Knees Straight

When the patient sits with his feet flat on the floor or on the foot plate of a wheelchair, he is receiving ROM to his ankles (heel cords are being stretched). *Note*: Standing and walking are the very best ROM exercises for heel cords. Do you see that if you take note of these activities during the day, there are many daily activities that will accomplish the ROM activities for you?

3. *Do specific stretching ROM on two-joint muscles.* Limitation of range of motion is usually present where a muscle is tight. The muscles most likely to tighten are those that bridge (cross) two or more joints.

For example:

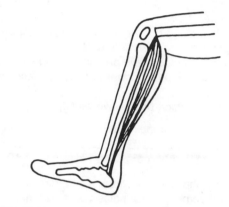

The Gastrocnemius

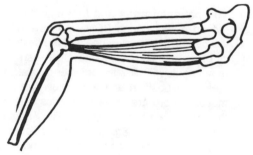

The Hamstrings

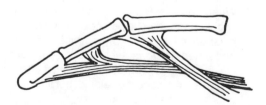

The Finger Flexors

Because of this, specific stretching ROM orders are often written for these areas. In most other areas general functioning in daily activities will fulfill ROM needs.

Test on Range of Motion

Before continuing to show you how to perform ROM activities, answer these questions to see if you understand the theory of ROM.

1. If your patient is bedbound and cannot move alone at all, what type of ROM would you do? _____
_____
2. At what time during the day would you do ROM with your patient? _____
3. ROM activities prevent _____of muscles and joints.
4. Is there a need for ROM activities when the patient is up and out of bed? _____
5. Your patient has some active strength. Would he or she be able to roll over in bed? _____
   Why? _____
6. Which muscles tend to be the tightest? _____

Answers:
1. *Passive ROM.*
2. *While bathing or other routine nursing activities.*
3. *Tightness and contractures.*
4. *No, not as much, and perhaps only in specific areas.*
5. *Maybe. The patient does not need full active strength and might be able to do some of the activity.*
6. *Muscles which bridge two joints.*

Did you answer these correctly? Review if you missed any.

Before showing you the specific directions, here are some general notes about performing ROM on a patient.

1. The patient's arms and legs should be moved gently during ROM, always within the patient's pain tolerance and the flexibility of the muscles and joints. Slow, careful movements will allow the muscles to relax in their new position and then allow further motion. There are some diagnoses where there is no pain and overzealous ROM could injure the patient, e.g., myositis ossificans.
2. Support the area to be treated. Support the extremity above and below the joint being moved to ensure true motion of the joint.
3. When passive ROM is given, the patient should be in the supine position to make it most effective. Self-ROM activities can be performed sitting or supine. Shoulder flexion, if done passively, is always most effective when the patient is supine, but it is also effective in the sitting position.
4. Do each exercise five to ten times once daily—do ROM on problem areas more frequently (three to four times).
5. Check the motion of the involved side against the normal side to evaluate full ROM of the joints.

6. If a patient is totally bedbound, do ROM activities on all extremities.
7. When the patient can do these motions alone, the motions are called active ROM.
8. By using the motions exactly as outlined and adding a weight or resistance, one then starts progressive resistive exercise (PRE) to individual muscles. PRE, especially when the muscle is strong enough to work against gravity, enhances the strengthening of the muscle.

Functional activities serve a triple purpose: to accomplish ROM, to build strength, and to accomplish a necessary activity. It is wonderful for a patient to be able to lift a ten-pound weight with his leg muscles, but if he cannot get out of a chair alone, then he is stuck. (Strengthening leg muscles using functional activities will be discussed later.)

Please continue now to learn how to do ROM. All these instructions can be very useful for giving home instructions for patients. They are also a ready reference for using ROM on patients later. They need not be learned in full detail now, but do perform each movement actively yourself while reading the material. This will help you later to evaluate ROM in the functional activities discussed.

Performing Range of Motion

The following pages show pictures and give instructions regarding passive range of motion activities. Two types of passive ROM will be compared. First you will see the nurse giving ROM to the patient who cannot do it alone, and then you will see a hemiplegic patient giving himself daily routine ROM to his upper extremity.

UPPER EXTREMITIES

Shoulder Flexion

ROM by Nurse

Starting Position: Keep arm straight.
Hold arm as shown across the wrist and at the elbow (1).

ROM: Lift the arm straight over the patient's head until the arm rests flat on the bed above the head (2), (3).
Reverse the motion and repeat (4).
Note picture 3: Bend the patient's elbow if there is not enough room on the bed for the motion.

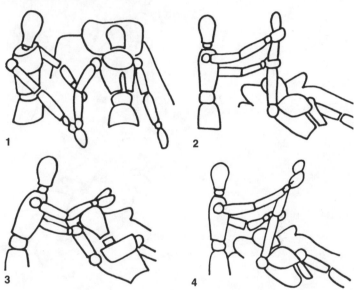

Hemiplegic Self-ROM

Starting Position: Keep the arm straight.
Hold wrist of affected arm with unaffected hand (1).

ROM: Raise the arm above the head (2).
Sit in a straight-backed chair so the patient does not tip body.

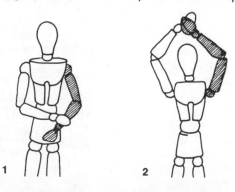

Shoulder Abduction

ROM by Nurse

Starting Position: Keep the arms straight by the side, palm of patient's hand facing his body. Hold the arm across the wrist and at the patient's elbow, as shown (1).

ROM: Keeping the arm flat on bed, slide the arm sideways away from the body (2). Keep moving the arm on the bed until the elbow touches the ear. Allow the arm to roll or turn over at about a 90° angle with the shoulder. Also bend the elbow as the arm comes up to the head if there is not enough room on the bed for the motion (3), (4).

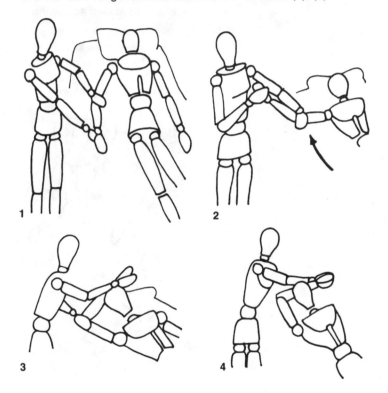

Hemiplegic Self-ROM

Starting Position: Assume cradle position by grasping the affected arm at the elbow and raise the arms to shoulder height (1), (2).

ROM: Holding the arm at shoulder height, move the arm from side to side (3), (4). Move only the arm—do not move the body.

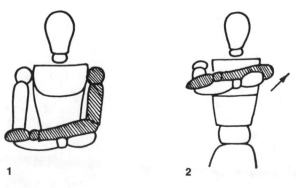

External-Internal Rotation

ROM by Nurse

Starting Position: Bring the arm out from the side, forming a 90° angle with the body. Keep the elbow bent to a 90° angle. Keep the upper arm on the bed. Press down on the shoulder toward the bed (1).

ROM: Move the hand gently back until the back of the hand touches the bed (2), (external rotation). Then move the hand forward until the palm of the hand touches the bed (3), (internal rotation).

Note: Be sure that the arm and shoulder remain in position.

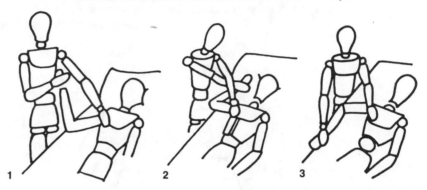

External Rotation and Horizontal Abduction

Hemiplegic Self-ROM

Starting Position: Interlock the fingers (1).

ROM: Lift the hand behind the neck (2), (3) (external rotation). Bring elbows forward, touch elbows together, and then move elbows backward (external rotation and horizontal abduction). Repeat from beginning.

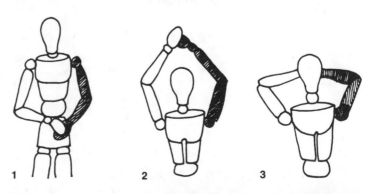

Also—in wheelchair.

Starting position: Position elbow of affected arm inside of wheelchair arm rest. With other hand grasp forearm of the affected extremity.

ROM: Push forearm away from body, being careful that arm remains stabilized against wheelchair arm rest.

Elbow Flexion and Extension

ROM by Nurse

Starting Position: Lay patient's arm down on the bed.
Place your hands one above elbow, one at wrist.

ROM: Bend arm to touch hand to shoulder. Then straighten arm completely.

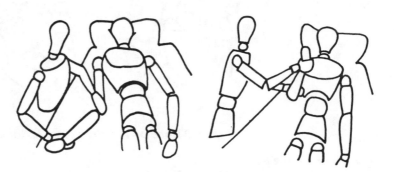

Hemiplegic Self-ROM

Starting Position: Grasp affected extremity at the wrist.

ROM: Same directions as above for ROM by nurse.

Supination and Pronation

ROM by Nurse

Starting Position: Rest upper arm on bed, bend elbow to a 90° angle. Hold upper arm against the bed, hold the patient's hand across the wrist (1).

ROM: Turn the palm of the patient's hand toward his feet (2), (pronated position); then toward his face (3), (supinated position).

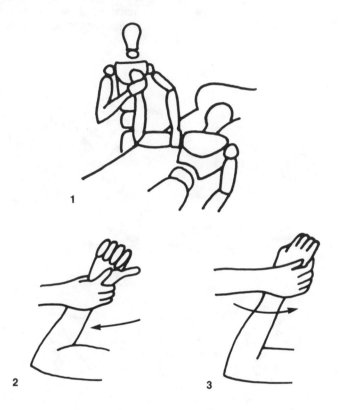

Hemiplegic Self-ROM

Starting position: Grasp affected arm just above the wrist, holding it on lap. Turn so the palm of the hand and wrist are facing up (1), (supinated position).

ROM: Turn in the opposite direction so the palm and wrist face down (2), (pronated position). Repeat movement.

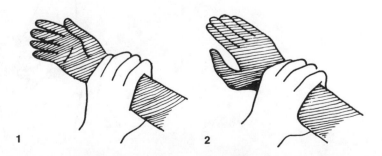

Wrist Flexion and Extension

ROM by Nurse

Starting Position: Stabilize lower arm at the wrist with one hand. Hold the patient's fingers and hands with the other hand (1), (2).

ROM: Bend wrist forward as far as it will go (3). Then make a fist. Move hand backward as far as it will go, and then straighten fingers (4). This produces ROM and stretching to both wrists and fingers as the muscles cross the wrist and finger joints. When a muscle bridges more than one joint, the muscle tends to tighten faster.

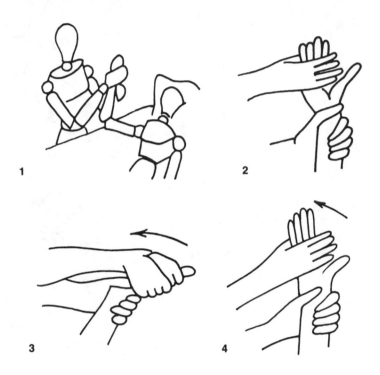

Hemiplegic Self-ROM

Starting Position: Interlock fingers of good and affected hands. Rest the affected wrist on the opposite knee.

ROM: Bend affected hand up and down.

Finger Flexion and Extension

ROM by Nurse

Starting Position: Stabilize the hand by holding the palm of the hand in a neutral position.

ROM: Bend and straighten all fingers at one time.

If the fingers are stiff, bend and straighten each individual finger. To move each joint individually, stabilize directly above and below the joint to be moved.

Hemiplegic Self-ROM

Starting Position: Place involved hand on lap or table, palm up.

ROM: Straighten involved fingers and then bend into a fist.

Thumb Abduction

ROM by Nurse

Starting Position: Stabilize the hand by holding the patient's fingers straight with one hand. Hold the thumb with the other (1).

ROM: Pull the thumb away from the palm, stretching the webbing between the thumb and index finger (2).

1

2

Hemiplegic Self-ROM

Starting Position: Place involved hand on lap in neutral position, thumb and index finger facing up. Place thumb and index finger of uninvolved hand between the thumb web of the involved hand.

ROM: Spread thumb and index finger of uninvolved hand so thumb web of affected hand is spread open.

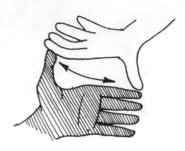

Thumb Opposition

ROM by Nurse

Starting Position: Same starting position as with thumb abduction (1).

Move thumb over to the little finger, making it describe a semicircle (2).

ROM: A good active exercise for this movement involves the patient making circles between the thumb and each finger (3).

1   2

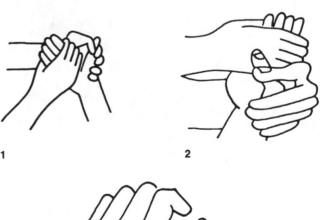

3

Hemiplegic Self-ROM

Starting Position: Place involved hand on lap, palm up. Move thumb over to the little finger.

LOWER EXTREMITIES

Hip Flexion

ROM by Nurse

Starting Position: Patient's leg flat on bed. Nurse holds under knee and under heel.

ROM: Raise knee toward chest, producing as much bending at the hip as possible. Allow the knee to bend slightly or within the patient's tolerance and comfort.

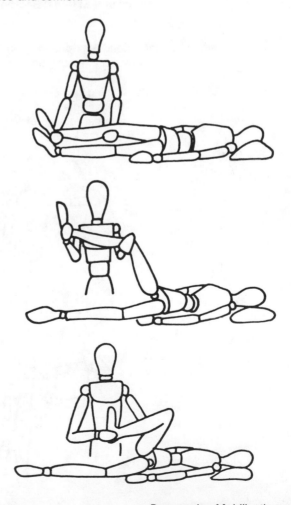

Hamstring Stretching—Straight Leg Raising

(This is one of the problem areas where the muscle bridges two joints [hip and knee].)

Starting Position: Patient's leg flat on bed. Nurse holds under knee and heel.

ROM: Keep the patient's leg straight. Gently lift leg up straight and as high as possible, hold for five count, lower the leg gently down to the bed, relax, and repeat. Move hands to hold the leg securely and comfortably.

Internal and External Rotation of the Hip

Method 1

Starting Position: Bend hip up to 90° angle and bend the knee to 90°. Hold patient under knee and under heel (1).

ROM: Keeping the hip and knee in place, turn the lower leg toward you (2), (internal rotation of the hip). Then turn it away from you (3), (4), (external rotation of the hip). Do not force this movement. It can injure the knee.

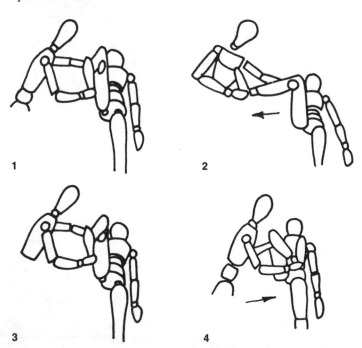

Method 2

Starting Position: Keep leg positioned flat on the bed and patient's toes and kneecap pointed upward toward the ceiling. Nurse places hands on top of patient's leg, one above the knee, one above the ankle.

ROM: Roll leg inward (1), (internal rotation). Then roll leg outward (2), (external rotation).

A patient can work actively on rotation using Method 2. Method 1 is very difficult to do actively.

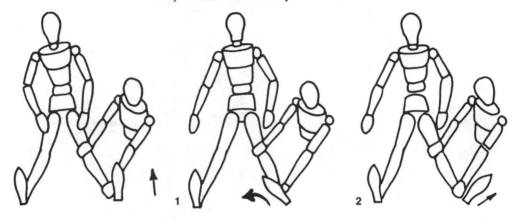

Start   1   2

Abduction and Adduction of the Hip

Starting Position: Patient's leg flat on the bed. Your hand under the knee and under the heel (1). Keep leg in "toes up" position as described on the preceding page.

ROM: Keeping the leg flat on the bed, pull the leg out toward you (2), (hip abduction). Then move the leg in toward the other leg (3), (hip adduction).

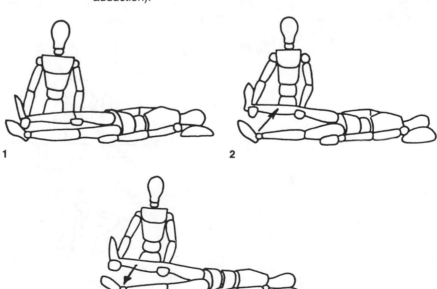

1   2

3

Knee Flexion and Extension

Method 1

Starting Position: Leg flat on bed. Nurse holds under patient's thigh and at the ankle, as shown (1).

ROM: Lift the thigh and slide the heel along the bed toward the buttocks, causing flexion at the knee (2). Pull out at heel and rest leg straight on bed (1). Repeat.

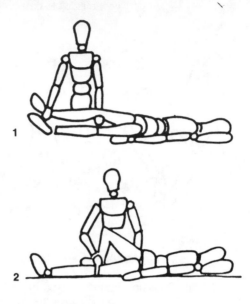

Method 2

Starting Position: Same as for method 1.

ROM: Put thigh in approximately 90° of flexion, bend knee, straighten knee five times, then return to start position. Move hands to hold extremity securely and comfortably. This method may also be used for hamstring stretching.

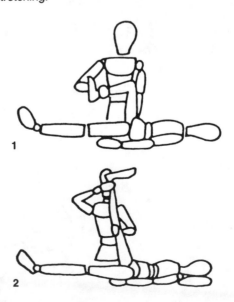

Dorsiflexion of Ankle (Heel Cord Stretch)

Starting Position: Stand facing the bed with feet spread apart. Patient's leg remains flat on the bed. Place one hand gripping heel as shown. Place other hand just above ankle; press downward toward the bed holding the leg flat.

ROM: Pull down on heel, keep your elbow straight, and lean toward the head of the bed pressing your forearm against bottom of the patient's foot. This pushes the foot up toward the leg or bends the ankle and stretches the heel cord (gastrocnemius muscle). Hold position firmly, count to five slowly, relax to the starting position, and repeat.

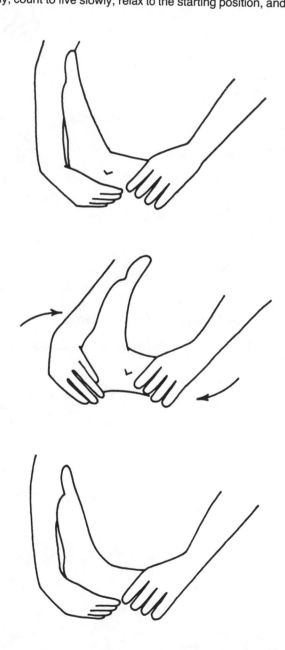

Inversion and Eversion of Foot

Starting Position: Patient's leg flat on bed. Put one hand on patient's leg to prevent internal or external movement of leg. One hand holds foot as shown.

ROM: Turn foot outward. **(1)**
Turn foot inward. **(2)**

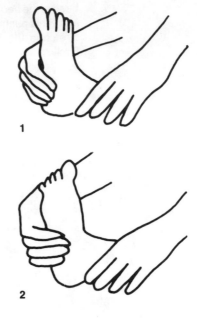

Toe Flexion and Extension

Starting Position: Hold foot as shown.

ROM: Bend all toes down. **(1)**
Pull all toes up. **(2)**

Flex and extend each toe joint individually if tightness or weakness of the toes has been determined (use the method described above for finger flexion and extension).

This completes the ROM exercises. Remember to evaluate your patient and pick out the exercises needed. As we discuss how to accomplish different functional activities in the remainder of this book, evaluate each activity for the ROM it produces.

In summary:

1. Maintain a periodic check on your patient's ROM. Do not let the patient get tight—it could retard or prevent independence.
2. Do not overemphasize ROM.
3. Do ROM in conjunction with other activities.
4. Get your patient active as soon as possible.
5. Use passive ROM only as a starting point.
6. Quickly use ROM as a strengthening process in conjunction with active ROM and functional activities.

Now the patient is ready to move on his own to be taught some functional activities. The next three activities will be discussed in dialogue form. I strongly suggest that you try each activity yourself as you proceed through the instruction. Remember that players in our dialogues are the nurse and the patient Mr. Jones.

Moving Up and Down in Bed

The nurse prepares the scene by

1. lifting the siderails
2. rolling the bed flat
3. turning down the blanket and straightening the sheets
4. checking Mr. Jones's pulse and any other cardiac symptoms

THE NURSE: Mr. Jones, I will tell you how to move up further in bed so that you will be able to do it yourself. O.K.?

MR. JONES: That's great! What do I do?

THE NURSE: Reach upward with your arms to hold onto the headboard. Bend your knees and hips, and place your feet flat on the bed. Now pull with your arms and push with your legs simultaneously. This will allow you to move up

toward the head of the bed. There, you moved a little. Do it again. It might take you more than one try to get there.

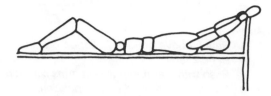

Now to move down in bed, Mr. Jones, just reverse the technique. Check Mr. Jones's pulse.

The patient can also reach for the edge of the mattress, the siderails, or a trapeze. Be sure he reaches above his head.

Or the patient can get into a quarter or half sitting position and use his hands and elbows and arms to push, as illustrated below.

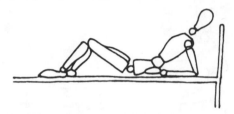

Find a bed and follow the nurse's instructions. Could you move up in bed according to these instructions? Remember to adapt techniques within the patient's limited physical abilities, e.g., a stroke patient would use only uninvolved upper and lower extremities. A hip fracture patient would *not* use the fractured hip unless it was approved for weight bearing.

To give assistance, hold the patient's feet so he can push easier with his legs or help the patient to move his buttocks by sliding your hands under them. Always be aware of your own body mechanics.

If patients are not cooperative, keep working with and encouraging them. This is difficult work for the patients, but as they become stronger, it becomes easier for them. Furthermore, most patients become so pleased with their progress that they try harder.

Test on Moving Up and Down in Bed

Try to answer these questions to see if you learned how to move up in bed.

1. Describe briefly, step by step, how to move up in bed.
    a. _____
    b. _____
    c. _____
    d. _____

2. To pull effectively with his arms, the patient must reach _____ his head.
3. How does a patient move down in bed? _____
4. How would a hemiplegic move up in bed? _____
_____

Answers:
1. a. *Reach above head to headboard or use elbows to push.*
   b. *Bend knees.*
   c. *Push with feet and pull with arms simultaneously.*
   d. *Repeat until moved up into position.*
2. *Above.*
3. *Reverse the technique for moving up in bed.*
4. *Follow the same instructions, but use one arm and leg.*

Moving Sideways in Bed

Bed Activities

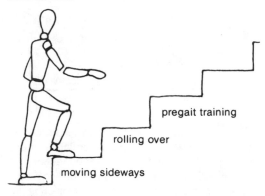

pregait training

rolling over

moving sideways

moving up

Now that Mr. Jones can move up in bed, he will use some of the techniques from that activity and learn to move sideways in bed. Let us assume that Mr. Jones will be moving toward the right side of the bed. The nurse prepares the scene again by

1. lifting the siderails
2. rolling the bed flat
3. turning down the blanket and straightening the sheets
4. checking Mr. Jones's pulse and any other cardiac symptoms

THE NURSE: First put your right hand on the siderail, Mr. Jones, just at the level of your shoulder. Don't reach too high.

Now bend both your knees, and put your feet flat on the bed. Lift your hips off the bed by pushing on your feet. Raise them just enough to clear the bed.

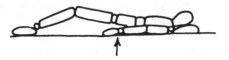

While you have your hips off the bed, shift your hips to the right, then put them down on the bed and relax. Now, move your head and shoulders over toward the right; scooting them is fine. You can pull with your arm, too, if necessary.
Good job, Mr. Jones.

Check Mr. Jones's pulse.

A hemiplegic patient might have difficulty moving his involved leg in bed. To move it in bed, the patient should place the uninvolved foot under the involved ankle. The patient then lifts the involved leg just enough to clear the bed and moves the uninvolved leg as needed for the particular activity. Likewise, the upper extremity is moved by the uninvolved upper extremity by grasping it at the wrist.

We sometimes call the activity of lifting up the buttocks "bed pan" exercises. Patients seem to understand the movements better with a picture of the bed pan routine in their minds. To assist a patient with this activity, you can do any one or a combination of the following:

1. Hold the patient's knees and feet in the flexed position.
2. Give the patient assistance to clear his buttocks off the bed. Do this by sliding your hand under the buttocks.

3. In conjunction with (2), give the patient assistance in shifting his hips to the side. Stand on the same side toward which he is moving. After putting your arm or arms under his buttocks, pull toward you.

Consider the motions necessary to move sideways in bed and you will see the strengthening process in action. Briefly, bending hips and knees into position strengthens hip flexor muscles and hamstrings; raising the hips off the bed strengthens the buttocks, back, and abdominal muscles; and pulling with the arms strengthens hand muscles and many arm muscles, especially the biceps. Each functional activity described in this chapter, when analyzed, strengthens particular muscle groups.

Find a bed and follow the nurse's instructions. Could you move over in bed according to these instructions?

Test on Moving Sideways in Bed

After you practice the maneuver, please answer these questions:

1. Describe briefly, step by step, how to move over in bed.
    a. _____
    b. _____
    c. _____
    d. _____
    e. _____
2. How does a hemiplegic patient move his involved leg sideways? _____
_____
3. What are bed pan exercises? _____
_____

Answers:
1. a. Put hand on the siderail at shoulder level.
*   b. Bend knees.*
*   c. Lift hips off bed.*
*   d. Shift hips sideways.*
*   e. Pull shoulder over.*
2. By putting the uninvolved foot under the involved ankle.
3. Lifting the hips off the bed.

Rolling over in Bed

Bed Activities

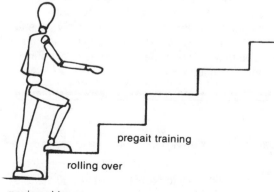

pregait training

rolling over

moving sideways

Preparations for this activity are the same as those for the two previous activities. Remember to check the pulse. The nurse stands on the left side of the bed. Mr. Jones is lying on his back.

THE NURSE: Mr. Jones, I will want you to roll over on to your right side. You are lying in the middle of the bed now. Please move sideways toward me [to the left] so you'll have more room to roll over in the bed. Move just a little off center. Now cross your left leg over your right leg as far as possible. Cross your left arm over your chest and reach for the siderail or mattress. You can also hold onto the mattress or railing with your right arm, if you wish. Pull with your arms and roll over. Good job! Check Mr. Jones's pulse.

Crossing the "left leg over the right leg" as far as possible shifts the buttocks toward the right and starts the patient into the roll. If the patient is a hemiplegic and you are rolling him, put the good foot under the bad ankle to cross the legs. (See how many activities have this same motion? Your patients should learn this activity early.)

Sometimes the patient cannot roll over. In that case, try having him swing his arm and/or leg across. This will create some momentum, which will help. (Notice that we are using the patient's body mechanics here. The heaviest part of a patient is his hips. By crossing his leg and arm in the direction to be turned, they are used as lever arms to lift the hip weight.)

Assistance might be needed when the patient first starts the activity, but as the activity is done, the patient will become stronger and able to do it easier.

Find a bed and follow the nurse's instructions. Could you roll over in bed according to these instructions?

Test on Rolling over in Bed

Please answer the following questions.

1. Describe briefly, step by step, how to roll over in bed.
   a. _____
   b. _____
   c. _____
   d. _____
2. How are the patient's body mechanics used to help him roll over in bed? _____
   _____
3. If you are rolling to the left, which leg is crossed over the top of the other? _____

Answers:
1. a. *Move toward the left side of the bed—just off center.*
   b. *Cross leg in the direction you are going—left over right.*
   c. *Cross left arm over chest and reach for the siderail.*
   d. *Pull over.*
2. *By using his legs as lever arms to shift the weight of his hips.*
3. *Right leg over left.*

   How did you do? If you answered all questions correctly, you are doing fine. Let's continue.

We have now discussed all activities performed in bed. We've determined that Mr. Jones has some mobility. He's rather easy to handle in bed now, as he is able to help himself.

Special Note: The nurse taught Mr. Jones these activities during the course of the day while giving him general nursing care. She taught him to move up in bed when he slid down too far, and she taught him to roll over while changing his sheets. Many hours are saved after patients are taught to do these activities themselves. After they learn, they do not need to ring the bell again to be moved in bed; they can do it alone. Your Mr. Jones can learn too!

Unit Review Test on Bed Activities

To check your understanding of this unit, please complete the following test. Write your answers in the space provided.

1. In which muscle groups is limitation of range of motion most likely to occur? _____

2. Range of motion activities accomplish two things. Name them.
   a. _____
   b. _____
3. Describe two different methods of using the arms to move up in bed.
   a. _____
   b. _____
4. Mrs. Williams has a broken right hip. What steps would she take to move toward the left side of the bed?
   a. _____
   b. _____
   c. _____
   d. _____
   e. _____
   f. _____
5. In which two joints might tightness occur if pillows were placed under the knees?
   a. _____
   b. _____
6. How does a hemiplegic or a hip fracture patient move his involved leg in bed?_____
   _____
7. Your patient is bedbound and unconscious. Testing for range of motion has shown that all joints except the ankle are limber. How would you proceed with range of motion activities?
   _____
   _____
8. Why is it important to use good bed positioning with your bedbound patient?_____
   _____

Now that you have answered these questions, compare your responses with those given below.
1. *Ones that bridge two or more joints, e.g., gastrocnemius, hamstrings, finger flexors.*
2. *a. Limber muscles and joints.*
   b. Initial strengthening.
3. *a. Pull on headboard, mattress, trapeze.*
   b. Get into quarter to half sitting position and push with arms.
4. *a. Put left hand on siderail at shoulder level.*
   b. Bend left knee.
   c. Lift hips up off bed.
   d. Shift hips to the left.
   e. Pull shoulders over.
   f. Move right leg over sideways.
5. *a. Hips.*
   b. Knees.
6. *Puts the foot of the uninvolved leg under the ankle of the involved leg, lifts the leg slightly, and moves it with the uninvolved leg.*
7. *Position the patient properly. Do passive ROM along with bathing. Do passive ROM on ankle whenever in the room with patient.*
8. *To prevent deformities that might prevent patient independence later.*

If you answered eight correct, a perfect score! Turn to pregait training section. If seven correct, you are still doing great. Turn to pregait training section. If five or six correct, this is satisfactory; but please look up and review your errors in the text before continuing. If zero to four correct, sorry, poor score. Please review the bed activities section.

What else can Mr. Jones learn to do independently? Have you observed that each functional activity employs some action that the patient has learned in a previous activity? That's Progressive Mobilization—the Independence Staircase.

PREGAIT TRAINING

This unit is called *pregait training*. Let's watch Mr. Jones learn to sit up and stand up.

Assuming a Sitting Position

Mr. Jones is going to sit at the edge of the bed. Here, even more than with bed activities, it is important to check for cardiac symptoms and pulse responses. Dizziness is probably the most common occurrence when the patient first sits up.

Doctor S. orders "Dangling 5 minutes 2 × daily." Let's see how the nurse and Mr. Jones handle this one. The nurse prepares the scene by doing the following:

1. rolls the bed flat
2. stands at the right side of the bed
3. takes Mr. Jones' pulse
4. checks that he is wearing his shoes

THE NURSE: O.K., Mr. Jones, you have learned to move easily in bed. Now put together all those things you have learned and move to a sitting position at the edge of the bed. First, move sideways toward this edge of the bed. Roll over onto your right side. Good. Now slide your right arm underneath you with your elbow bent. That's tough. Maybe I can help you get it back there. You see you'll have to use it to push with in a minute.

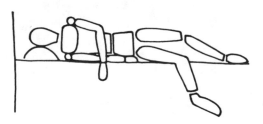

Now do these two things at the same time. Drop your legs off the bed and start pushing up with your right elbow.

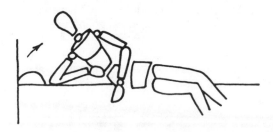

After your weight has been transferred onto your right elbow, shift your weight to your right hand and keep pushing until you are upright.

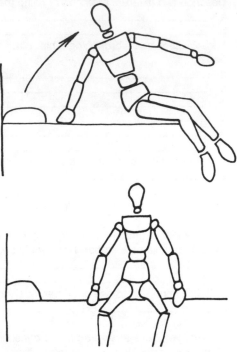

That's it. Are you dizzy? Your pulse is good.

A stroke patient should always roll onto the uninvolved side to sit up. It is much easier for him that way.

If the patient needs help, assist him as necessary, but encourage him to do as much as he can alone. Three varying degrees of assistance might be as follows:

1. Help a patient move his legs off the bed.
2. Place your hand under the patient's head and help push his body up.
3. Put your arm under the patient's shoulder and help push him up to a sitting position (see picture below).

As soon as the doctor states that it is all right to have your patient sit, refer to the Sitting Tolerance Schedule (Table 12-1). If the patient cannot move into a sitting position alone, provide all the necessary help. Just get the patient to sit!

Be sure to watch your body mechanics. Notice the difference between this method of assisting Mr. Jones and the method used by the nurse and Mr. Smith in the section above entitled "Tool 3: Using Proper Body Mechanics." This is the correct way to sit up even the largest or most involved patient.

You should go on to the next activity, sitting balance, but we will pause and check to see if you understand the sitting up procedure.

Practice: Find a bed and follow the nurse's instructions. Could you sit up according to these instructions?

1. *Describe briefly, step by step, how to sit at the edge of the bed.*
   a. _____
   b. _____
   c. _____
   d. _____
   e. _____
2. *If the patient needs help, where would you assist him?* _____
   _____
3. *What is the most common occurrence when the patient sits up for the first time?* _____
   _____
   _____
4. *Which way should a stroke patient roll to get into a sitting position?* _____
   _____

Answers:

1. a. *Move toward edge of the bed.*
   b. *Roll onto your side.*
   c. *Put your arm underneath you.*
   d. *Drop legs off bed and push up with arms at the same time.*
   e. *Push until sitting.*
2. *At the legs, head, or shoulders.*
3. *The patient gets dizzy (blood pressure drops).*
4. *Onto his uninvolved side.*

If you feel that you can do this activity, go on to the next discussion.

Sitting Balance

versus

When the patient is in a sitting position, it is important that he has good sitting balance. This means that he should be able to sit unsupported, even against resistance.

Have you ever had a patient who kept falling over when sitting on the edge of the bed? This is called poor sitting balance. To help a patient achieve good sitting balance, two factors must be considered: (1) good body position and (2) practice.

Position: The patient should

1. sit level on the bed—bed flat—weight even on both buttocks
2. position feet flat on the floor—wide base of support (notice the principle of body mechanics here)—shoes on
3. place arm, or arms, where he can push on them to maintain a good, erect position (initially, you may have to let him hold onto the edge of the bed to keep his balance or you may have to assist him).

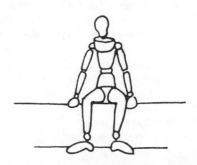

Practice: To work with the patient, stand in front of him. By doing this, you can help him move his hands or body as needed and can demonstrate what an upright position looks like. Also, in this position, you will not be tilting the bed with your own weight. (Did you ever sit on a bed and find yourself sliding toward the nearest person, who weighed more than you?) Give the patient all the advantage you can.

As the patient's sitting balance improves, he should be able to sit without holding onto the edge of the bed and should be able to move his arms around at will. He should practice reaching above his head, out to the side, out in front, etc. The patient should start by lifting his arms just a little and putting them back on the bed. Next time, he should raise them higher until he can do all the reaching activities easily and still maintain an erect position.

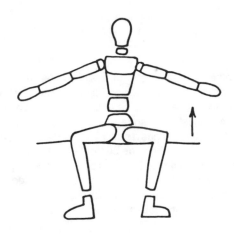

After the patient can do the above, the nurse should add resistance to the activity by pushing on the patient from either side, from the front, or from the back. (Let the patient know that you are going to do this exercise so he does not think you are just trying to push him over!) Good sitting balance is achieved when the patient can do all this. This achievement means that the patient has good trunk control. Often, much time must be spent sitting with the patient to achieve good sitting balance. It is very important to spend the time, because if the patient does not have enough trunk control to sit, he will not have enough trunk control to stand. A patient with poor sitting balance will forever be slumped over in a wheelchair. (See also Chapter 14 for obtaining good sitting balance in a wheelchair.)

A good time to practice sitting balance is when the doctor first prescribes "dangling." If you con-

sider the patient's sitting balance when he dangles, the dangling experience will be much more pleasurable.

Another important aspect of dangling is that it is the start of the "push" to build up your patient's sitting tolerance or his ability to stay out of bed for long periods of time (eventually all day). See again the Sitting Tolerance Schedule (Table 12-1). The more your patient is out of bed, the more opportunities for doing different activities; the patient will become stronger and more independent.

Can you see your patient climbing the Independence Staircase?

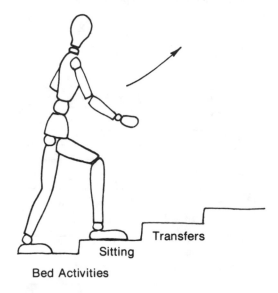

Transfers
Sitting
Bed Activities

Transfers

Your patient has come up quite far now on the Independence Staircase. The next step, transfers, is a difficult one. Often this is the highest level to which a patient can advance. If a patient can be independent at this level, he can function quite well in a home situation. He can cook, get around, get in and out of bed, get to the bathroom, etc. He is wheelchair independent. Acceptance of such a goal should not be considered "giving up." It is a reasonable alternative for the person who cannot be expected to walk functionally. Individuals commonly live independently at home, work at demanding professions, travel, and engage in sports—all from a wheelchair. Such persons accept no limitations on their horizons. With that in mind, independence in transferring is a big step, and we want Mr. Jones to learn how to move from his bed to a wheelchair.

Standing Transfers

Standing transfers in all situations (e.g., bed, toilet, regular chair, or car) are accomplished in basically the same manner as bed to wheelchair. The variations depend only on structural differences in the appliances. Set the scene by doing the following:

1. Roll the bed flat and check Mr. Jones's pulse rate.
2. Adjust the height of the bed so Mr. Jones's feet will touch the floor when he sits on the edge of the bed.
3. Put on his shoes. This is done so Mr. Jones has a good solid foundation. You do not want your patients to slip. If they do not have shoes on, have them transfer barefooted rather than wearing "slick" slippers. Do not transfer patients with just elastic stockings on their feet. They will certainly slip.
4. Bring in the wheelchair and check to see that it is a safe chair: good framework, brakes lock well, foot plates work properly, and it wheels easily. The wheelchair in this case is a standard wheelchair. (See Chapter 14 for fitting particular patients.)
5. Determine which side is Mr. Jones's stronger side. It is determined that Mr. Jones is stronger on the left. If the chair is placed on the patient's strongest side, the patient will have more confidence and find it easier to transfer.
6. Lift up the foot plates, removing obstacles that are in the way.
7. Place the chair on his left side, parallel to the bed, and in a position where the raised foot plates will be between Mr. Jones' feet and the bed.
8. Lock the brakes! This is so the chair will not roll when he puts his weight on it.
9. When all is ready, Mr. Jones sits up. His sitting balance is good. His pulse is stable.
10. Stand in front of Mr. Jones, near enough to help, but do not hinder his movements.

Remember body mechanics, of course. Be prepared. Now Mr. Jones is ready to move from his bed to the wheelchair.

THE NURSE: Mr. Jones, slide forward to the edge of the bed. Place both feet flat on the floor and spaced sufficiently apart for good balance. Place your right hand flat on the bed and your left hand on the right armrest of the chair (1).

1

Now lean forward slightly at the hips. Push on your hands, straighten your legs and trunk, and stand up (2).

2

Now start moving your feet toward the left. First left foot, then right, turning them so that you begin moving in a circle. Use small steps. Move your left hand to the other armrest. Keep turning until you are standing directly in front of the chair and feel the back of both legs against the chair. Put your right hand on the chair, too (3).

3

Lean forward slightly and sit down slowly. Lower yourself with your arms and legs. Slide back in the chair and sit squarely (4).

4

Put your feet on the foot plates. Good, you're there, safe and sound! To get back to bed, Mr. Jones, you would reverse the process, placing the chair again so that you would be moving toward your good side.

Mr. Jones's pulse is fine. He has responded well to the activity.

When Mr. Jones leans slightly forward before he stands, this movement centers his weight over his feet. Put your hands on Mr. Jones's rib cage to help him stand if he needs help. Your knees should be bent, back straight. Brace his leg or legs with your legs if he needs the support. (See illustration B, p. 80, for correct position to assist with transfers.) As Mr. Jones gets stronger, you will have to help him less and less. He will reach a point where you can stand farther away from him while he does the activity alone. Remember, *do not* give assistance unless needed.

If the patient is a stroke patient with no responses at all in the hemiplegic side or if the patient is a non-weight-bearing patient on one side, he should pivot on the uninvolved foot.

Now you should practice as if you were (1) Mr. Jones and (2) the nurse.

Test on Standing Transfers

Answer these questions.

1. Where does the patient push to stand up? _____
2. How does a stroke patient turn in a circle? _____
   _____
3. Where should the nurse hold Mr. Jones to assist him? _____
   _____
4. How should the wheelchair be placed in relation to the following:
   a. Mr Jones:_____
   b. The bed:_____
5. Name two safety measures regarding the wheelchair that are important for patient transfers:
   a. _____
   b. _____

Answers:
1. *On the armrest of the chair and on the bed.*
2. *By pivoting on the uninvolved leg.*
3. *Around the rib cage area. You should never pull up the patient's arm; this could cause damage, especially to a hemiplegic arm.*
4. a. *On his stronger side. The patient should always move in the direction of his good side.*
   b. *Parallel to the bed and between the bed and Mr. Jones's feet.*
5. a. *Locking brakes.*
   b. *Raising foot plates.*

If you answered these correctly you are doing well. Transfers done properly are very important to you and your patient. Be sure that you can do the standing transfer step by step and feel comfortable with the dialogue so you will be able to teach a patient.

Four-Person Transfers

If you find that you cannot transfer a patient yourself because of the patient's weight, disability, etc., seek additional help immediately. As many as four people can be used to help transfer a patient effectively using the following system.

Let us suppose that the nurse is helping to transfer Mr. Jones from his bed to a wheelchair. She places the wheelchair on Mr. Jones's strong side at a 30° angle to the bed. As the person in charge, she should assess carefully why she needs the additional assistance and then determine where to place the helpers for an effective transfer. She should recruit only the help needed. She does not want to lift the patient completely but to assist him where he is weak. She positions herself in front of the patient, bracing his knees with her knees, placing her hands around his rib cage, etc. (see Figure 12-9). The nurse is labelled person #1. She will help Mr. Jones to stand, allowing him to do as much as he can for himself but being prepared to help him when necessary. Her instructions to him throughout the transfer will be as previously described in the standing transfer. It is important that Mr. Jones knows the steps of the transfer and begins learning them even when he is very weak.

We have found many times that a patient can stand with the assistance of one person but cannot turn to sit down in the chair safely. If that is true of Mr. Jones, the nurse should call another person, labelled #2 in Figure 12-10, who would place his hands firmly on either side of Mr. Jones's hips and help him to turn. This person should stand between the bed and the wheelchair, with one knee on the bed for good body mechanics. Standing in this manner, person #2 might also be able to help lift or lower the patient a little. However, lifting from this position, though safe for moving hips, could injure person #2's back if he lifts too much weight. Therefore, if the patient needs considerable assistance to stand, recruit another helper (person #3) to get in the position shown in Figure 12-10. This person would kneel on the opposite side of the bed and could then lean Mr. Jones forward and help him to a standing position by lifting under his hips. In returning Mr. Jones to the bed, the person in this position could pull his hips back on the bed.

If Mr. Jones also has difficulty standing up out of the wheelchair or is too weak for the nurse (person #1) to lower him to a sitting position slowly, then another helper (person #4) should be placed behind the wheelchair (see Figure 12-11). From this position, person #4 can assist in standing or

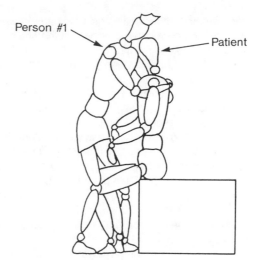

Figure 12-9 One-Person Transfer

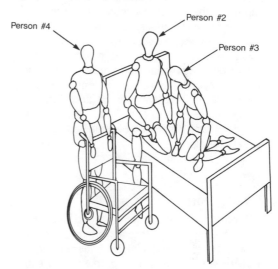

Figure 12-10 Positions of Assistants in Four-Person Transfer

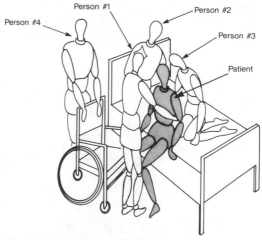

Figure 12-11 Four-Person Transfer

sitting the patient as well as help the patient lean forward and scoot forward or back in the chair.

Can you see the entire scene? Look at Figures 12-9, 12-10, and 12-11 and read about the transfer in the following paragraph.

The nurse (person #1) stands in front of Mr. Jones, ready to assist him to transfer from bed to wheelchair. Person # 3 helps scoot him to the edge of the bed, leans him forward, and puts her hands under his hips. On the signal from the nurse, person #3 helps Mr. Jones to stand by lifting up on his hips. Then person #2 places his hands on the sides of Mr. Jones's hips and helps the nurse turn Mr. Jones toward the wheelchair. When Mr. Jones has both of his legs against the wheelchair, person #4 places her hands underneath his hips and helps lower him and also scoots him back into the wheelchair. It is very important that everyone work as a team when transferring a patient in this manner.

If one of your patients needs to be transferred using helpers, remember to move the patient slowly, giving him adequate directions and time to try to do as much as he can for himself. You may need a lot of help with him at first, but as he practices the transfer he will be able to do more and more for himself and eventually may be able to transfer alone.

Continue reading for another functional type of transfer.

Sliding Board Transfers

If your patient cannot stand, sliding board transfers are ideal. This particular transfer serves well the paraplegic or quadriplegic patient or anyone who for some reason is unable to do a standing transfer. I have used it with patients who have had severe knee flexion contractures and hemiplegic patients who were too heavy or weak for me to assist to a standing position. This transfer is ideal for families when they are without the aid of a nurse or therapist.

To do this transfer, one first must have a wheelchair with removable arms (refer to Chapter 14 regarding removable arms) and a sliding board. Sliding boards are now standard rehabilitation items and can be purchased from most medical supply offices. If one needs to be manufactured, a 10- by 28-inch board made of a strong wood and varnished heavily will work well.

Imagine the nurse is preparing to transfer Mr. Jones using a sliding board. She positions the wheelchair as for a standing transfer. She locks the brakes, removes the foot rest closer to the bed (if possible), or lifts up the foot plate. She moves the arm of the wheelchair closer to the bed. Mr. Jones is sitting at the edge of the bed. He should be wearing shoes and his feet should be touching the floor. Because bare skin sticks, he should also be wearing slacks or pajamas so he can slip easily on the sliding board. The nurse directs the patient to lean over to the side away from the wheelchair and she puts one end of the sliding board under his buttocks. She puts the other end of the sliding board on the chair seat.

The nurse stands in front of Mr. Jones and blocks his knees with her knees and puts her hands around his trunk (or she could use a belt around his waist to balance him). She directs him to lean forward slightly. He should then push with his arms, lift his buttocks slightly off the board, and slide over toward the wheelchair. The nurse encourages him to use all the available muscle strength in his legs and in his arms. She then might need only to pull on his belt to help him. The nurse and Mr. Jones repeat this action until the transfer is completed. She allows him to place his hands along the sliding board or wherever he can on the wheelchair to move himself most effectively. Many patients can learn to do this transfer independently, especially paraplegic patients.

If Mr. Jones cannot help at all, the nurse might need to press against his knees and pull him forward toward her, creating a rocking movement that will allow her to slide him sideways on the board and into the wheelchair. She should always remember her body mechanics.

If a sliding board is not available, a pillow can be placed over the wheelchair tire to span the gap between the bed and the wheelchair and protect the patient from the wheelchair parts. Then a transfer similar to a sliding board transfer can be performed.

Using a pillow to transfer is more difficult than using the sliding board, because the sliding feature of the board is eliminated and the patient must lift his hips up enough to shift his buttocks sideways toward the wheelchair. Though this method is more difficult, it is possible to perform and is safer for the patient and nurse than standing a person unable to stand. For the patient who can lift his buttocks up easily and shift his hips but cannot stand, this method works well. If he can use a pillow, a sliding board is not needed.

After the patient can move easily across to the chair, he can often discard pillows and sliding boards and lift himself across into the chair.

Test on Sliding Board Transfers

Please answer the following questions to test your understanding of sliding board transfers.

1. Describe the type of wheelchair needed to perform a sliding board transfer. _____

2. Name two reasons for using a pillow for this type of transfer. _____

3. Does a patient have to be able to lift his hips to use a sliding board? _____
   Why? _____

4. What type of patient would use a sliding board? _____

Answers:
1. *One with removable arms and, preferably, removable legs.*
2. *a. It spans the gap between the wheelchair and the bed.*
   b. It protects the patient from the wheelchair parts.
   c. It eliminates the need for purchasing a sliding board if the patient can initially use this method or can progress from using a sliding board to using this method.
3. *No. You can pull him over on the sliding board or use a rocking motion to slide him over.*
4. *One who could not come to a standing position due to paraplegia, quadriplegia, weakness, weight, or the limited strength of the assistant.*

Note: You have just learned a number of different transfers. It is important to evaluate your patient carefully to decide which method to use. Always choose the method most appropriate for the patient at the time. As the patient progresses with rehabilitation, the method of transferring him should be changed accordingly.

Wheelchair Mobilization and Weight Shifting

Wheelchair Mobilization

THE NURSE: Unlock the wheelchair brakes, Mr. Jones. There are two. When unlocked the brakes do not touch the wheels. [You might need to teach your patient to do this. Refer to Chapter 14 regarding wheelchair brakes.]

Place your hands on the steel rims and push forward and evenly on both wheels. The wheelchair will move straightforward.

To turn to the left, push only on the right wheel. To turn to the right, push only on the left wheel.

To go backward, pull backward evenly on both wheels.

If the patient is a stroke patient and has function only on one side, he must use the arm and leg on that side to wheel the chair. This is accomplished in the following manner:

1. Raise the foot plate on the uninvolved side and place the patient's foot on the floor (with shoes on).
2. Put the uninvolved hand on the wheel.
3. Push (as above) with the uninvolved hand and "pull" with the uninvolved foot.

"Pulling" with the foot is done by extending the knee, placing the heel of the foot down firmly on the ground, keeping it on the ground, and forcibly flexing the knee. The patient can "pull" the chair along in this manner. (Sometimes patients use their toes to pull.) Likewise, the foot acts as a rudder to straighten the chair out as one goes along. Because of the use of the foot, it is very important for this particular type patient to be in a chair which allows his whole foot to touch the floor easily. (See Chapter 14 regarding hemi wheelchairs.) If his foot does not touch the floor, the patient cannot wheel the chair.

Major Safety Note: Always lock the brakes and raise the foot plates when the chair has stopped and the patient intends to get out of it.

Weight Shifting in the Wheelchair

It is important that patients be able to shift their weight in the wheelchair for two reasons:

1. Pressure must be taken off the buttocks to prevent decubiti from prolonged sitting. (Patients should shift weight at least every fifteen minutes. See also Chapter 9.)
2. Patients must be able to lift their buttocks so they can reposition themselves in the chair.

Wheelchair Push-ups

Wheelchair push-ups are designed to accomplish the two above mentioned goals as well as to strengthen the arms. Wheelchair push-ups are most valuable for paraplegic patients who have absolutely no sensation in the buttocks area.

Repeating the push-up 10 to 50 times at one session turns the push-up into an exercise which strengthens the patient's triceps and shoulder depressors. These muscles are particularly important for crutch gait. Obviously the exercise would be good for any patient you are teaching to crutch walk or walk with a walker.

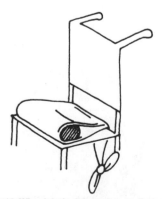

Figure 12–12 Wheelchair Adaptation to Prevent Slipping

Method:

- Place one hand on each armrest, elbows bent.
- Keep the shoulders level, lean forward slightly, push on the hand and straighten the elbows, lifting the hips off of the chair.
- Hold to count of five.

Holding the hips off the chair allows the circulation to flow freely in the buttocks and allows the patient's position in the chair to be changed.

A hemiplegic patient also must be able to shift weight in the chair, but because of the lack of use of one side of his body, a wheelchair push-up is impossible. However a modified push-up can be done.

Method:

- Use one hand on the armrest.
- Place feet on the foot plates.
- Lean forward slightly, bending at the hips. (Do not lean so far forward as to fall out of the chair or tip it over.)
- Push with arm and both legs as much as possible to lift the hips.

Note: If you have a patient who continually slips down in the wheelchair, this is what you can do to help him get back into position:

1. Stand in front of him and put his feet on the foot plates. Pulling his trunk toward you, bend him at the hips. Have him push with his hands or one hand and with his legs. As he is pushing, you push against his knees. He will slide back in the chair.
2. Have him sit on a towel in the wheelchair. You stand behind the wheelchair. Position the patient forward (bend him at the hips). Hold onto the towel and pull it toward you. This will pull his buttocks back in the chair.

To move a patient in a wheelchair successfully, the main point to remember is to have him lean forward. To prevent the patient from sliding out of the wheelchair, keep his hips in a flexed position and his buttocks at the back of the wheelchair. A method used to accomplish this when standard restraints do not work is to fold a sheet in half, with the end of it hanging through the back of the chair. Place a rolled pillow on the front of the chair on top of the sheet. Wrap the rest of the sheet firmly over the pillow and put the end of the sheet through the back of the chair. Tie the ends of the sheet to the wheelchair (Figure 12-12). Lift the patient into the wheelchair so that his knees rest on the pillow and the patient's buttocks are against the back of the chair.

Test on Wheelchair Mobility and Weight Shifting

Please answer the following questions about wheelchairs.

1. If you want the wheelchair to turn to the right, which wheel do you push? _____
2. How do you know that the brakes are locked? _____
_____
3. What is the most important point to remember when fitting a hemiplegic with a wheelchair?
_____
4. What are two ways wheelchair push-ups can help patients?
   a. _____
   b. _____
5. What is the main point to remember in repositioning a patient in a wheelchair? _____
_____

Answers:
1. *The left wheel.*
2. *The brake touches the wheel and the wheels do not move!*
3. *That his foot touches the floor. Otherwise he will not be able to use his uninvolved hand and foot to push the chair.*
4. *If you answered any of the following, you were correct:*
   a. *Prevent decubiti by weight shifting.*
   b. *Help patients slide back in the chair.*
   c. *Help strengthen arms.*
5. *Direct the patient to lean forward.*

Please review if you were unsure about any of the answers. Otherwise, continue to the next section.

Standing

Stand-ups (an essential exercise)

Transfers and standing activities go hand in hand. As a patient's standing (both strength and balance) improves, his transfers get better; and as his transfers get better, his standing improves.

Practically speaking, we can transfer patients out of bed who cannot stand alone, because we help them as much as they need to be helped. If we do it in the manner discussed in the transfer section, the patients learn to help themselves in the process. You can help them control their trunk and legs. However, for patients to progress to independent transfers and to walking, they must be taught to stand and balance themselves. Even if a patient cannot walk, the ability to stand is still extremely helpful, as it will enable standing transfers, pulling up pants, toileting, reaching, and numerous other functions. Recall that earlier we said that a patient who could lift ten pounds with his leg muscles but could not stand up from a chair was stuck. The purpose of this exercise should thus be obvious. We will now discuss exer- cises to increase stand-up ability, strength, and balance.

The exercise is called *stand-ups*. It is as simple as it sounds. The instruction to the patient to get him to perform the exercise is "Stand up." The act of standing up is remarkable in what it accomplishes. When a patient stands up, he is strengthening every muscle in his body to a certain degree. He uses his leg muscles to get up and his trunk muscles to retain a good, erect position. The main accomplishment is in the strengthening achieved in the thigh muscles (especially the quadriceps). The exercise is also a general conditioning program for the heart, lungs, and autonomic reflexes that maintain the blood flow to the head. Standing is very important to patients' ability to walk later.

The equipment needed for the stand-up exercise includes (1) a chair, (2) a table, (3) some books, firm pillows, or pieces of wood to build up the height of the chair, (4) a patient (Mr. Jones), and (5) an assistant (the nurse or anyone who wants to help the patient).

More than any other exercise, this exercise utilizes the psychological need of patients to be encouraged and to be successful. Success breeds success. Stand-ups, if done correctly, can produce high patient motivation and independence. This is accomplished by adjusting the exercise equipment so the patient can get into the standing position alone. By being able to accomplish an activity alone, the patient feels successful and is motivated and encouraged.

It is important to emphasize that the stand-up exercise and gait activities to follow must be done with as little help as possible from the nurse or any other assistant. This is to assure that the patient's own efforts provide the necessary antigravity contractions. Pushing a patient to progress too quickly, not using a step-by-step approach in his treatment plan, and physically helping him too much can produce failure. "Physical support may actually create passivity and dependence. A patient who is suported well beyond his needs learns to depend upon that support!"[2]

The following instructions for the stand-up exercise and gait activities will explain how to assist the patient safely without allowing him to depend on you for support.

1. Raise the height of a chair seat with pillows, phone books, newspapers, etc.

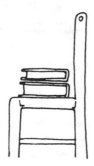

You may use captain's chairs with wooden "risers" fitted in them. These risers are boards that are either two inches in height or shaped to the chair seat and fitted together with corresponding pegs and holes to assure safe stacking of the risers (see illustrations below). The risers should be of hollow construction so as to be light enough to handle easily.

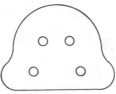

Riser top view

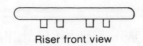

Riser front view

2. Estimate the height of the chair needed to allow the patient to stand alone. A good height at which to start can be determined by measuring the patient's leg from the knee to the foot and making the chair height one and a half times that length. Suppose the patient's leg measures 18 inches from the knee to the foot. One and a half times that amount is 27 inches, so start with a chair approximately 27 inches high (floor to seat). The angle of the knee will be approximately 130°.

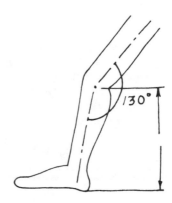

3. Sit the patient on this chair facing the table.
4. Check the patient's pulse.
5. Put the patient's hand, or hands, flat on the table.
6. Put the patient's feet on the floor (shoes on). They should touch fairly well.
7. The patient should be sitting at the edge of the chair. If seated too far back, he will find it more difficult to get up (refer to transfer and body mechanic principles).

8. Have the patient lean forward slightly, push down with his hand slightly on the table, straighten his knees and back, and stand-up. Hands should be used mostly for balance. The work should be done by the legs, not the arms.

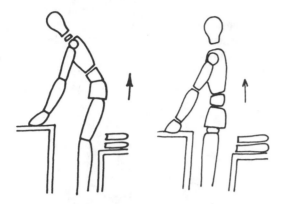

The patient should be able to stand alone, with absolutely no help from you.

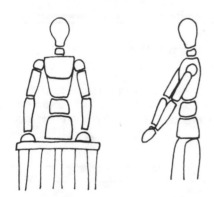

With this accomplishment, the patient is encouraged. He will be pleased with himself and ready to work harder. He now knows that he can stand up alone. He knows that he can succeed. With that important point established, you can proceed with the exercise.

If you determine that at the initial starting height the activity was too easy for the patient, let him know that he is doing well, that the stand-up was too easy and that you are going to lower the seat about an inch or so and he can try the exercise again. Keep lowering the seat until it is just moderately difficult for the patient to stand up alone. When you have found this level, the patient can begin the stand-up exercise. Repeat the exercise as follows: (1) patient stands up, (2) remains standing about ten seconds, (3) sits slowly, (4) sits about fifteen seconds. Repeat the exer-

cise 10 to 20 times at one session. The number of repetitions should correspond to the patient's tolerance. Someone very weak would do less than 10 repetitions. Later, as endurance increases, the repetitions could be increased to as many as 30. This exercise also builds endurance. The exercise should be done two to four times daily, spaced at even intervals, e.g., 8 A.M., 12 noon, 4 P.M., and 8 P.M. The more stand-ups a patient does, the stronger he becomes.

In a hospital, the bed can be raised to an appropriate height to do stand-ups effectively.

As the patient gains strength, the chair should be lowered gradually until the patient can stand from a regular chair by himself. He will then have strong legs.

We have found that strong legs are especially important with stroke patients or patients with hip fractures. Because of the added work put on the normal leg to compensate for the weak leg, it must be "super strong" to allow effective walking. We have seen this strengthening method work over and over again for almost any condition that requires leg strengthening. It works primarily, we feel, because it is simple to do, has a strong motivating effect, and the instructions are simple to follow. The directions can be explained easily by demonstrations, gestures, or tactile assistance, which allows even very confused or aphasic patients to understand the exercise.

Standing Balance

During the standing phase of the stand-up, the patient should also practice standing balance. At first, he should keep his hands on the table for balance. Then, have him lift his hands off the table, raise them sideways and overhead while maintaining his balance. The patient's ability to complete this exercise will increase with practice and gradual increase of strength. Later, resistance can be given to the patient by pushing him unexpectedly from side to side, forward and back. This will stress his balance and will increase his ability. (See the section on sitting balance for this exercise.)

Extra notes on standing, stand-ups, and standing balance:

1. After strength, endurance, and balance are gained, the patient should be instructed to continue the exercise at least daily to maintain the strength in his legs.
2. If a patient has a fractured leg, place a block of wood under the *uninvolved* foot. This helps him keep his weight off the fracture.

4. To evaluate when a patient is able to stand, test his quadriceps strength. If he can hold against some resistance, he can probably stand. Also, try to stand him. If he can stand, it is obvious that he can perform the exercise. If he cannot stand, use the standard PRE exercises until his leg strength increases sufficiently so that he can stand.

5. If the patient's balance is very bad, have him assume a wide base of support on the table with his hands.

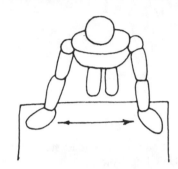

3. If a patient is too weak to perform the stand-up exercise alone, adjust the chair as high as possible and provide assistance until he can stand alone.

Test on Standing, Stand-ups, and Standing Balance

Try to answer the following questions.

1. Place two to three books in a chair. Sit on them and place your hands on the table according to the stand-up exercises. Hold one foot off the floor. Stand up and sit down ten times. Now remove both books and repeat the same exercise. Which way was easier? Can you see that it is easier to stand up from a higher chair? _____

2. This is Mr. Jones's first attempt at stand-ups.
   How much would you elevate the chair? _____
   _____
   _____

3. If Mr. Jones is having terrible standing balance problems, what could you do? _____
   _____

4. How many times a day should a patient do stand-ups to make the program effective?
   _____

5. What muscles are most strengthened by the stand-up exercises? _____
   _____

6. How long and how often should a patient continue these exercises after going home? _____

7. Why are stand-ups so effective?
   a. _____
   _____
   b. _____
   _____

8. What is the most important single goal of the stand-up program? _____
   _____

Answers:

1. *The second way should have been easier.*
   Was it?
2. *One and a half times his leg length from knee to foot—or whatever amount is needed to allow him to stand up alone.*
3. *Spread his hands apart on the table.*
4. *Two to four times a day (four would be better).*
5. *Quadriceps and other thigh muscles.*
6. *For a stroke patient, at least once a day for the rest of his life.*
7. a. *They motivate the patient.*
   b. *They are easy to do.*
8. *That the patient be able to stand up alone.*

I realize that there was a great deal of information in this section. After answering the questions you may want to reread the information. This is a very important section, for the stand-up exercise can be used with many different patients.

Stairclimbing

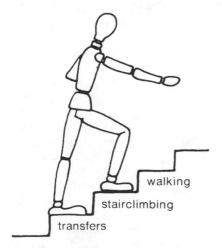

walking

stairclimbing

transfers

quadriceps strength as much as stairclimbing does. EMG studies prove this is true. Using stairclimbing as an exercise, the patient

1. learns to shift his weight when picking up his feet
2. learns to place his feet properly
3. learns to take small even steps
4. gains additional strength in his legs
5. learns to maintain his balance when one leg is off the ground (if he is a hemiplegic, stairclimbing will improve his reflexes and the spasticity in the quadriceps muscle)

Additionally, when you tell a patient that he is going to start moving his feet, looking up a flight of stairs is not as frightening as looking down a long hall. The eye to floor distance is much less on stairs than on the level (see illustrations below).

Stairclimbing, or "Up with the good foot, down with the bad."

You might be surprised to find stairclimbing as our next step to independence. It would seem that stairclimbing should be taught after walking. (It should be taught last for a patient using crutches.) But for the hemiplegic patient or one with weak or uncoordinated legs, stairclimbing *used before walking* adds certain abilities.

Generally, stand-ups increase the strength of the quadriceps muscles and increase the ability to stand and balance. The exercise is done with both feet on the floor.

Generally, stairclimbing increases the strength of the individual quadriceps muscle and increases the ability to stand and balance while the body is in motion. Walking does not increase

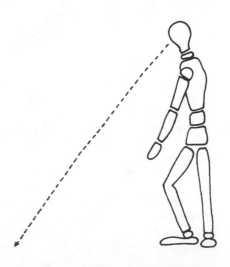

Usually our patients go down the stairs forward, but if a patient is frightened or very weak, walking down backward gives him the same "eye to floor" confidence, eliminates the turning procedure on the stairs, and places the involved hip in a more extended position to help facilitate the action of the gluteus maximus muscle.

In the rehabilitation center, we use the stairs progressively, as we do stand-ups, by starting the patient on two-inch stairs and advancing through four-inch to six-inch stairs as his strength and ability increase. This progression is good if the facilities are available; otherwise, you can use the normal stair (six-inch), foot stool, or curb and give more assistance, lessening the assistance as the patient improves.

It is always easier to teach stairclimbing by demonstrating it first. Now let's see how the nurse and Mr. Jones approach this exercise. The nurse sets the scene:

1. She uses a six-inch staircase with a railing on both sides.
2. She wheels Mr. Jones up to the staircase in his wheelchair and locks the wheelchair.
3. She demonstrates stairclimbing to Mr. Jones.
4. She takes his pulse.

(The instructions here are for a patient with one involved leg, two good arms, and use of two railings. A hemiplegic patient would only use the railing on his uninvolved side. Also, if only one railing were available, a person would use only one hand on that railing.)

Note: *Good leg* refers to the uninvolved or strong leg; *bad leg* refers to the involved or weak leg. In the drawings, the solid foot represents the bad foot. The little saying "Up with the good foot, down with the bad" really helps patients remember how to climb stairs!

THE NURSE: Okay, Mr. Jones, now you will climb the stairs. Stand up from your chair. Push on the armrests—don't pull on the railing. Stand up straight and get your balance. Good.

Going Up

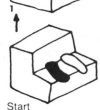

Start

Now place your hands on the railings. Keep your "bad" leg straight. *Step up with your "good" leg first*. Place your foot totally on the stair. Now push on your hands (don't pull) and step up with your bad leg to the same step. Get your foot all the way on the step and have your feet spread evenly.

Now get your balance.

Move your hands higher on the railing and repeat the same process for the next step. Take one step at a time until you arrive at the top of the stairs.

Turn around by taking small steps in a circle.

Going Down

Start

Stand facing down the steps with both feet close to the edge of the step. Place your hands on the railings slightly ahead of your feet. This is for balance. *Step down with your bad leg first*, lowering your weight slowly with your good leg.

(Feet should be about six inches apart.) Do you have your balance, Mr. Jones?

O.K., now quickly put your good foot down beside your bad foot.

Regain your balance again, and repeat the same process for each step.

Some patients' legs are about equal in strength and they can step one foot over another. This will aid in strengthening both legs. A hemiplegic patient should always go up and down stairs one at a time. When going down stairs, the patient should always lean slightly forward, since the tendency is to fall backward, not forward. If the patient descends the stairs backwards, he should follow all instructions given, only step down backwards.

To assist the patient, you should be behind him when he is going up the stairs and in front of him when he is going down. Use a wide base of support, with one foot on each step. Be close enough to the patient to balance him if necessary or hold him if he starts to fall.

Remember your body mechanics!

If you are working with a patient and he begins to fall, hold him as close to you as possible to help him rebalance himself. If it is evident that he cannot regain his balance and will fall, you should hold him close, keep your back straight, bend your knees, and lower him to the floor or sit him down on the step.

Try to answer the following questions.

1. How many stairs should a hemiplegic patient climb at a time?_____
2. Coming down the steps, the patient should position himself so that both of his feet are _____ to the edge of the step.
3. The patient should always keep his hands _____ of his feet for balance.
4. The patient should step up with his _____ foot first and down with his _____foot.
5. For safety, when assisting a patient, you should be _____ him when going up the stairs and _____of him when coming down the stairs.
6. Name two things which are accomplished by doing stairclimbing as an exercise.
   a. _____
   b. _____

Answers:

1. One.
2. Close.
3. Ahead.
4. Good or uninvolved; bad or involved.
5. Behind; ahead.
6. If you answered any two of these, you were correct:
   a. The patient learns to shift his weight.
   b. The patient learns to place feet.
   c. The patient gains strength in his legs.
   d. The patient learns to maintain balance when one foot is off the floor.
   e. The patient learns to take small steps.
   f. It develops quadriceps spasticity in a hemiplegic patient.

Now let's see what *stairclimbing with crutches* would look like.

The same method of stairclimbing would be used with a patient with a fractured leg or a hip fracture who could not bear weight. In such a case, crutches would be used. Crutches are to be considered with the bad or involved foot.

Methods Using Crutches

Use of two crutches going up: Step up with good or uninvolved leg first, then bring crutches and bad or involved leg up. Do not step on the involved leg.

Use of two crutches going down: Stand close to the edge of the step, put crutches down, and put bad or involved leg down, then quickly put the good or uninvolved leg down. Do not step on the involved leg.

Notice that crutches are spread apart enough for balance and are placed in the middle of the stair. A patient's balance will be better if he places the bad or involved foot on the step but does not put weight on it. Stairclimbing can also be done in a non-weight-bearing fashion by using one crutch and the railing. Use the same method, except that when the second crutch would be moved, move the hand on the railing instead.

The "solid" foot represents the bad or involved foot.

Two-Crutch Method

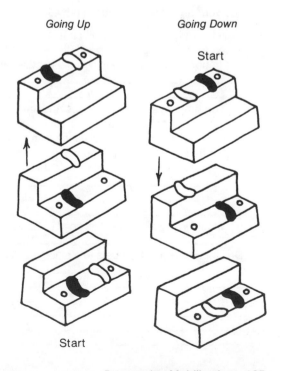

Going Up

Going Down

Start

Start

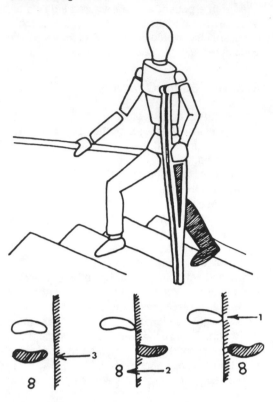

Crutch-Railing Method

The nurse and Mr. Jones have climbed stairs. They are nearly to the top of the Independence Staircase. Before proceeding to the test for this unit, please reread the section "Where to Start Progressive Mobilization." Is it clearer? Please take the test now on pregait training to see if you will be able to take your Mr. Jones this far up the Independence Staircase!

Test on Pregait Training

Place your answers in the space provided.

1. Crutches are moved along with the _____leg.
2. When stairclimbing, step up with the _____leg first and down with the _____leg first.
3. It is important that a patient be able to stand alone during stand-ups. Why? _____
   _____
   _____

4. a. You have evaluated Mr. Jones and have decided that he has no muscle tightness, could move about in bed alone, and could get to sitting position alone. He has good sitting balance. He needed moderate assistance with transfers because he could not stand up easily from the bed. His knees buckled when he moved his feet. What exercises on the Independence Staircase would you use with Mr. Jones? _____
   _____
   _____
   _____

   b. Would you walk him at this point? _____
   _____

5. Describe how a patient gets to a sitting position at the edge of the bed. _____
   _____
   _____
   _____
   _____
   _____
   _____

6. If Mr. Jones has a weak left side, on which side of him would you position the wheelchair for a transfer? _____
   Why? _____

7. When a patient gets in or out of a wheelchair, what is the most important factor to remember?
   _____
   _____

8. What is the most important factor to consider about a wheelchair if a stroke patient is to wheel himself? _____
   _____
   _____

9. Stairclimbing accomplishes five goals. Name two.
   a. _____
   b. _____

10. Describe briefly how you would proceed with stand-up exercises (name the equipment and outline the method). _____
    _____
    _____
    _____
    _____
    _____
    _____
    _____
    _____
    _____
    _____
    _____

11. What muscle groups strengthen most with the stand-up exercise? _____
    _____
    _____

12. Mr. Smith has considerable weakness in the muscles on his involved side. He has poor trunk control. When he sits, he leans toward his involved side. What exercise should you use to correct this? _____
    _____
    _____

Now that you have answered these questions, compare your responses with those given below.
1. *Bad or involved leg.*
2. *Good or uninvolved leg; bad or involved leg.*
3. *It encourages and motivates him and makes him feel successful. Remember, "success breeds success." The patient's muscles are functioning without assistance.*
4. a. *Transfer training and stand-up exercises.*
   b. *No, because his legs need to be strengthened first.*
5. a. *Moves toward edge of bed.*
   b. *Rolls onto side.*
   c. *Puts arm underneath.*
   d. *Drops legs off bed and pushes up with arms at same time.*
   e. *Pushes until sitting.*
6. *On the right side, so he can move toward his good side.*
7. *Lock the brakes!*
8. *The wheelchair must be low enough so the patient's feet can touch the floor.*
9. *If you named any two of these, you were correct:*
   a. *The patient learns to shift weight.*
   b. *The patient learns to maintain balance on one foot.*
   c. *The patient learns to place feet properly.*
   d. *The patient teaches himself to take small even steps.*
   e. *The patient gains additional strength. (Stairclimbing also improves reflexes and spasticity in the quadriceps muscle for the stroke patient.)*

10. *Use chair with books, etc, to elevate it. Place in front of a table. Elevate chair so patient can stand up alone from it (one and a half times length of leg from knee to foot, or 130° angle of the knee should accomplish this). Have patient place both of his hands on the table. Stand up unassisted for about 10 seconds then sit for approximately 15 seconds. Repeat ten times, increasing the number as the patient's endurance increases. Practice standing balance at the same time.*
11. *Quadriceps.*
12. *Sitting balance exercise.*

When you are satisfied that you understand the information in this unit, please continue.

You and Mr. Jones have one more step to climb on the Independence Staircase of Progressive Mobilization. *The patient needs to learn to walk.*

Please proceed to the next section to find out how to help the patient do this.

GAIT TRAINING, OR "HOW TO TEACH YOUR PATIENT TO WALK"

Safety First: Five Rules

Safety Rule 1: Make Sure That You Are Ready to Teach Your Patient to Walk and That Your Patient Is Ready

It is very important that you have prepared your patient well for walking. Preparation means that he is able to perform *all* the activities discussed in the other three units of this chapter. It means that he has taken *every* step necessary on the Independence Staircase.

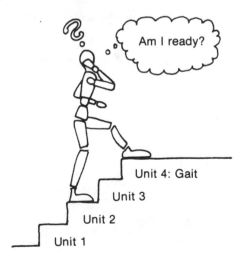

Unit 4: Gait
Unit 3
Unit 2
Unit 1

Could you get from the bottom to the top of a flight of stairs without climbing the steps in between? Of course not. To determine if Mr. Jones is ready to walk, ask three important questions.

Question 1: Mr. Jones, can you sit? Show me.

Help!

If your patient looks like the left picture, proceed. If he looks like the right one, go back and teach him how to sit alone with good sitting balance.

Question 2: Mr. Jones, can you stand up? Do you have good strong legs? Show me.

No, ugh!

If your patient looks like the left picture, proceed. If he looks like the right one, go back and teach him how to stand and strengthen his legs.

Question 3: Mr. Jones, can you stand and balance alone? Show Me.

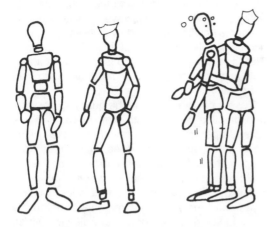

If your patient looks like the left picture, proceed. If he looks like the right one, go back and perfect his standing balance.

It is important that your patient at least be able to stand and balance himself before he tries to walk. It is best that strengthening, balance, and endurance building exercises be continued in conjunction with the walking program so the patient will develop as much strength as possible.

We are cautioning you to prepare your patient properly for walking because if you do not, walking will prove to be taxing, unsafe, depressing, and perhaps futile.

You should use all the units of this chapter properly. Be sure that your patient is ready for each step on the Independence Staircase. If you have prepared your patient well, walking or gait training can be a rewarding and fun experience for both of you. Can you recall a moment when you saw a child take his first step? Let your patient know you are proud of him. It really helps!

Safety Rule 2: Choose Safest Gait

In general, provided that the patient has been well prepared and given the proper walking aids, his instincts about walking will be correct as to safety and technique. As long as safety is not sacrificed, it is all right to experiment with modifications in his walking patterns. Where there is a choice between the speed or the appearance of gait and its safety, always choose the gait which is the safest.

Safety Rule 3: Take Proper Cardiac Precautions

When you walk a patient, you should monitor his pulse and watch for other cardiac signs during exercise. Do you remember the importance of this

procedure? Review the first section of this chapter if you do not.

Safety Rule 4: Ensure that Patient is Wearing Good Shoes

"A building is as good as its foundation." Your patient should be wearing good shoes. Shoes that slide off the patient's feet (scuffs, etc.), high heels, and slippery soles can lead to falls and sprained ankles. Your patient already has some kind of difficulty walking or he would not be here for your help; do not add to his problems. See that he has good shoes. Tied oxfords with rubber heels are best for men and women.

Safety Rule 5: Guard Patient Correctly

You are responsible for the patient's safety when he is walking. Described here is the safest and most appropriate way to prevent falls during walking. If you have prepared your patient well for walking by following safety rules 1 to 4 above, you will have eliminated most of the following hazards. But even then you must anticipate them and be prepared to guard accordingly.

Most patients, particularly stroke victims, will fall toward their weak side if they are going to fall. Patients can also fall forward or backward. They fall primarily because their muscles are weak and their legs "crumble" under them or because their balance is poor. Weakness in various muscles often makes it difficult to maintain the proper position for walking.

Following is a description of how you should look while guarding. In our example, Mr. Jones's left side is the weaker. *Stand on his left side* and *just a little behind him*. Put your right hand on his belt or walking belt and your left hand on the front of his shoulder. In this position you can push back on his shoulder and push forward on his hips to straighten him up or you can pull him against yourself. If you cannot hold him, you are in a good position to ease him *gently* to the floor. Remember to use good body mechanics. If a patient is falling, you can do more harm to your back and the patient by straining to hold him up than if you ease him to the floor. Back injuries will not help anyone. You should never hold a patient only by the arm or let him hold onto you, because if he suddenly starts to fall, you will both fall over.

As your patient's walking ability improves, gradually release your hold on him by taking your hand from his shoulder, and then from his belt, until he is on his own. However, always stand in the same position to catch him if necessary. Practice using this position until it feels comfortable. This is very important. If you do not feel comfortable and balanced, it will be hard for you to help your patient effectively.

Take a partner, stand in the guarding position, and practice walking with him. Keep your feet spread apart for good balance and take a step each time your partner does: Coordinate your steps with his. Practice until you feel comfortable.

When guarding a patient, be careful that you do not hold onto him so much that he does not have freedom of movement. Remember that you are there to teach and assist him to walk, not to drag him around the room! If he leans on you too much, he will learn to depend on that support and will not learn to support himself for independent walking.

Test on Safety Rules

Please answer the following questions regarding safety during gait training.

1. Name three activities that your patient should be able to do before he can walk.
   a. _____
   b. _____
   c. _____
2. Why should you prepare your patient well for walking? _____
3. If Mr. Jones's pulse is 122 while sitting in the wheelchair, is he safe to walk? _____
4. State what type of shoes are best for patients to wear. _____
5. Describe the guarding position for walking. _____
6. Can this section of the Progressive Mobilization package be used completely alone? _____
   Why or why not? _____

If you answered as follows you were correct:
1. *a. Sit alone—good sitting balance.*
   b. Stand up easily—good leg strength.
   c. Balance alone—good standing balance.
2. *Otherwise he might fail and the effort involved in walking would be taxing, unsafe, depressing, and futile.*
3. *No, his cardiac status is not stable.*
4. *Tied oxfords with rubber heels.*
5. *Stand on the patient's weak side, to the side and a little behind. Place one hand on the belt, the other hand on the front of the shoulder.*
6. *No, because the patient must be able to perform all the steps or activities on the Independence Staircase in order to succeed with gait.*

Normal Gait

Ideally our attempts at gait training are designed to teach our patients to walk as normally as possible. Often due to the disorder, the patient is not able to perform these normal movements. For you to determine what normal is, a brief discussion of normal gait follows. Recall that this book is not intended to be a physical therapy text, and gait is discussed here only as it applies to our needs.

During normal gait, each leg alternates between the *stance phase*, during which the leg is on the ground, and the *swing phase*, during which the leg is brought from behind to the forward position. Each phase has distinct characteristics, many of which are very important to teach the patient so he will be able to walk effectively and efficiently. Each step is discussed in the order that it occurs during normal gait.

Stance Phase

1. *Heel Strike*. Normally we hit the floor with our heel first and with our foot dorsiflexed (left picture below). Patients occasionally will attempt to touch with their toes first and are usually best encouraged to follow the normal pattern. This is especially important to consider during crutch walking. If the patients strike the floor with their toes first, normal action of the foot cannot follow; their gait pattern becomes awkward, unstable, and inefficient. When the foot hits the floor, it should be pointed straight ahead, with the knee in full extension and the leg slightly abducted (feet apart) (right picture).

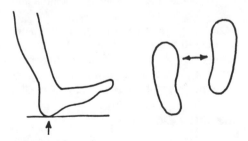

2. *Stance*. After the heel strike, the patient rolls over onto the ball of his foot, and bends slightly (about 15°) at the knee. He then fully extends the knee. He must be able to stand straight on that leg. A strong quadriceps muscle or an assistive device might be needed to produce this stance position and allow the patient to walk. If the knee "buck-

les" at this point, the other leg cannot be lifted off the floor.

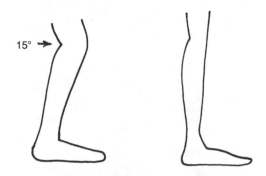

Also during the stance phase, the trunk must be maintained in an upright position to enable forward movement of the other leg. This is accomplished by the action of the gluteus maximus muscle. If the gluteus maximus is not functioning when the involved leg is in stance position, the trunk falls forward. To compensate for this weakness, the patient must be instructed to stand very straight with his shoulders back and his pelvis forward. You might need to assist your patient in maintaining this position initially. Review the guarding position. You will notice that you are standing in a perfect position to assist the patient with this problem. (See illustrations below.)

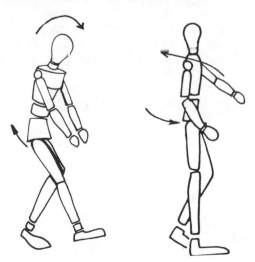

3. *Push Off*. The patient then pushes off with his toes and the ball of his foot, bends his knee slightly, and simultaneously bends his hip slightly.

The push-off action illustrated below proceeds into the swing phase.

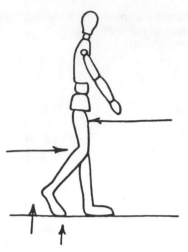

Swing Phase

The other leg is now in stance phase.

1. With the hip and knee bent, the ankle and foot held at about a 90° angle, and the body weight shifted onto the other leg, the leg begins to swing forward.

   If a patient cannot perform one, two, or more of these normal movements the leg can be called "a functionally long leg." This means simply that the patient for some reason cannot "shorten" the length of his leg by the normal movements discussed above to swing that leg past the other one. The leg will often feel "glued to the floor." Reasons for a functionally long leg may be long leg casts or braces, stiff knee joints, weak ankles (drop foot), weak or nonfunctioning hip flexors, plantar flexion contractures, etc. What to do about the problem of a functionally long leg will be discussed in the next section ("Assistive Devices").

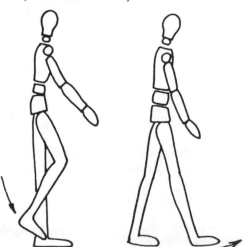

2. When the leg swings past the other leg, the knee extends by a combined action of the hamstrings (to control the speed of the extension) and the quadriceps muscle (to produce full extension of the knee). All steps produced are equal in length. (If the quadriceps and hamstrings do not function properly here, the patient will not produce full extension of the knee and not swing the leg completely past the other leg; also, when heel strike occurs, the knee might "pop" back into forced hyperextension.)

3. With the knee straight, the foot dorsiflexes beyond a 90° angle and the patient's leg is again in a position for heel strike. The gait pattern repeats.

As one can imagine, each patient will present a different problem regarding his gait pattern. One patient might be able to dorsiflex his foot for heel strike and to clear his foot during swing phase but not be able to flex his hip; another might be able to do both but not extend his knee. It is our responsibility to help each patient become as normal as possible and to find ways that each can walk regardless of his inability to follow the normal gait pattern precisely. We might need to strengthen a particular muscle or muscle group to correct the gait problem, substitute an assistive device for the inability to perform a certain movement, or instruct the patient to use walkers, crutches, or canes. Whatever we decide to do to help the patient, remember two points:

1. We must produce a gait that is as safe and functional as possible.
2. We want the patient to become as normal as possible within the limits of his diagnosis.

Continue reading now about assistive devices and how to use walking aids to help the patient become as normal and functional as possible. Recall previous units, which discuss ways of strengthening muscle groups to achieve this.

Assistive Devices

Lifts

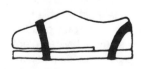

A *lift* can be placed on the patient's good or uninvolved leg. This makes the uninvolved leg longer than the involved leg and in theory compensates for the "functional" longer length of the involved leg. The patient can then swing the involved leg past the uninvolved one and produce a more normal gait.

Lifts can be made from any rigid material by tracing the patient's shoe shape, cutting it out, and taping it to the bottom of the patient's shoe with masking tape. The height of the lift depends on how much length needs to be added to the good leg in order to allow the other leg to swing through. Start with a quarter-inch lift and add height until the patient can move his leg. Try not to exceed three-quarters of an inch, because this could disturb his balance. On the other hand, do not be afraid to add more if it is absolutely necessary, especially with a long leg cast or a stiff knee. As the patient's gait improves, try to decrease the height of the lift. You may be able to abandon it later as the patient learns to move his leg. If it is obvious that the patient should always have some type of lift, a shoe repair shop can add the height he needs.

Can you see how this would help your young patient with a long leg cast to use crutches, or your stroke patient to use his cane? Or help a patient with a weak hip flexor and hip musculature move his leg forward? We have discovered that lifts make it easier for a patient to walk and it takes less energy. You may want to consider this factor when you are treating a patient with low endurance. Walking, especially with a disability, like a hemiplegia, takes a lot of energy.[3]

Braces

Have you ever seen a patient (most likely a stroke patient) who dragged his toe when walking? Such a patient is said to have a "dropped foot." It is usually due to muscle weakness or lack of muscle function in the ankle. The patient cannot move his ankle up and down or from side to side. Dropped foot causes great instability in the foot and a functional long leg. These problems can make gait difficult or impossible. A short leg brace provides an easy remedy. It stabilizes the ankle at the 90° angle and holds it from moving improperly from side to side. The patient can then move his leg properly and without fear of a twisted ankle.

Two basic types of short leg braces are available. One is a standard brace with metal uprights (see illustration A below). This brace is attached to a sturdy shoe, preferably an oxford type. The other is made of plastic and fits into the shoe. This is called a *corrugated polypropylene below knee orthosis* (see illustration B). Both are available through certified orthotists, who are trained to fit and manufacture braces. It is important that these fit properly so as not to rub the skin and cause pressure sores.

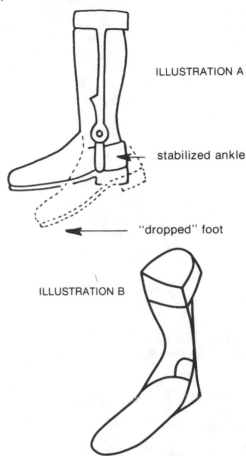

ILLUSTRATION A

stabilized ankle

"dropped" foot

ILLUSTRATION B

A brace is not necessarily a substitute for a lift, nor is a lift a substitute for a brace. One or the other or both might be needed by your patient. Experiment and decide. Let the patient have some input into the decision as well. Remember, the patient's instincts concerning safety of gait are generally good.

Knee Immobilizers

If the patient cannot keep his knee sufficiently extended during the stance phase to allow proper swing on the other side, a knee immobilizer will enable him to do so. A knee immobilizer can be purchased from your local medical supply vendor. For it to be effective in keeping the leg straight, the knee immobilizer must have heavy stays and a strap across the patella.

The knee immobilizer is a temporary device; used as such it permits early gait training and stimulus to the quadriceps muscle. If the ankle dorsiflexors are weak or absent as well, the knee immobilizer can be used in conjunction with a short leg brace.

At intervals, attempts should be made to remove the knee immobilizer as the patient's leg becomes stronger. When the knee remains sufficiently straight during the stance phase, the knee immobilizer can be removed completely. If it is apparent that the patient will not be able to keep his knee extended sufficiently during the stance phase, a long leg brace with a knee lock could be needed.

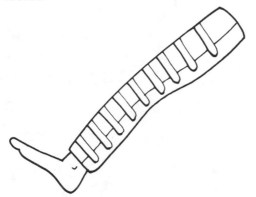

Notice that the use of a knee immobilizer or a long leg brace with a locked knee will produce the functional long leg discussed above, and a lift on the good foot should be used to help compensate for it.

Remember these points! We have had patients come to the rehabilitation center because they could not walk. All we did was to provide them with a lift or a brace and their walking problem was solved. Do you see the value of knowing what the patient needs?

Walking Aids

Crutches, Walkers, Canes, or You

How do we know whether a patient needs a walking aid and, if so, what kind? Table 12-3 can be used as a quick reference for determining your patient's needs. Study it carefully. When using any walking aid, the patient should

1. lean hard on it to get the full benefit of the device
2. lean on it less as he progresses in ability (except, of course, with crutches or walkers for non-weight-bearing fractures)
3. move it with the weak leg

TABLE 12-3 Walking Aids

TYPE	DESCRIPTION	WHICH PATIENTS SHOULD USE THEM	COMMENTS
Walker			
a. Standard Walker 	Rubber tips Can be adjusted to proper height	Patients with general weakness Patients with two good arms The older patient Patients with general mild balance problems Patients with a fractured hip, leg, or foot Patients with weak leg or legs	The walker must be lifted when moved. It is very stable.
b. Gliding Walker 	Same as above except it has metal plates on tips instead of rubber	All the above plus patient with poor forward and backward balance; parkinsonism; arthritis	The walker may be pushed or slid on floor. The patient with poor forward and backward balance does not have to lift this walker. When he does have to lift a walker, he tends to fall backward.
c. Roller Walker	Front legs have wheels	All the above plus patient who needs walker mainly for balance; patient who does not need support from walker	The best roller walker locks when it is pushed on firmly.

TABLE 12-3 continued

TYPE	DESCRIPTION	WHICH PATIENTS SHOULD USE THEM	COMMENTS
Crutches			
a. Crutches 	Wooden or steel Adjustable Rubber tips	Younger patient with fractured hip, foot, etc. Patients should have two strong arms Patients should have good balance	Not recommended for older patients. Crutches are only as stable as the person using them.
Canes			
a. Walkcane 	4 legs Rubber tips Adjustable	Hemiplegic patient Patient with only one good arm Patient who has a lot of lateral instability (keeps falling to one side—hemiplegic patient primarily) Patient who needs to take weight off of an involved foot, e.g., sprained ankle, weakness Patient with general balance problems	This cane provides much more stability than a regular cane. Recommend it as the first device used in progress toward independence without a cane. Use in hand opposite the involved leg. When used strictly for balance problems, use it in the hand which is most effective for the patient. Let him try it and see!
b. Walkcane with glider tips 	Same as above except has glider tips	All the above	Even better with balance problems; it can be pushed (see walker with gliders).
c. Quad canes  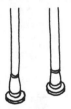		Patients with same problems as listed under walkcanes but less severe	Gives less support than a walkcane does. Used as the second device in progress toward independence without a cane. Quad canes come with wide or narrow bases. Wide-base quad canes offer more stability than those with narrow base. Can be part of progression toward use of regular cane.

continues

TABLE 12-3 continued

TYPE	DESCRIPTION	WHICH PATIENTS SHOULD USE THEM	COMMENTS
d. Cane		Patients same as above but even less severe	Pictured here is the best type of cane. It is the most stable of all regular canes. Gives less support than a quad cane. Use as a third device to independence.

You

TYPE	DESCRIPTION	WHICH PATIENTS SHOULD USE THEM	COMMENTS
a. Guarding	You are in the position described in Safety Rule 5, or just allow the patient to hold your hand	Patient with very mild balance problems Confused patient Patient who just progressed from a cane Patient who needs a little support for confidence	Sometimes people need to use a cane. They cannot understand what to do with a walker. They may fall over a walker and this is unsafe.
b. Standby	Walk in guarding position but do not touch patient	Patient is doing better than above	Almost to independence.
c. Let him walk alone		Patient is doing better still	Independence!

Test on Gait Training

You have been given a lot of information that is basic to gait training. Refer back to it as you continue to learn the techniques of teaching a patient to walk. Here are some questions to review your understanding of this material.

1. What patient would need a lift? _____
2. In normal gait, do you land on your heel first or your toes first? _____
_____
3. Your patient has poor forward and backward balance. Which walking aid would you use? _____
_____
4. You should move the walking aid with the _____leg.
5. Which cane would you use for a patient who needed a lot of support laterally? _____
_____
6. Where would you stand to guard a patient? _____
_____
7. Should you change a patient's gait pattern that is safe but does not look normal? _____
Why or why not? _____
_____
8. What causes a functional long leg? _____
_____
_____

Answers:

1. *A person with a functional long leg.*
2. *Heel first.*
3. *A walker—preferably a glider walker.*
4. *Weak.*
5. *A walkcane.*
6. *On the weak side, and a little behind him.*
7. *No, you should never sacrifice safety for appearance.*
8. *Weak leg muscles, stiff joints, tight muscles, or long leg braces.*

If you answered correctly, you are doing well. Use this information as we continue. If you made some errors, review the material before you proceed.

The nurse is setting the scene for "how to stand a patient from a chair," but before we continue, look at the way we have divided the remaining instruction:

1. How to stand a patient from a chair.
2. How to measure a patient for a walking aid.
3. How to use a walking aid.
4. How to turn around using a walking aid.
5. How to back up and how to sit down in a chair.

We're at the top of the Independence Staircase and we're anxious to learn this step!

How to Stand a Patient from a Chair

Set the scene:

1. Mr. Jones' shoes are on. He is wearing good ones.

2. His chair is stabilized with wheelchair brakes locked (for greater stability, also push chair against a wall).
3. All stools or foot plates are out of the way so he will not trip or hit his legs against anything.
4. His pulse is taken; cardiac signs are good.
5. His walking aid (walker, crutches, or cane) is in its appropriate position (to be discussed later).

THE NURSE: Mr. Jones, slide forward in your chair and put your feet flat on the floor (left picture).

Note: If the patient cannot slide forward in the chair, instruct him to stretch out his legs in front of him, lean back against the chair, and push his back against it. This will allow his hips to slide forward (middle picture). Then he can pull his body forward by grasping on the chair arm or seat (right picture).

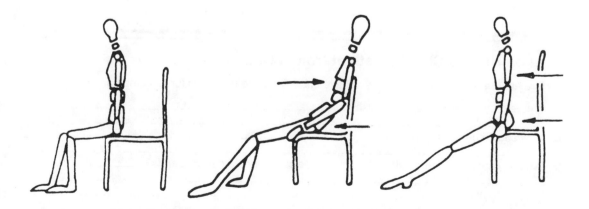

THE NURSE: Now put both hands on the arms of the chair (illustration 1 below) or put one hand on the walker or crutches and one hand on the chair (illustration 2 below).

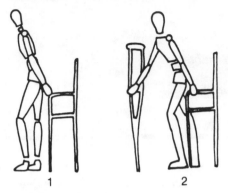

1   2

Lean forward a little, push with your arms, straighten your legs and back, and stand up straight.

Now put both hands on the walking aid (if appropriate)—either one at a time or both at once.

Get your balance. You are ready for the next step.

Note: On occasion, you may need to vary this method of getting a patient out of the chair. For example:

1. If he has a long leg cast or hip fracture, he cannot put both his legs under him.
2. If the patient has only one arm, he can only push with the one arm. Be sure it is on the chair.

Two variations using walking aids are as follows:

1. To stand up with a regular cane, hold the cane in one hand while using both hands on the chair.
2. To stand up with crutches, hold both crutches in one hand by the handgrips. Put the other hand on the arm of the chair and follow the original procedure. (See illustration 1 and 2 above.) When you are standing, take one crutch and put it under the opposite arm. Then turn the other crutch into position. The patient should be standing as shown in illustrations 3, 4, and 5 below.

   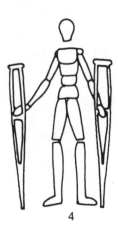   

3   4   5

Test on How to Stand a Patient from a Chair

Here are a few questions to see if you have understood the directions for standing up.

1. Where do you tell Mr. Jones to push? _____

2. How should he position his legs? _____

3. What is important to remember about the wheelchair when a patient stands? _____
_____
_____
_____

Good. Now you have your patient standing. How does the walking aid look? Is it all right? Too tall? Too short? How to answer these questions will be discussed in the next section.

How to Measure Walking Aids

The proper measurement of a walking aid is important if the patient is to walk properly. Here are five rules that apply to measuring equipment.

1. *Measurements should be taken standing.* You can estimate the measurements of walking aids before the patient stands, but the final measurement must come when the patient is standing. That is why we discussed standing first!
2. *Trust the patient's instincts.* You do want the walking aid to fit the patient correctly and "by the book," but how the patient feels is equally important. If the fit is close to what is theoretically correct and the patient is holding the device properly, let the patient try it his way.
3. *Be sure the legs are even.* Adjustable walkers and canes can be adjusted by pushing in on the button and sliding the tubing in or out to make the walker or cane shorter or longer, respectively. A "wobbly" walking aid is worse than none. Adjustable crutches have screws and wing nuts which are pulled out to move the handgrips or lengthen the crutches. Be sure that these are replaced tightly. Do not leave any space showing between the different pieces of the crutches, or the screws could break.
4. *Be sure parts are clean.* Always check the rubber tips on walkers, crutches, and canes. They should be clean and not worn. They should have suction ability and lots of tread; worn rubber tips can cause slipping accidents.
5. *Be sure patients have shoes.* Always measure the patient with shoes on, preferably the shoes that he will wear for walking.

Keep these rules in mind while you learn how to measure walking aids.

Walkers

1. Place walker in front of patient and partially around him.
2. He should stand straight, shoulders relaxed.
3. His elbows should be almost straight.
4. Let him try the walker. See if he can push on it easily without bending over.
5. Keep readjusting the walker until it feels right and he can use it well.

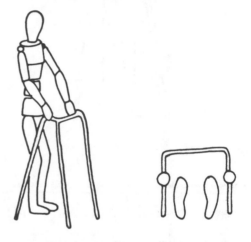

Note: Often people adjust walkers too high. When this occurs, the patients get very tired trying to lift their body weight with their arms.

Practice: If a walker is available, try one that is too high for you. Then try one which is too low, and finally one that fits. Do you not agree that the walker is harder to use when it is too high or too low?

Crutches

1. Have the patient hold the crutches with the tips about six inches from each foot and out to the side in a good comfortable weight-bearing position.

2. He should stand straight, shoulders relaxed.
3. The axillary pads should lie against the ribs about three to four finger widths from the axilla or armpits.
4. The handles should be positioned so the elbows are flexed about 30°, or even with the greater trochanter.

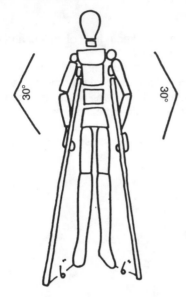

Again consider comfort and use.

Note: NEVER let the patient press down on the axillary pads. Weight bearing on the axillary pads could paralyze his arms from pressure on the nerves that run in the axilla. All weight should go onto the hands, not the armpits!

Canes

1. Patient should stand straight, shoulders relaxed, with one hand on the cane.
2. Hold the cane in a good weight-bearing position (approximately five to six inches ahead and to the side of the patient's foot).

3. The hand holding the top of the cane should rest so the elbows are flexed about 30°, or even with the greater trochanter.
4. Consider the patient's feelings about his ability to push on the cane.

Test on Measuring Walking Aids

Do you think that you could measure a patient for a walking aid now? Try to answer the questions below to be sure.

1. How far from the armpits should the top of the crutches be? _____
   Why? _____
2. What position should the elbows be in for crutches, canes, and walkers? _____
   _____
3. What should be your final criteria for walking aids? _____
   _____
4. Briefly describe how the rubber tips on a walking aid should look. _____
   _____
   _____
5. Walking aids should be measured when the patient is _____and wearing _____

Check here to see how you did on the questions.
1. Three to four finger widths, so the patient does not lean on crutch tops with his armpits.
2. Flexed about 30°, or even with the greater trochanter.
3. That the patient feels comfortable and that he can use the walking aid easily.
4. Not worn, good suction, clean, lots of tread.
5. Standing; shoes.

Now that Mr. Jones is standing and measured with his walking aid, we are going to watch him and the nurse walk down the hall.

Using Walking Aids

Walking with a Walker

THE NURSE: Are you ready Mr. Jones? Now remember you have broken your right leg and cannot put any weight on it. However, you can place your foot on the floor while you walk. We are going to use a standard walker.

You stood up very well, Mr. Jones. Do you feel balanced? Practicing those stand-ups and standing balance exercises has helped. You are getting very strong.

Stand straight and look straight ahead. Pick the walker up, and place it forward a little. Put your right foot forward, and place it on the floor. No weight, please. Push *hard* on your hands and, lifting all of your weight, step forward with your left foot, placing it next to the right foot. Repeat these same actions for each step.

1. Move walker forward

hand

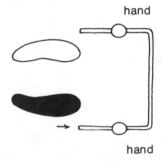

hand

2. Move right foot (involved foot)

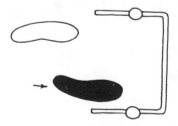

3. Move left foot (uninvolved foot)

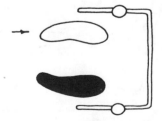

Repeat

Note well the following points:

1. Remember your guarding position and body mechanics.
2. Be sure the walker is always ahead of the patient. Do not let him step up against the front bar of the walker because this is an unstable position for the walker.
3. If the patient has poor forward-backward balance, use a walker with gliders so he does not have to pick the walker up off the floor.
4. If the patient has a weak leg or a partial weight-bearing fracture, use the same method described, with this exception: have the patient put some weight on his leg as well as his hands. As the weak leg becomes stronger, he gradually increases the weight on his leg and decreases the weight supported by his hands. For a fractured leg, this progression should be guided by a physician.
5. Some patients will have to hold their leg off the floor. If they are confused and touch their foot to the floor, even lightly, they may end up with all their weight on that leg. Sometimes a lift on the uninvolved leg is helpful because this will make the involved leg much shorter and they will remember not to step on it—plus the lift will make it easier to move the fractured leg.

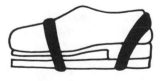

Answer the following questions.

1. *Should you let a patient step up to the front bar of the walker?* _____
   _____

   Why or why not? _____
   _____

2. Name the sequence of the movements carried out with the walker. First, _____
_____; then
_____; then
_____; then
_____; then repeat.
3. The patient must _____with his arms.

Answers:

1. No—because the walker is unstable in that position.
2. Move the walker; move the involved leg; push on the walker; move the uninvolved leg.
3. Push hard.

Walking with Crutches

THE NURSE: Balance with crutches is very important, Mr. Jones. Press on the crutch handles so you become accustomed to pushing on them. Remember, when you walk, do not push on the crutches under your armpits.

Mr. Jones, you have a cast on your right leg so you cannot put your foot on the floor. Hold it up off the floor.

Do you see the triangle that your crutches are making with your feet?

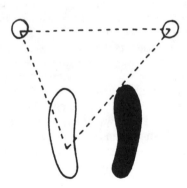

The triangular position of feet and crutches makes you stable on them. *Never* line the crutches up with your feet. This position is like walking on a tight-rope.

Always keep your triangle either forward or backward.

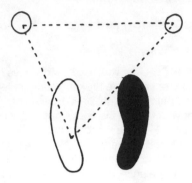

Forward

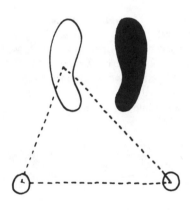

Backward

When you are walking, Mr. Jones, hold up your right foot, put both crutches forward, push on your hands, and step past the crutches with your left foot, landing on your heel first (heel strike) for balance.

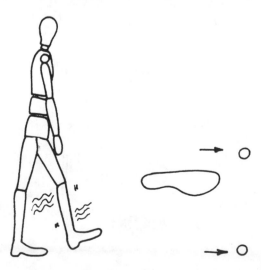

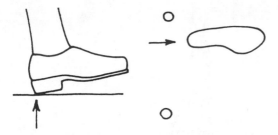

See the backward triangle now? Repeat these steps again. Use momentum from one step to the next to make the crutch walking easier. In other words, repeat one step immediately after the other. If you stop after each step, walking with crutches will be very hard work!

If Mr. Jones could put weight on his involved foot, you would tell him to (1) move his crutches forward; (2) step forward with his involved foot up to the crutches, then; (3) step past the crutches with his uninvolved foot, landing on his heel first.

Start:

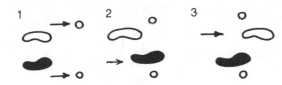

As he becomes stronger, he will move the crutches and the involved foot all at once (three-point crutch gait).

Start:

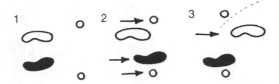

If the patient cannot step past the crutches, he might use them like a walker. He would only step up to them and not past them. If this were the case, I would recommend that your patient use a walker instead of crutches. *Remember*: Do not place crutches and feet in a single line.

All these examples are designed to be used with patients who have a weak or a non-weight-bearing leg. There are other variations of crutch gaits that can be used as your patient's legs become stronger or as he is able to bear considerable weight on his involved leg. These gait patterns resemble cane walking and are shown below. Follow the arrows to determine when to move each foot (Figures 12-13 to 12-15).

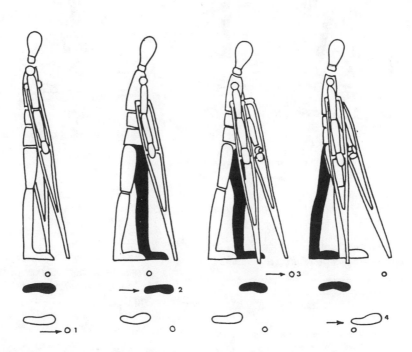

Figure 12-13 Moving one crutch or one foot at a time.

Four-point crutch gait (opposite crutch first pattern). This crutch gait is very stable.

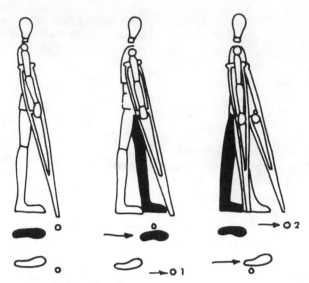

Figure 12-14 Moving one crutch and one foot together.

Two-point crutch gait (crutch and opposite foot together pattern). This gait is faster than moving one crutch and then one foot separately, as in the four-point crutch gait.

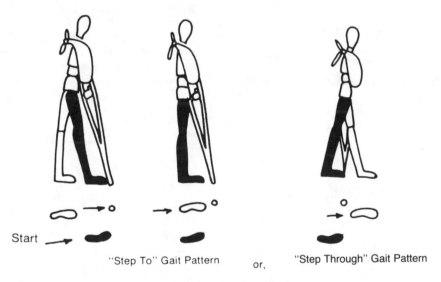

Start

"Step To" Gait Pattern   or,   "Step Through" Gait Pattern

Figure 12-15 Using only one crutch and moving one crutch and one foot together.

(See section on walking with canes for information on how to do this.)

Answer these three questions to see how you are doing.

1. *What two important facts about walking with crutches must always be related to patients?*
   a. _____
   _____
   b. _____
   _____

2. *When you take the step with your uninvolved foot you should land on your _____ first. Why?* _____
   _____

3. *Move the crutches with the _____ leg.*

Answers:
1. a. *Never put weight on crutch tops—this puts pressure on nerves in armpits.*
   b. *Do not place crutches and feet in a single line.*
2. *Heel. The balance is better.*
3. *Involved (or bad).*

Did you get them all correct? Continue when you are ready.

If a patient has both legs paralyzed (paraplegia), he would most likely need long leg braces and crutches to walk. To begin, the patient would first need to assume the *para-stance* position. This means that he stands with his pelvis forward and his back arched. His crutches would be placed in front of him to maintain his balance (see A in Figure 12-16).

To take a step, he would push on the crutches and swing both legs past the crutches (see B in Figure 12-16). When he lands on his heels, he immediately assumes the para-stance position again, moves his crutches forward, and is ready to repeat the process (see C in Figure 12-16).

If the patient fails to assume the para-stance position after each swing and instead allows his hips to flex, he will "jack-knife" (his trunk will fall forward) and he will lose his balance and fall (see D in Figure 12-16). You must guard the paraplegic patient carefully while he is walking to prevent this from occurring. Standing in the position described and illustrated on p. 130 will help prevent this from happening. See E in Figure 12-16 for the proper position for guarding the patient.

I have included this brief description of how to walk a paraplegic patient who has already been taught to walk on crutches. The techniques in teaching him to do this are best carried out by a physical therapist in a rehabilitation setting. Training a paraplegic to walk is a difficult and complex task. For further help, see the references listed for further information on gait exercises for para-

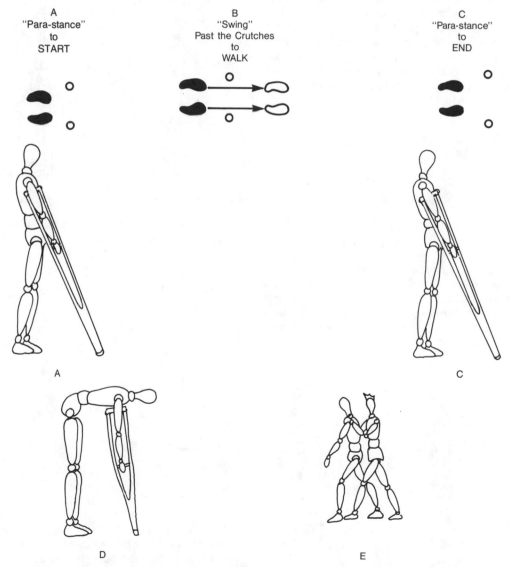

A
"Para-stance"
to
START

B
"Swing"
Past the Crutches
to
WALK

C
"Para-stance"
to
END

A

C

D

E

Figure 12-16 The parastance position is important for stability.

plegics. Remember that you have already learned how to help these patients get fitted in appropriate wheelchairs, perform range of motion, work on sitting balance and sitting tolerance, move in bed, do wheelchair pushups, etc. You have a lot to contribute to their care.

Now back to your Mr. Jones. Let's teach him to walk with a cane.

Walking with Canes

Cane gait is very similar to crutch gait and is further along in the progression toward independence. The three types of canes discussed here (walkcanes, quad canes, and regular canes) are also used progressively.

If a patient needs a great deal of support you would start with the walkcane, because it has four widely spaced legs. As the patient becomes stronger, he can progress to a quad cane (which gives less support) and then to a regular cane.

As with crutches, there should always be a triangle with the cane and the feet. In addition, the cane should always be used in the hand opposite the weak leg.

Canes give patients lateral support. A good example is the patient with a left hemiplegia. He would tend to fall to the left. Good use of the cane in the right hand would encourage him to lean to the right, making him more stable in a lateral direction.

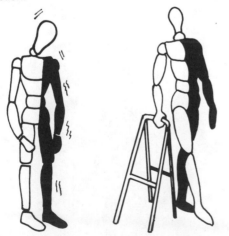

If Mr. Jones has had a stroke and needs to use a walkcane, these would be his instructions from the nurse. (Remember good body mechanics and the guarding position.)

THE NURSE: Mr. Jones, move the cane forward and out to the side. Put your weight on it, shifting the weight off the involved leg. Move your involved leg up even with the cane. Be sure that your feet are spread apart. Then press on the cane and, putting as much weight as possible on your involved leg, step past the cane with your uninvolved leg.

This could be called *cane first gait* (step-through gait pattern).

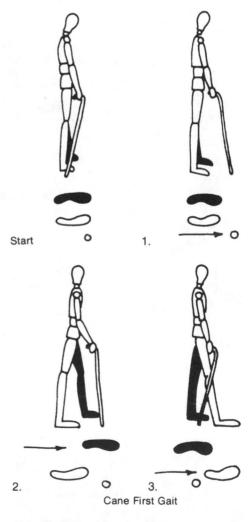

Start   1.

2.   3.

Cane First Gait

If your patient's balance or strength is not good enough to step past the walkcane or cane, teach him a *step-to gait*. But be sure to keep the walkcane well ahead of the feet.

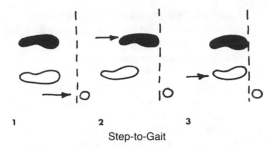

Step-to-Gait

A strong, well-coordinated patient should move the cane and his involved foot forward at the same time and then step past the cane with his uninvolved foot. This could be called the *cane together gait*.

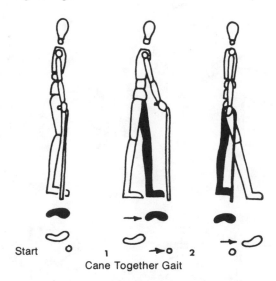

Cane Together Gait

Remember, when using any of these walking aids, try to have the patient walk as normally as possible without sacrificing safety (Safety Rule 2, p. 129). At first, your patient will not be able to walk very far, but as he practices, his endurance will increase, and he will be able to walk further. Encourage your patient to walk a little further every day!

Here are some review questions:

1. *Which cane gives the most stability?*
   _____

2. *Your patient has a left hemiplegia. In which hand should he hold the cane?* _____
   _____

3. *Repeat the sequence used for cane gait.*
   a. _____
      _____
   b. _____
      _____

c. _____
   _____

4. *Canes give stability in which direction?*
   _____

Check your answers.

Answers:

1. *The walkcane.*
2. *The right hand.*
3. a. *Move cane forward and out to the side.*
   b. *Step forward with the involved foot—even with the cane.*
   c. *Step past the cane with the uninvolved foot.*
4. *Laterally.*

How to Turn Around Using Walking Aids

The method of turning around is the same regardless of which walking aid Mr. Jones uses. In this instance, Mr. Jones is using a walker.

THE NURSE: Mr. Jones, always turn toward your good side. Move the walker around in a small circle, using the same gait pattern as for straight walking. (Keep the uninvolved foot on the inside of the circle.) First move your walker and turn it a little. Then step with your involved foot; now move your uninvolved foot. Repeat until you are turned around.

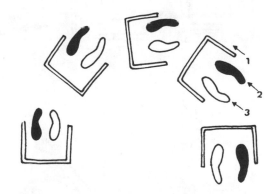

Good, Mr. Jones. That was a nice turn.

For safety, the patient should not pivot on the good or uninvolved foot—he should walk in a circle, as shown above. Be sure he keeps his feet spread apart when turning. If the feet get too close together, the patient is likely to lose his balance and fall over.

How to Back Up and Sit Down in a Chair

Set the scene:

1. The wheelchair is locked (or the regular chair is stabilized).
2. The foot plates are up and out of the way.
3. Mr. Jones will use a walker in this episode.

THE NURSE: Walk up close to the chair (bed, toilet, etc.) and turn around again. Be sure that the foot plates of your wheelchair are out of the way and that the wheelchair is locked. Turn around until your back is toward the chair. Now, back up with your walker. Move your walker backwards toward you. Press on your hands. Step back with your good foot, then move your bad foot back. Repeat these steps until you feel the back of both of your legs against the seat of the chair. (See illustration below.)

Be sure that the chair is stable. Are the brakes locked? Let go of the walker with one

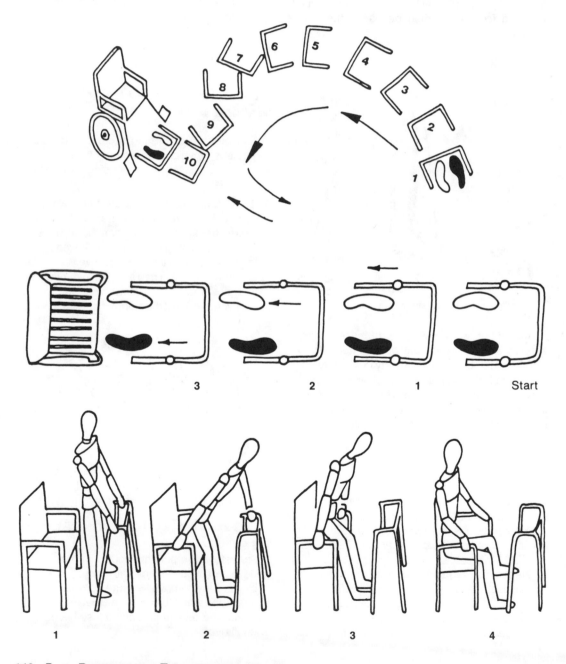

hand, and reach back to the arm of the chair. Holding firmly to the wheelchair with that hand, reach back with the other hand. Using both your arms and legs, lean forward a little and ease yourself down into the chair. Slide back in the chair until you are in a comfortable position.

There you are safe and sound, Mr. Jones! Let me check your pulse. It is good.

Described above is the correct way to turn around and sit down in a chair using a walking aid. No deviations from this method should be allowed when a patient is using crutches or a walker. Turning around is probably the most hazardous time for a patient who is walking. If he does not perform the turning process carefully, his feet get too close together, he loses his balance and falls. Many broken hips have occurred when patients have turned to sit down into a chair.

Sitting Down with Crutches

If Mr. Jones had been using crutches, to sit down he would first take the crutches from under his arms and put them both in one hand. Then holding onto the handgrips, he could reach back with the other hand to the chair and continue as described above. This method is the reverse of standing up with crutches.

Turning to Sit When Not Using Walking Aids

If the patient is not using any walking aid or is using a quad cane or a regular cane, a second method of turning around to sit down in a chair is appropriate. Suppose the patient has paralysis of his arm and leg on the left.

1. The patient walks up close to the chair and faces it.
2. He places his cane to the side, being certain he has placed it so it will not fall in his way.
3. He holds onto the left arm of the chair with his uninvolved right hand.
4. He assures himself that his balance is good.
5. He then reaches across with his right hand and grasps the right arm of the chair. He turns his feet carefully in a small circle, first moving his right foot, then his left, being certain that his feet are spread apart. His good or uninvolved side is always closest to the chair.
6. He continues to turn until he feels the chair touching the back of both of his legs and then proceeds to sit down.

Our Mr. Jones has completed the entire walking process from getting up properly, to walking properly, to sitting down properly. He has really made it to the top of the Independence Staircase!

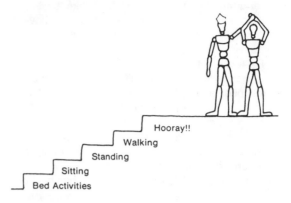

Hooray!!
Walking
Standing
Sitting
Bed Activities

You and Mr. Jones have really done well. Let's see how you do with these questions.

1. Which direction should a patient turn if he is using a walking aid? _____
   _____

2. Name two ways that a patient should move his feet when using a walking aid to turn or back up.
   a. _____
   b. _____

3. List the sequence of steps for a patient to use when sitting down in a chair.
   a. _____
   b. _____
   c. _____
   d. _____

4. When sitting down, what precaution should be taken with the wheelchair? _____
   _____

Answers:
1. *Toward his strongest or good side.*
2. a. *Same pattern as straight gait.*
   b. *Feet spread apart.*
3. a. *Turning around.*
   b. *Backing up until he feels the back of the chair against the back of his legs.*
   c. *Reaching back with one hand, then the other.*
   d. *Leaning forward and sitting down.*
4. *The brakes should be locked.*

Did you do well? Do you understand now how to walk a patient? If you have answered the questions along the way, I'm sure you do. Before we close, here are a few last-minute notes about walking.

At first the patient may only be able to walk a short distance and not have the strength or energy to turn or back up at all. In that case you should simply walk him forward as far as he can go and then bring a chair up behind him to sit in. But no matter what type of patient, *always* have him use the proper standing and sitting procedure.

Patients with poor lateral balance (usually stroke patients) have difficulty understanding the concept of leaning to the good side. This problem is most evident when a patient is using a cane, but it also occurs with other walking aids.

Here is the solution: *Use two people*. One does the instructing, encouraging the patient to lean on the cane or lean to the good side. The trick to getting the patient to do this is to hold him by the belt or under the arm and pull him toward you, forcing him to lean on his good side. The other person should stand in the guarding position but *not* touch the patient or talk to him. All the emphasis should be on the good side.

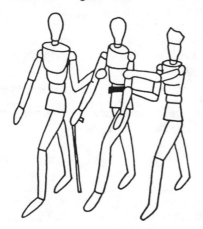

For patients with weak legs, assistive devices should be used progressively in the following order (imagine that the patient's legs are gradually getting stronger with exercise):

1. a walker or crutches
2. a walkcane (start here for a stroke patient)
3. a quad cane
4. a cane
5. stand-by assistance from you
6. independence

Some patients might not make it beyond step 1 or 2 of the progression. But if they are doing their best and it is appropriate for their diagnosis, they have certainly succeeded (and so have you in teaching them).

Didn't it make you feel good to see the nurse and Mr. Jones in our book make it to the top of the Independence Staircase? You and your Mr. Jones can get there too! We have given you the information you need!

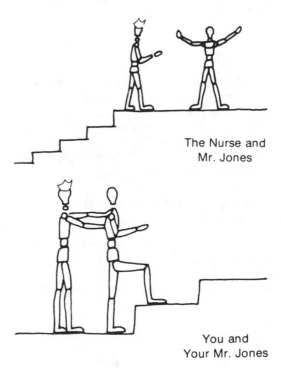

The Nurse and
Mr. Jones

You and
Your Mr. Jones

Unit Review Test on Gait Training

Now that you have finished all sections of this chapter, we would like to summarize the experience by giving you a few case histories to test your ability to develop a treatment plan. Remember to use the Independence Staircase and write down all the procedures you could follow with each patient to reach his particular goal. This will show you that you can help your Mr. Jones to independence. If you have trouble with this exercise, remember that the material is right here to review.

1. Mrs. Brown is a 67-year-old female with a fractured right hip. She had it pinned ten days ago. Her physician, Dr. Allen, tells you that he wants her to walk. What would you do? _____

_____

_____

_____

_____
_____
_____
_____
_____
_____
_____
_____
_____
_____
_____

2. Today is May 3. Mr. Beech had a stroke on May 1. Mr. Beech is alert, cooperative, and has normal strength on the right and fair strength on the left. His vital signs are normal. Dr. Anderson prescribes Progressive Mobilization activities. What would you do? _____

_____
_____
_____
_____
_____
_____
_____
_____
_____
_____
_____
_____
_____
_____

Your answers should be similar to these:

1. *Tell Mrs. Brown that you are going to help her walk. Take her pulse. Evaluate her arm strength. Evaluate her leg strength on the good side. See if Mrs. Brown can move her own involved leg. Check if she can move in bed alone, move sideways, sit up. Teach her anything with which she needs help. Be sure she has good shoes. Check sitting balance. Teach her how to transfer into the wheelchair without putting weight on her right leg. Check her standing ability. If it is good, proceed directly to using a walker. If not, do stand-ups and practice standing balance. (She could use crutches also, but at this age a walker is better.) Teach her to walk with the walker without putting weight on her right leg.*

2. *Tell Mr. Beech that you are going to begin activities with him that will allow him to regain his strength. Check his pulse. Check his range of motion, especially on his involved side. Do range of motion exercises as appropriate. Do active exercises to the left, with emphasis on the ankle. Check his pulse after each activity and, if stable, continue. Ask him if he is tired. If not, continue. Check out his movements in bed and sitting balance. Be sure he has shoes. Check him for transfer ability and teach him transfers if necessary. Transfer toward the right side. Check out his stand-up ability. Teach him stand-ups. Give him a walkcane on the right side. If he can walk with it easily (cane with opposite leg), try him with a regular cane, or none. As long as you keep checking pulse and other cardiac signs, you can progress this patient very quickly.*

Do your answers match? If they do not, please review the questions and answers again and keep in mind the Independence Staircase.

This is the end of your formal study in this area. You will find that as you use this method, you will continue to learn. Each patient is different and each session with your patient will be a learning experience.

We have taken what is specifically called a functional approach to the rehabilitation of patients, especially stroke patients. In your future studies you will encounter other more complex methods of rehabilitation which are also effective. Research studies have shown, however, that the functional approach shown here is a faster means to independence and equally as effective in the long term.[4] In these days of high medical costs, early rehabilitation of the patient—producing a shorter hospital stay—is an important consideration.

May we challenge you now to use the methods of treatment you have learned here? It is very rewarding to teach your patient, to be able to let go of his hand, and to see him walk independently. The nurse helped Mr. Jones to independence. Go ahead and help *your* Mr. Jones to independence.

NOTES

1. R. Sine, "Stroke Rehab. Program: Simple Exercise Plan," *St. Mary's Hospital Medical Staff Newsletter*, January 1980, pp. 1–2.

2. Ibid.

3. S. Olney, T. Monga, and P. Cosfigan, "Mechanical Energy of Walking of Stroke Patients," *Arch Phys Med & Rehabil* 67, no. 2 (1986): 92–98.

4. J. Lord and K. Hall, "Neuromuscular Reeducation versus Traditional Programs for Stroke Rehabilitation," *Arch Phys Med & Rehabil* 67, no. 2 (1986): 88–91.

SUGGESTED READINGS

Hirschberg, G., and C. Lewis, *Rehabilitation: A Manual for the Care of the Disabled and Elderly*. Philadelphia: Lippincott, 1976.

Kisner, C., and L. Colby. *Therapeutic Exercise: Foundations and Techniques*. Philadelphia: F.A. Davis, 1985.

Kottke, F., G.K. Stillwell, and J. Lehmann, *Krusen's Handbook of Physical Medicine and Rehabilitation*. Philadelphia: Saunders, 1982.

Liss, S. Rehabilitating the Stroke Patient, *Texas Medicine* 69 (1973): 84–90.

Nixon, V. *Spinal Cord Injury*. Rockville, Md.: Aspen, 1985.

Palmer, M., and J. Toms. *Manual for Functional Training*. Philadelphia: F.A. Davis, 1986.

13 Self-Care Training: Hemiplegia, Lateralized Stroke Program, Parkinsonism, Arthritis, and Spinal Cord Dysfunction

Mahendra Shah, O.T.R.
Ruth Avidan, O.T.R.
Robert D. Sine, M.D.

INTRODUCTION AND OBJECTIVES

As the patient is engaged in his self-care activities under the supervision and care of the nursing personnel, you will have a direct effect on his attitude and performance. In order to contribute to the patient's maximal independence, it is of utmost importance that you understand the value of self-care training and know about the different self-care techniques and how to apply them.

Suppose you had a patient who was physically handicapped or mentally confused and couldn't attend to his personal needs:

1. Would you feed, shave, and dress him so he would be comfortable and content?
2. Would you instead evaluate the patient's potential, teach him the proper techniques, and encourage him to do as much as he could for himself?

Under the first approach the patient assumes a passive role. He realizes that you too have given up hope, and consequently he will slowly slip into a dependent, depressing, and debilitating existence. Once this existence is established, it becomes very difficult or even impossible to teach the patient self-care activities. The second approach, however, will give the patient a chance to learn to adjust to his disability by spending his energy on things that he can change and allow him to aim at the goal of reaching his own maximal independence. The level of independence he can attain is limited only by his physical, emotional, and mental deficits.

The self-learning units in this chapter describe eating, personal hygiene, and dressing techniques as they apply to three common diagnoses, namely, hemiplegia, arthritis, and Parkinson's disease. However, this knowledge can be applied to many other disabilities once the principles are understood. The diagnosis, symptoms, and causes are also of vital importance, since they provide us with clues concerning

1. what the patient will be able to do
2. how he will do it
3. the problems to be anticipated
4. the patient's progress
5. the precautions to be taken
6. an outline of the self-care techniques
7. the proper way to approach the patient and his family

The overall objective of this chapter is to familiarize you with self-care training in preparation for your clinical training under the supervision of a registered occupational therapist.

HEMIPLEGIA

It is important that the person who takes care of the hemiplegic patient knows how to help him in his self-care activities. Understanding the residual effects of hemiplegia, the proper way to approach the patient, and using the appropriate treatment techniques will promote the patient's physical, mental, and emotional independence. Review of Chapter 1 is important for an intelligent approach to the techniques discussed here.

Hemiplegia is a very broad subject. This package contains only the most basic and pertinent information regarding self-care training. The learning material is designed to provide a brief introduction to hemiplegia, to discuss the most common problems relevant to this condition, to guide you through the major training procedures, to expose you to a variety of self-help devices, and to present the proper way to approach the patient.

Unit Objectives

The goal of this unit is to prepare you in the basic techniques and procedures for training hemiplegic patients in self-care activities.

Specifically, once you complete instruction in this unit you should be able to

1. understand the principles of the "lateralized stroke program"
2. apply these principles to teaching the hemiplegic activities of daily living
3. recognize the problems and limitations of hemiplegic patients and identify possible solutions
4. select appropriate self-help devices and teach patients how to use these in activities of daily living
5. identify procedures to promote patient independence through the use of positive reinforcement and patience

The Lateralized Stroke Program

Note: It is imperative that the reader be thoroughly familiar with the Hemiplegic Syndromes, Chapter 1, before reading this unit.

Functions of the brain which are considered "lateralized" are those that are exercised within one of the cerebral hemispheres more than the other. Generally, we use the term to refer to "cognitive" functions, that is, functions that enable us to receive, process, and use incoming information. Since stroke patients have suffered severe injuries to one of their cerebral hemispheres, they tend to behave as if they are processing informa-

tion mostly with their intact hemisphere. Thus, cognitively, there are two separate hemiplegic syndromes calling for two separate programs.

A traditional stroke program treats patients with right and left hemiplegic syndromes in much the same manner. The addition of speech therapy may be the only recognition given to the functional asymmetry of the cerebral hemispheres.

The *lateralized stroke program* is devised to deal with the cognitive deficits and discrepancies seen between right and left stroke syndromes. When using this program, you must not only be able to recognize the patient's deficits but also be familiar with his residual capacities. It will be the residual capacities that will be the key to restoring functional activities.

We have devised "general" and "lateralized" guidelines. The general guidelines are to be used in working with either left or right syndromes and are on the order of general principles. The lateralized guidelines are more specific and are to be applied to the specified syndrome.

The general guidelines are principles that may guide any instructional program where cognitive and/or perceptual deficits exist. These principles are set out as guidelines so that they are emphasized and may be kept in mind while you are working with patients. If these guidelines are forgotten, you may find your patient is not learning functional activities—he is learning frustration and depression. If the patient appears inattentive or "poorly motivated" (it's unlikely a patient will want to be dependent if he really believes he can be otherwise), look to see if your own technique is inappropriate instead.

General Guidelines

1. Instructional material must be presented in a format acceptable to the patient's intact perceptual and intellectual capacities.
2. The patient must be taught to use complementary functions to compensate for his deficits.

Discussion. The first general guideline implies that we must communicate along open perceptual channels. That's obvious enough when the perceptual deficit is clear. No one attempts to teach the blind using written material or the deaf by lecture. It is not difficult, however, to find examples of health care professionals giving verbal instructions to the severely aphasic patient or presenting diagrams to the spatially deficient left hemiplegic. The perceptual deficits in strokes are more subtle than those we may be used to.

The first guideline also implies that the information must be presented in a form that can be processed by the patient. Few of us would give complex material to the demented patient. However, since the two hemispheres process information quite differently, information which is acceptable to the left hemisphere may be impossible for the right hemisphere to process and vice versa. We must keep in mind that we are presenting to the intact hemisphere and must keep information presented appropriate to that hemisphere's capabilities.

The second general guideline emphasizes that the training of the stroke patient will proceed most quickly and surely if we draw on his residual abilities and do not dwell on his deficits. The guideline may be applied in the physical sphere as well as the cognitive one. The patient with a hemiplegic upper extremity may be taught one-handed activities of daily living with the intact arm quickly and easily and reach full independence. Such training given early may avoid much of the depression and preoccupation with the hemiplegic arm too often seen in stroke patients.

Far more subtle application of the principle, however, calls for its emphasis in dealing with cognitive functions. The left hemiplegic's loss of spatial ability may be compensated for by verbal cuing. Spatial ability is not distributed evenly throughout the population. There are those of us who have a good nonverbal sense of direction and like to read maps and hate to ask directions. Others hate maps but easily recall long detailed verbal directions and happily find their way from point to point. These individuals are verbally cuing themselves through space. This technique may be utilized by left hemiplegics. The patient may be taught to verbally cue himself in finding his way back to his room or pulling on a shirt. He may also cue himself verbally to compensate for left inattention.

The right hemiplegic may use his ability to "read" the situation, facial expression, and body language to compensate for his receptive aphasia. Patients get so good at this that family and attendants often believe they understand all that is said despite a complete aphasia. The parallel in everyday life is our similar use of such body language cues when we don't trust what is being said (e.g., statements read by hostages, courtroom presentations, courting professions, political speeches, etc.).

More subtle still is the application of the principle to the disparate modes of thought present in the respective hemispheres. The left hemiplegic may not get the "whole picture," but he can analyze particulate information in a sequential form. He should be encouraged to do so by breaking up information into small pieces and ordering them sequentially. The right hemiplegic is even less likely to make errors of judgment if he is allowed free access and exploration of a "real" (not simulated) problem so that he can exercise that poorly understood but most important form of thought termed *appositional*.[1] Again, there is the parallel in normals in the use of nonverbal thought commonly termed *horse sense*.

The stroke patient is uniquely suited for these principles, since most functions in one hemisphere have a parallel complementary function in the other hemisphere which may be used in place of the lost function. The patient's strengths and weaknesses must be recognized and the principles applied intelligently "with both hemispheres" if success is to occur.

The lateralized guidelines in Table 13-1 are specific as to side. They are offered to help you model your own lateralized stroke program. An attempt is made to explain some of the rationales and findings upon which they are based, but space prohibits detailing the extensive studies that have clarified functional hemispheric asymmetry.

The examples of activities which follow the guidelines will show you how they actually are applied.

What to Do about the Severely Paretic Arm

In order to reach functional independence quickly and assure the patient of some success while avoiding failure and depression, most techniques will involve training the normal arm. This will occur to the extent of giving the appearance of ignoring the hemiplegic arm. When there is some neurological recovery in the affected arm, the affected arm is used as an assistive hand, mainly to stabilize objects. With additional recovery, the patient will be able to use the affected hand for performing tasks that require gross dexterity and coordination. The patient or his family might ask why more therapy is not directed toward the affected arm. They reply should be, "It isn't known how much recovery in the affected upper extremity will take place. Consequently, if we encourage the use of the unaffected arm in self-care and ADL early, the patient will have a chance for utilizing his potential toward a realistic goal and reaching his maximal independence." At the same time, the affected arm will be exercised in therapy and/or by the patient himself as needed. A *sling* might be used for the affected extremity.

TABLE 13-1 Lateralized Guidelines

GUIDELINES FOR LEFT HEMIPLEGIA

1. Present material on the right side. Objects to be worked on should be presented singly. Nothing that may be distracting should be further to the right of the object to which attention is to be directed.

2. Verbal instructions should be put simply and briefly.

3. Work areas should be quiet, with a minimum of distraction.

4. Material should be broken into small steps, then presented in logical sequence.

5. Encourage verbal self-cuing to facilitate focusing and training and particularly to compensate for spatial ability deficits and hemi-inattention.

6. Pictures are a poor learning aid.

7. Do not accept the patient's assertions of adequate function.

8. Despite the patient's reasonable verbal assurances of good judgment and concern for his personal safety, rely on observation to determine his level of activity.

9. No attempt should be made to confirm learning by copying or constructing pictures.

10. Facial expressions of approval or disapproval are not to be relied upon as "reinforcers."

11. "Music room" listening as an activity is apt to be a poor reinforcer.

RATIONALE (Directed to Residual Capacities in Right Hemisphere)

1. Each hemisphere directs attention toward the opposite visual field. A hemispheric lesion disturbs the normal balance. The normal hemisphere, uninhibited by the damaged hemisphere, directs attention to the opposite side. The effect is of "neglect" or "agnosia" for the side of the hemiplegia, created by a biasing of attention to the contralateral side.

2. Verbal input may heighten left hemispheric activity, thereby increasing contralateral biasing of attention.

3. The left hemisphere is more easily alerted than the right, but habituates more rapidly. The effect is of easy distractibility and short attention span.

4. The left hemisphere utilizes sequential logistic learning.

5. The linguistic mode is the complementary mode to right hemispheric spatial superiority. It is an extremely versatile mode capable of compensating for numerous cognitive deficits.

6. The left hemisphere has poor ability to recognize and synthesize figures.

7. Left hemiplegics often react with denial to their disability.

8. Patients with left hemiplegia tend to demonstrate poor judgment, impulsive behavior, and confabulation.

9. Right hemispheric lesions produce spatial agnosias. Such practices are likely to be unrewarding.

10. The left hemisphere recognizes facial expression poorly. The lack of patient response may be interpreted as "poor motivation."

11. Pitch appreciation is a right hemisphere function.

GUIDELINES FOR RIGHT HEMIPLEGIA

1. Use verbal communication only when you are sure it is completely understood; if it is not, cease use of speech altogether.

2. Use the *real* situation for a functional activity. If this is not practical, use simulated situations, pantomime, and gestures, in that order.

3. The right hemiplegic can benefit from prolonged intermittent instruction; he may benefit if allowed to remain in therapy and observe other patients' activities.

4. Use facial expression freely to express approval, disapproval, humor, etc.

5. Present material as a whole; different parts may then be gone over separately and reiterated.

RATIONALE (Directed to Residual Capacities in Left Hemisphere)

1. Use of poorly understood speech can be distracting and may defer the use of other methods of communication. Adequate communication should not be sacrificed in hopes of providing speech therapy.

2. The right brain best appreciates the reality in contradistinction to symbolic reconstruction such as speech, reading, mathematics, and gesture.

3. The right hemisphere maintains its ability to "alert" over a prolonged period. It may be expected to learn from observation.

4. The right hemisphere is superior in recognition of facial expression.

5. The right hemisphere learns best in context and is able to synthesize parts.

Table 13-1 continued

6. Position material so it is presented from the left side.	6. The right hemiplegic has contralateral biasing of attention, although it is not as well recognized nor as troublesome as it is in left hemiplegia (see left hemiplegic guidelines). It may be that the right hemiplegic compensates with his ability to synthesize whereas the same loss compounds the problem of the left hemiplegic.
7. The patient may enjoy music, sing, and play musical instruments.	7. The right hemisphere is superior in appreciation of pitch.

Evidence exists to show that a sling does not promote contractures or retard the return of neurological functioning.[2] A sling may be used

1. to prevent shoulder subluxation
2. to relieve pain in the arm, especially in the shoulder
3. to prevent swelling and deformity, especially in the forearm and hand
4. for patients who ignore the affected side or have poor sensation on this side, thereby protecting the arm from hot and sharp objects and from getting it caught in doors, wheelchairs, etc.

Not all hemiplegic patients will gain full independence in self-care and activities of daily living (ADL), but remember that even if a patient is only partially independent, it may mean a great deal to him. Let the patient do as much as he can for himself and by himself. It is also important for a patient to be able to feel comfortable about accepting assistance in activities that are beyond his capabilities.

Test on the Lateralized Stroke Program

You have just finished an important section. Let's see if you understand and remember the basic facts. Circle the correct answer to the following statements.

1. You should postpone self-care training and ADL until the affected extremity gains some neurological recovery. True or false?
2. With a deficit in visual perception, the patient will have difficulties performing self-care activities. True or false?
3. You can motivate the patient by doing his self-care activities for him. True or false?
4. A patient who ignores the left (or the right) side of space will be helped by putting his bed so that his good side is to the wall. This encourages the patient to "scan" to the hemianoptic side. True or false?
5. A lost function is a function that cannot be replaced, and one must work to restore it. True or false?
6. Use every opportunity to talk to the aphasic patient, particularly giving instructions. True or false?
7. Patients need to be challenged to learn like everybody else. True or false?
8. Despite a severe impairment encompassing all symbolic usage (speech, numbers, and even appropriate use of some objects), the right hemiplegic often attains good overall function because he retains good judgment. True or false?

Answers:
1. *False.*
2. *True.*
3. *False.*
4. *False. Positioning the bed this way will isolate the patient, possibly to the extent of producing sensory deprivation.*
5. *False. Complementary functions may be used to compensate for each other.*
6. *False.*
7. *False.*
8. *True.*

As always, if you missed any answers, that suggests you have not read the text in enough depth. Try again before you proceed. If you were 100 percent correct, begin the next section on feeding procedures.

Feeding

Feeding training is one of the most important activities in self-care training of hemiplegic patients. It gives them independence in one activity while they are dependent for everything else during the early phase of rehabilitation.

When the patient has difficulty swallowing, the task of feeding training becomes more complex. In recent years, several sophisticated methods of teaching swallowing have been described. These are very valuable, especially when there is cranial nerve damage. Thorough evaluation and training in swallowing (dysphagia training) done by an occupational therapist may resolve this problem. A few simple measures are described below.

1. If a nasogastric tube is in place, it might have to be removed before training can begin. Residual soreness and swelling can inhibit swallowing for several days. The patient may have to be supported with IVs during this interval. If the nasogastric tube is replaced too hastily you may invite repeated failure.

Figure 13-1 Plate Guard

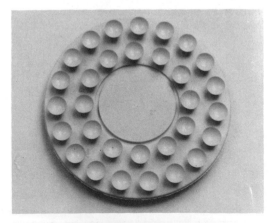

Figure 13-2 Suction Holder

2. Positioning the patient properly is of utmost importance in order to decrease risk of aspiration. The patient must be sitting up and the neck should be slightly flexed. Backward tilting of the neck should be avoided to prevent the opening of the airway.
3. Prior to feeding, appropriate mouth care should be provided to keep the oral cavity clean. This also induces salivation. After feeding, all the food should be removed from the mouth to minimize chances of aspiration.
4. Soft food is easier to swallow than fluids. Pureed food or firm gelatin should be tried before water. Food is easier to swallow when placed at the back of the mouth on the "well" side.

Feeding the Right Hemiplegic

One of the guidelines is to use the real situation for functional activities. As the right brain (which is the intact hemisphere) best appreciates the reality, feeding training should be done at mealtimes.

The use of self-help devices is highly recommended whenever necessary. Success in early stages helps prevent frustration on the part of the patient as well as the staff and reinforces independence. The set-up and procedure are described below.

Set-up:

1. The actual mealtime should be used as much as possible.
2. The whole tray should be placed in front of the patient. The patient may not recognize the spoon or fork (due to visual agnosia). Initially only one utensil should be used at a time.
3. The person helping with feeding should be in front.
4. The patient can eat in a room with other distractions or people—he can benefit a great deal by observing others.
5. The use of a plate guard (Figure 13-1) will help the patient in getting food on the utensil and prevent it from falling off the plate. Generally the right hemiplegics are acutely aware of and do not like sloppiness. When they see food falling on the table, it upsets them.
6. In order to prevent the plate from moving, a wet washcloth, suction holder, or "dycem" may be used (Figure 13-2).
7. Initially the food may be cut for the patient, as one-handed cutting techniques take a

little time to learn. If the method described below under "Self-Help Devices for Feeding" is used often enough at mealtimes and shown to the right hemiplegic patient, he will learn to use it quickly.

8. Allow sufficient time for feeding.

Procedure:

1. Keep verbal instructions to a minimum.
2. Place the dish to the left of the patient.
3. Give the fork to the patient and let him hold it in his hand.
4. Guide his hand to the food and assist in scooping and bringing his hand to his mouth. The patient will generally follow through with the chewing and swallowing.
5. Repeat the procedure a few times, allowing the patient to do most of the activity.
6. Use facial expressions freely to express approval and disapproval, and give gestural feedback.
7. When finished with one dish, take the fork away and let the patient take a rest to avoid perseveration.
8. The patient may neglect the right side of the mouth, but becomes aware if food drops to his lap or table.
9. Proper mouth care should be given after the feeding.
10. Use built-up-handle utensils as necessary (Figure 13-3).

Feeding the Left Hemiplegic

The left hemiplegic usually exhibits a short attention span and gets distracted very easily. Therefore these patients will learn best in a quiet area and with a minimum of distraction. It is disastrous to put a left hemiplegic in the dining room with other patients. Very likely, by the end of the hour he will have talked about everything but left his food untouched. If you ask, "Well, Mr. Smith, how come you have not finished your lunch?" he will have a very convincing answer! This situation can best be avoided by (1) having the patient eat all meals in a quiet area and (2) having the person who is helping feeding find adequate time to spend with the patient and not try to do too many other things at the same time.

The set-up and procedure are described below.

Set-up:

1. Present one dish at a time on the right side.
2. Present one utensil on the right side at a time. There should be no distracting objects further to the right.

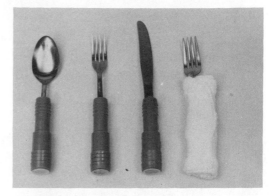

Figure 13-3 Built-Up-Handle Utensils

3. The person helping with feeding should be far to the right side.
4. Contrasting colors for the dishes and tray may help in figure-ground discrimination.
5. Use adapted equipment, such as a plate guard, as needed.

Procedure:

1. Give very brief and simple verbal instructions broken down into steps. Try one step at a time. You must avoid "overfeeding." For example, one might present a bowl of cereal and a spoon to the patient with instructions like this: "Good morning, Mr. Smith. How are you? It is time to eat your breakfast. I want you to use this spoon to eat the cereal—can you see it?" With instructions like this, the left hemiplegic will have difficulty focusing and his attention will wander. The correct instruction would be something like this: "Mr. Smith, please use this spoon for cereal." Then, either point to the spoon or give it to the patient. Once the patient is done with the cereal, take the bowl and spoon away and present another dish.
2. The left hemiplegic is likely to continue talking rather than to eat. Keep refocusing attention on the activity.
3. Ask the patient to slow down or stop every so often, as the patient is likely to exhibit impulsivity.
4. Use verbal feedback as opposed to gestural feedback. Facial expressions of approval or disapproval are not to be relied upon as reinforcers. The left hemisphere (which is the intact hemisphere in left hemiplegics) recognizes facial expressions poorly. The lack of patient response to the facial expression is likely to be interpreted as "poor motivation." These patients may occasionally respond poorly to change in tone of voice as well.

5. The patient is likely to neglect the left side of the mouth and may not be aware even if food drops to his lap.
6. If the patient neglects the left half of the dish, it could be given a one-quarter turn so that he can see the food.
7. The patient should not be left alone during feeding training.
8. Proper mouth care should be given after feeding.

Figure 13-4 Cutting One-Handed

Figure 13-5 Facing Opening, Thumb on Flap

Figure 13-6 The Two Flaps Pulled Back

Self-Help Devices for Feeding

Cutting Food. Cutting food with one hand isn't easy, but it *is* possible if you have a sharp knife, tender meat, and the "know-how." In order to cut food, hold the knife the way you ordinarily do, placing your index finger on the top part of the blade. Place the tip of the sharp edge on the distant part of the food to be cut, apply pressure on the blade, and rock the knife up and down. After each cut, proceed with the tip and repeat the rocking motion until you cut all the way through (Figure 13-4).

Opening Jars. Stabilize the jar by putting it between your knees or place it inside a drawer and lean against it with your hip.

Opening Milk Cartons:

1. Place the carton so you face the opening side. Bend each flap all the way back with your thumb while your fingers hold the back of the carton (Figure 13-5).
2. Bend both flaps back at the same time (Figure 13-6).
3. Push the outer edges of the flap together, thumb against the rest of the fingers, to form a spout (Figure 13-7).

Spreading Food on Bread:

1. Use soft food from a container.
2. Grasp the handle of the knife with your thumb, placing the ring and little fingers under the handle (Figure 13-8).
3. Place the index finger on the flat side of the blade.
4. Place the knife on the bread and with the middle finger hold bread against the plate while spreading the food.

Figure 13-7 Two Flaps Pushed in to Form a Spout

Let's do a quick review of eating procedures and self-help devices. Try to answer the following questions.

1. *After the peas spread all over the table, you realized that you should have used a plate guard. True or false?*
2. *The food was too soft and the patient had trouble spreading it on bread. True or false?*
3. *In order to cut food the patient needs an adapted knife. True or false?*
4. *For the patient with hemianopsia, you should initially place the food on the affected side; after additional training, you should place it in front of the patient. True or false?*

Answers:

1. *True.*   3. *False.*
2. *False.*   4. *False.*

If any of the answers were incorrect, please review this section again. If your answers were correct, please continue to the next section.

Personal Hygiene Procedures and Self-Help Devices

In completing the section on eating, you should have recognized the importance of sequence. Here, too, we will start with the tasks that are easy for the patient to perform and learn and we will finish with the more difficult ones.

Combing Hair. Short hair is easy to handle. Long hair can be kept in place with an elastic band. The left hemiplegic patient may find it difficult to handle the comb at the back of the head and may also tend to neglect the left side. You may have to make him aware of the fact that he has not combed the left side, and in some cases it is better to do the left side yourself initially and let the patient do the right side. The right hemiplegic may not recognize the comb and may put it in his mouth! However, if you demonstrate the activity a few times and if it is done with morning care, he will pick up the activity quickly.

Shaving. Rechargeable electric razors are best for hemiplegic patients. Again, following the general guidelines described earlier, the patient can become independent in this activity. Demonstrate the activity to the right hemiplegic and guide his hand as needed. The left hemiplegic needs to be cued continuously and the activity should be broken down into steps, e.g., do the sides first and then the chin area.

Figure 13-8 Spreading Food

Make-up. This is a difficult activity for both left and right hemiplegics. If the aphasia is severe, the right hemiplegic may fail to recognize the lipstick and/or powder compact and may not know what to do with these objects. The left hemiplegic might have difficulty in applying the lipstick properly. However, some patients might be able to manage make-up activities after training.

Lipstick can be turned out or in by gripping the case between the middle and ring fingers with the base of the lipstick directed upward. Rotate the base using the thumb and index finger. This can be learned with practice. Some patients may find it easier to hold the base of the lipstick between their teeth with the case sticking outside the mouth and then rotate the case with the hand.

A powder compact can be glued or attached at the base to a stable surface, thus making it easier to open.

Antiperspirant. With practice, a spray can be handled with one hand for both underarms.

Toothpaste and Toothbrush. Unscrew toothpaste by holding the tube with three fingers and use the thumb and index fingers to screw and unscrew the cap. Some patients may prefer to stabilize the tube gently between their knees and use the free hand to unscrew the cap (Figure 13-9). Patients with dentures can use an adapted toothbrush with suction cups (Figure 13-10). Attach the toothbrush to the sink and, grasping the dentures in the hand, brush the teeth. Some patients prefer to rinse the dentures and soak them in denture cleanser.

Fingernails. Use a one-handed brush for cleaning nails (Figure 13-11) and use a file taped onto the table for filing nails. The affected hand has to be held by the unaffected hand or another

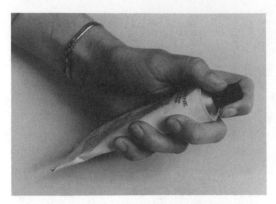

Figure 13-9 Unscrewing Toothpaste One-Handed

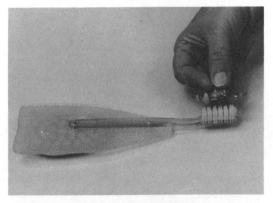

Figure 13-10 One-Handed Toothbrush for Dentures

Figure 13-11 One-Handed Brush for Cleaning Fingernails

file can be used for filing the affected hand on the patient's lap. For toenails use a clipper.

Bathing. Patients with severe receptive aphasia or perceptual deficits may need maximum assistance in bathing during the early phases of rehabilitation. Patients should be supervised in bathing unless a patient has good motor, perceptual, and speech recovery and is able to understand and follow instructions with good judgment.

The patient should be taught to test warmth of water with the unaffected arm. Always turn on the cold water first and turn off the hot water first. A patient with poor sitting balance will require help when washing lower body parts. Let the patient do as much as he can by himself, but at the same time remember safety.

A sponge bath by the sink can be done by the patient with the washcloth and a long-handled sponge and the soap on a rope around his neck. The patient should be seated, preferably in a locked wheelchair or an armchair.

In the shower, use a steady chair with a back and with suction cups attached to its legs. The faucets should be within easy reach. Special equipment for the shower and the tub will contribute to safety. The equipment may include (1) non-skid tapes on the shower floor, tub bottom, and top edge of the tub; (2) nonslip grab bars attached to the walls at the side of the shower or tub; and (3) a portable shower hose.

Don't leave a patient alone when he is bathing unless he is able to function independently.

Now that you have read the above procedures carefully, you should have no trouble answering the following questions:

1. *A hemiplegic patient can be trained to become independent in personal hygiene activities. True or false?*
2. *Bathing should be one of the first procedures to be taught. True or false?*
3. *You should praise every effort and every little success. True or false?*
4. *You should encourage the patient to do everything himself, even if it is potentially unsafe. True or false?*
5. *Bathing will require special transfer techniques and special equipment. True or false?*
6. *Inability to recognize the space and part of the body on the affected side because of perceptual problems will affect the learning process and hinder progress. True or false?*

Answers:

1. True	*3. True*	*5. True*
2. False	*4. False*	*6. True*

If you missed any, please review this section again. If your answers were correct, proceed now to the next section on dressing procedures.

Dressing Techniques

It is recommended that patients wear street clothing daily. As the right hemiplegic patient best appreciates reality, he is more likely to respond to dressing training in the morning, preferably after a shower or bed bath. This enhances the patient's motivation to learn and his attitude toward independence. (If the dressing training is done during the later part of the day, the patient may have difficulty in accepting it.)

As in any other activity the patient should be encouraged to do easier tasks and assistance should be given for the more difficult tasks.

Given below is a list of recommended clothing styles which will make self-dressing easier for the patient.

1. If possible, initially use clothes that open completely in the front.
2. Use dresses, skirts, and pants that slip easily over the hips.
3. If possible, use clothing with a loose fit.
4. Use rayon and nylon jerseys, which are easier to handle.

Right Hemiplegic Training

Set-up:

1. Patient should be sitting up if possible.
2. Garments should be placed to the left side of the patient and within easy reach.

Procedure:

All clothing articles, including self-help devices, should be placed within easy reach of the patient. Now, let's consider the sequence for training the patient to dress himself.

Buttoning. In the early stages let the patient do unbuttoning with one hand. Buttoning the regular buttons with one hand is difficult, especially when one-handed coordination is poor. Failure, with its attendant frustration, should be avoided. Therefore, if the patient has difficulty with buttoning, assistance should be given.

Putting on a Shirt. Patients with right hemiplegia respond best to demonstration. Initially let the patient observe you while you are dressing him. Patient may assist spontaneously.

1. Place the shirt on the patient's lap with collar toward knees and label showing. Put affected arm across and into the armhole (Figure 13-12).

2. Pull sleeve up to the elbow and over the affected shoulder. Throw shirt around the back (Figures 13-13 and 13-14). After doing this once or twice, you might guide patient's left hand over the right hand and let him pull the sleeve. When a patient can successfully manage all or part of the activity, give gestural feedback with facial expressions of approval.
3. Direct the unaffected arm downward and put into the armhole. Button shirt from bottom to top. The button of the unaffected hand's cuff should be secured by an elastic thread and kept buttoned at all times. Button the cuffs before the garment is put on if the cuffs are wide enough for the hand to get through.

Remember: When you put on a shirt or a coat, put the affected arm in first.

Taking off a Shirt:

1. Unbutton the sleeve and the shirt front. Push the shirt off the affected shoulder using the strong hand (Figure 13-15).
2. Remove the sleeve from the unaffected shoulder and work the unaffected arm out of the sleeve (Figure 13-16).
3. With the unaffected arm pull the sleeve below the elbow and then pull off the cuff from the affected arm (Figure 13-17).

Remember: When taking a shirt or coat off, the unaffected arm comes out first.

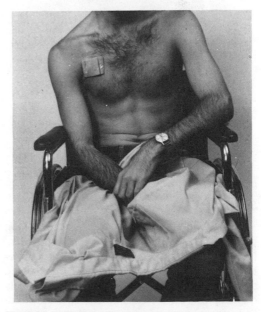

Figure 13-12 Placing Shirt on Patient's Lap

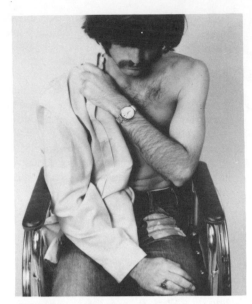

Figure 13-13 Inserting the Paretic Arm

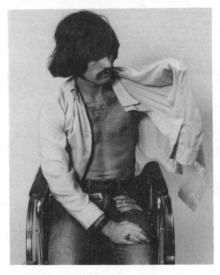

Figure 13-14 Inserting the Well Arm

Left Hemiplegic Training

Set-up:

The left hemiplegic responds best in a quiet surrounding with as little distraction as possible. Dressing activities should be attempted on a one-to-one basis away from other people. The training should be broken down into small steps and only one step at a time should be attempted. Instructions should be brief and simple. Attaching a rib-

bon to the right sleeve of shirt and pants makes it easier for the patient to recognize the right sleeve. The patient should be in a locked wheelchair if sitting and should not be left alone until the session is completed. The patient should be approached from the right side.

Buttoning. The left hemiplegic may be able to button and unbutton easily with one hand; however, very often the buttons and buttonholes may not match. The patient's attention should repeatedly be refocused on the activity and verbal self-cuing should be given. For example, one might say to a patient, "Mr. K., I want you to unbutton the bottom button." Often the patient attempts to unbutton the easiest button he can reach. His attention and the right hand should then be directed to the bottom button and to the fact that there are no more buttons below it. The patient should be asked to button the remaining buttons in a sequence ending with the collar button.

Taking off a Shirt. It is much easier if the training starts with undressing. In most instances, the left hemiplegic will take off the right side and will neglect to take off the left side. This can be helped by guiding his hand to the left side and assisting him to pull the sleeve. While doing this one might say, "Mr. J., after pulling off the right sleeve, you need to pull off the left sleeve." If his attention lapses, have the patient repeat your instructions aloud. This approach facilitates verbal self-cuing and his attention is refocused. This is one of the major differences between right and left hemiplegic training. When the shirt is completely off, it should be taken off the patient's lap so that he is aware that indeed he did take the shirt off.

Putting on a Shirt. Teaching the left hemiplegic to put his shirt on may be quite frustrating, time-consuming, and minimally successful when significant perceptual deficits are present. The task should be broken down into small steps and the patient should be told the logical sequence starting from left to right.

1. Put the left arm in the left sleeve. (The person who is helping should put the patient's left arm in the left sleeve. While this is done, the patient should be told, "Mr. D., first the left arm goes into the left sleeve.")
2. Throw the shirt around the back and let the patient know that this is the second step.
3. Ask the patient to put his right arm through the right sleeve.

After trying this method several times, the patient should be taught to make sure that each step

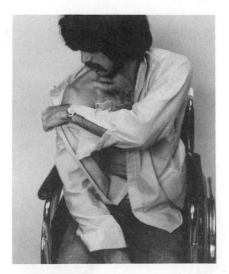

Figure 13-15 Removing the Shirt

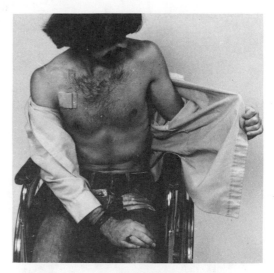

Figure 13-16 Undressing the Well Arm

is accomplished before starting the next step. For example, you might ask Mr. D. to check and make sure that the left arm is in the sleeve before he puts the right arm through the right sleeve.

As the patient makes progress, he can push the left sleeve above the elbow and throw back the shirt; assistance can be decreased to a minimum, i.e., putting the left hand into the left sleeve.

Other Self-Help Dressing Activities

In the following pages additional dressing activities for hemiplegics are described. The principles and guidelines described earlier should be used when applicable.

Putting on Undershirt or Slip (Method 1):

1. Put the affected arm through strap or sleeve by placing the affected arm on your knee and pulling the strap or sleeve over the hand and up to the elbow (Figure 13-18).
2. Put unaffected arm through strap or sleeve (Figure 13-19).
3. The unaffected arm should hold the garment at the head opening and slip it over the head and adjust it (Figure 13-20).

Putting on Undershirt or Slip (Method 2):

1. Gather the piece of clothing in the unaffected arm and slip it over the affected arm. Slip it over the head (Figure 13-21).
2. Put the unaffected arm through the strap or sleeve and adjust the piece of clothing (Figure 13-22).

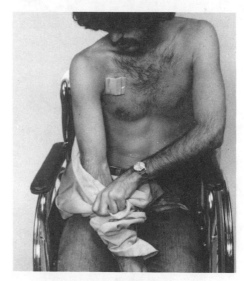

Figure 13-17 Undressing the Paretic Arm

Taking off Undershirt or Slip:

1. With the unaffected hand grasping the shirt from the back, pull forward and over the head.
2. Remove the unaffected arm from the shirt.
3. Remove affected arm from the shirt.

Please answer this question: You are about to teach Mr. K., who is a right hemiplegic, to put on his undershirt. Which hand should be put in first? If you said the right hand, you are correct.

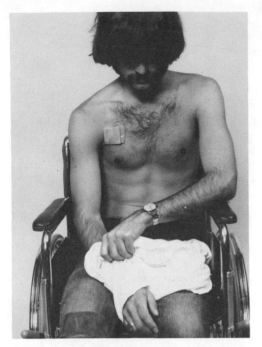

Figure 13-18 Donning the Undershirt

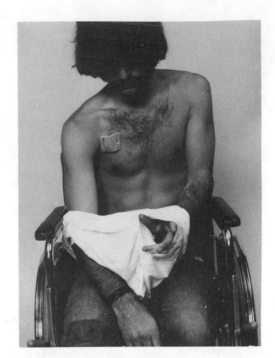

Figure 13-19 Inserting the Well Arm

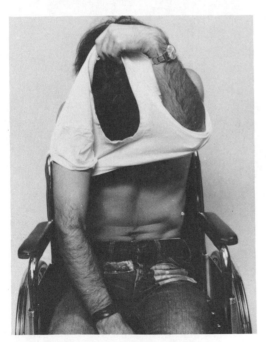

Figure 13-20 Donning an Undershirt (Method 1)

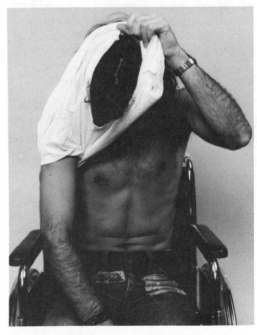

Figure 13-21 Donning an Undershirt (Method 2-step 1)

Putting on and Taking off Shorts, Underpants, and Slacks:

If the patient has good sitting and standing balance, he can dress while sitting on a regular chair or on the side of a steady low bed. If the patient has poor sitting and standing balance, he should dress while sitting in a locked wheelchair. If the patient is too heavy or too weak, it is easier to dress the lower extremities in bed.

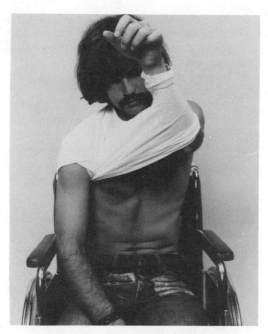

Figure 13-22 Donning an Undershirt (Method 2-step 2)

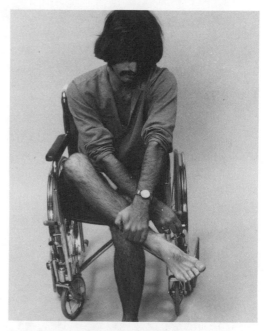

Figure 13-23 Preparation for Donning Pants or Shorts

Putting on Shorts or Pants:

1. Sitting down, the patient picks up his affected leg with his unaffected hand and places it over his unaffected leg (Figure 13-23).
2. Patient holds pants, bends down, and puts the pants on the affected leg (Figure 13-24).
3. Patient uncrosses legs, puts the unaffected leg into pants.
4. Patient pulls pants up to his knees, stands up (with the unaffected leg placed in the midline of the body), and pulls them up by raising the hips, using the unaffected leg.

Taking off Shorts or Pants:

This is done by reversing the procedure above, undressing the unaffected leg first.

Putting on and Taking off Bra:

This is a rather difficult activity. Bras that open in front may be used to make it easier. Using velcro fasteners in front will also help. The following procedure should be used if a regular back fastening bra is used.

1. Panties should be put on first.
2. Use patient's regular back-fastening bra.
3. A regular clothespin will be required.

Figure 13-24 Donning Pants

4. If the patient's right side is affected, place the hooks in front and turn the bra inside out. Use the unaffected arm to fasten one end of the bra to the panties with the clothespin (Figure 13-25).

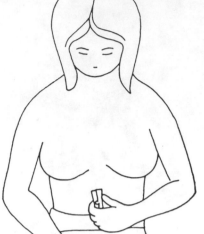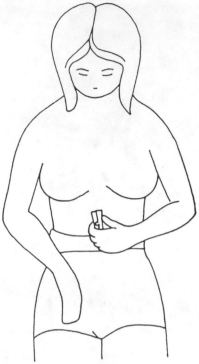

Figure 13-25 Donning a Bra One-Handed

5. Pull the other end around your waist with the unaffected hand, making sure that the right side of the bra is out. Hook the bra with the unaffected hand (Figure 13-26).
6. Take the clothespin off, turn the bra around into proper position.
7. With the unaffected hand put the affected arm through the strap and pull up over the shoulder.
8. Put the unaffected arm through the strap and pull the strap up (Figure 13-27).

Taking off Bra:

1. Pull the strap off the affected shoulder down to the elbow, repeat the procedure with the unaffected shoulder, and get the arm out.
2. Use the unaffected arm to pull the affected arm out.
3. Turn the bra around waist so that the hooks are in the front.
4. Unhook by holding the thumb against the rest of the fingers.

Remember: Have a patient with poor balance sit in a steady armchair or locked wheelchair.

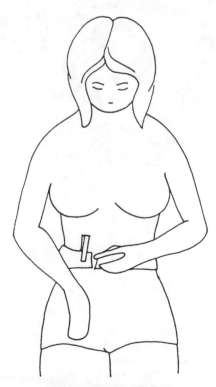

Figure 13-26 Hooking a Bra One-Handed

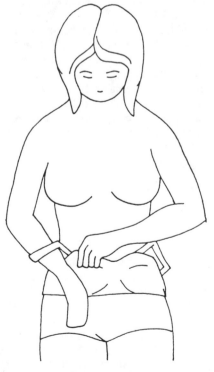

Figure 13-27 Positioning Bra

Putting on Socks (Method 1):

For the hemiplegic, it is easier to put on socks than to put on hosiery. A footstool can be helpful.

1. Have the patient sit in an armchair or a locked wheelchair. Using his strong hand, he places the affected leg over the unaffected leg, or places it on a stool.
2. The top of the sock is opened by placing the hand in the cuff and spreading the thumb away from the rest of the fingers (Figure 13-28).
3. The sock is placed over the toes and pulled over the foot (Figure 13-29).
4. Repeat the procedure with the unaffected leg. Make sure that there are no wrinkles.

Putting on Socks (Method 2):

Again, begin by crossing the legs. Turn the socks inside out and push the toe part in. Place the toe part over the toes, and pull the sock over the heel and up the ankle.

Putting On and Taking Off Shoes and Braces:

1. Shoes with buckles are easier to handle than those with shoe laces.
2. Elastic shoe laces are not recommended for spastic feet.
3. Velcro on the brace's closure is easier to handle than a buckle.
4. Insert-a-Foot Shoe Aid* can be handled more easily with one hand than can a long shoehorn. This device is slipped over the shoe heel before putting the shoe on and the foot slips into the shoe without effort. When the foot is in the shoe, the device is slipped out (Figure 13-30).

Putting on Shoe:

1. Sitting down, place the shoe aid over the shoe heel.
2. With the strong hand, pick up the affected leg and place it over the unaffected leg. Hold the shoe and brace by the top of brace. If no brace is involved, hold the shoe tongue.
3. Place the shoe in front of the leg and slip the foot into the shoe as far as possible (Figure 13-31).
4. With the strong hand, put the foot down on the floor and push down on the knee until the heel gets into the shoe (Figure 13-32).

*Available at Be OK Self-Help Aids (see source list at end of chapter for address) or can be made in an occupational therapy department.

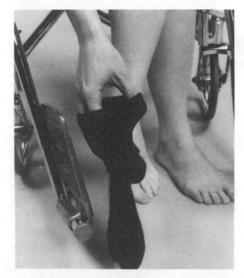

Figure 13-28 Opening Sock

Figure 13-29 Putting on Sock

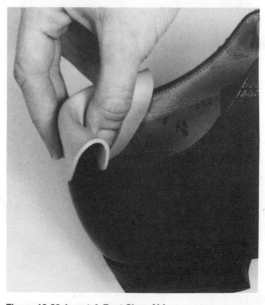

Figure 13-30 Insert-A-Foot Shoe Aid

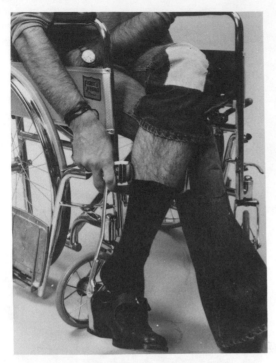

Figure 13-31 Putting on Shoe

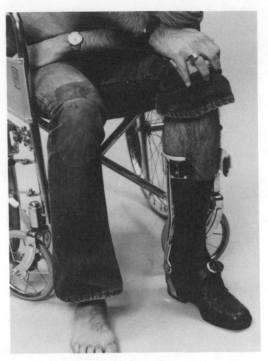

Figure 13-32 Slipping in Heel

5. Pull out the shoe aid and buckle the shoe and brace.
6. Place the shoe aid in the second shoe. Put the shoe on the floor or a stool.
7. Slip the foot in, pull the device out, and buckle the shoe.

Fastening Shoe:

1. *One-Handed Tying* (Figures 13-33 and 13-34). This method requires good carry-over and good hip flexion to reach the shoe.
2. *Velcro Closures.* These are easily made by sewing a 2-inch piece of Velcro loop and a 3-inch piece of Velcro pile together. Then secure this to the shoe by sewing through the eyelets and at the bottom near the sole. Secure a metal or plastic "D" ring or rectangle to the opposite side with a piece of Velcro sewn through the eyelets (Figure 13-35).
3. *Elastic Shoe Laces.* These are also available but are not recommended for patients with spasticity.

Review the material on dressing procedures by answering the following questions:

1. *A right hemiplegic should put the left hand in first when putting on a shirt. True or false?*

2. *Putting on socks is one of the easier tasks. True or false?*
3. *When a left hemiplegic takes his pants off, he takes off the right leg first. True or false?*
4. *When Mr. J., a right hemiplegic, took off his coat, he should have taken his left arm out first. True or false?*
5. *Mrs. B. has left hemiplegia with poor sitting balance. She should dress mainly from a locked wheelchair. True or false?*
6. *Putting on a bra requires a clothespin and a special procedure. True or false?*
7. *To put on the brace and shoe, you should cross the affected leg over the unaffected leg and place the shoe in front of the leg. True or false?*
8. *Hemiplegics should use a long shoehorn for putting on their shoes. True or false?*

Answers:

1. *False.*   4. *True.*   7. *True.*
2. *False.*   5. *True.*   8. *False.*
3. *True.*   6. *True.*

If you missed any of these questions, please review the appropriate material before you proceed. When you are confident that you understand these procedures, continue to the next section.

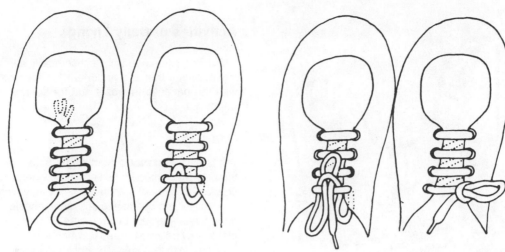

Figure 13-33 One-Hand Bow (Method 1)

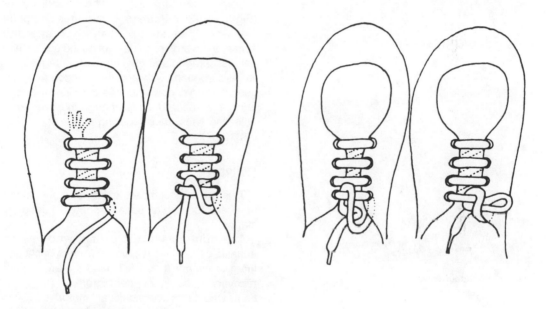

Figure 13-34 One-Hand Bow (Method 2)

Figure 13-35 Velcro Closure

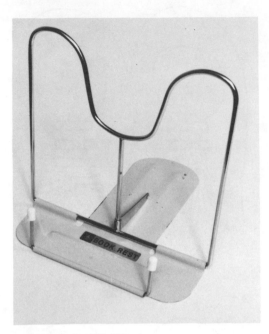

Figure 13-36 Book Holder

Figure 13-37 Cutout Window

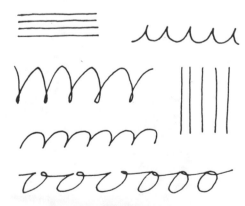

Figure 13-38 Writing Examples

Activities of Daily Living

In this section, we will discuss briefly some of the activities that are important for keeping up with the patient's interests and for keeping him happy.

Reading

It is frustrating for a hemiplegic patient to attempt to read when he has aphasia or perceptual problems. The left hemiplegic may have problems in reading due to neglect, hemianopsia, and other visual-perceptual problems. The left hemiplegic may be able to keep up with the news, etc., by listening to the radio. The right hemiplegic may have problems in reading as well as understanding spoken words. He might enjoy *familiar* television shows.

Some patients might benefit from a book holder (Figure 13-36). Patients sometimes complain that when they start reading again after the stroke, the words and lines get mixed up, so they get discouraged and give up reading. A piece of white cardboard with a cutout window may be useful. The window exposes one line at a time and the cardboard is big enough to cover other adjoining lines, thus reducing distractions (Figure 13-37).

Writing

This is a very complex activity and should not be attempted with an aphasic patient in the early stages.

The right hemiplegic patient who has no aphasia or who has recovered from aphasia can learn to write with the left hand if there is poor recovery in the right upper extremity. Those patients who do recover significant motor function in the upper extremity—such that isolated motions are present throughout the right upper extremity—can learn to write again with the right hand.

A clipboard is good for stabilizing the paper. The patient may have to start with a felt tip pen and prewriting exercises, e.g., horizontal and vertical lines along the paper, circles, half circles, etc. (Figure 13-38).

The prewriting activities improve dexterity and coordination. As the patient progresses, he will be able to print his name and eventually write it. With practice, the patient can be functional in this activity.

The left hemiplegic who is right-handed is able to write; however, there are different kinds of problems with these patients. Left hemiplegic pa-

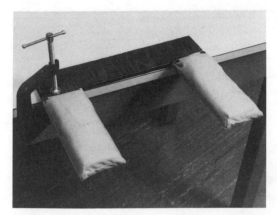

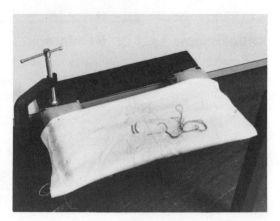

Figure 13-39 Embroidery Frame

tients will have difficulty in copying. They also find it difficult to concentrate due to their short attention span. However, with self-cuing these patients might be able to manage simple writing activities.

Telephone

A phone amplifier is like a two-way loudspeaker and allows both hands to be free. It does not require installation or wires. Pushbutton phones with automatic dialers may help in decreasing dialing problems.

Card Playing

A card holder and automatic card shuffler for the one-handed person are available from Be-OK Self-Help Aids and Fashion-ABLE.

Sewing

One-handed patients needn't stop their hobby of embroidery or doing the tasks of sewing buttons and repairing clothes. Use a simple frame made out of plywood with padded cushions on both ends (stuffed with old stockings or any other soft material). The horizontal piece should be clamped to a table with a C-clamp and the material to be worked on stretched and pinned to the cushions. Sewing is done by working the needle up and down. To thread the needle, stick it in the cushion with the eye up (Figure 13-39).

Homemaking and Work Simplification

Homemaking and work simplification are very important for disabled men and women, especially for those who have to be at home by themselves and must manage as much house-

work as possible. There are many techniques, procedures, and pieces of special equipment that the one-handed person can learn to use.

If you are interested in learning about these procedures and devices, listed below are two excellent references which should be helpful to you.

1. *Mealtime Manual for the Aged and Handicapped*, prepared by the Institute of Rehabilitation Medicine, New York University Medical Center. Essandess Special Editions, a Division of Simon & Schuster, Inc., 630 Fifth Avenue, New York, N.Y. 10020. Available on order from bookstores or from Fashion-ABLE. Spiral bound, or paper-on-board.
2. The American Heart Association, 44 E. 23 St., New York, NY 10036.

Before going on to the section review test below, try to answer the following questions.

1. *A patient who eats, dresses, and attends to personal hygiene independently will have a better self-image. True or false?*
2. *The self-help device for sewing is expensive. True or false?*
3. *When the patient complains that words and lines get mixed up when he is reading, you should suggest changing his glasses. True or false?*
4. *It does not make sense to train a patient to use both hands in writing if the affected hand is not gaining enough recovery for holding a pen. True or false?*

Answers:

1. *True*
2. *False*

3. *False*
4. *False*

Unit Review Test on Hemiplegia

Please circle the correct answer or answers for each item.

1. Hemianopsia can be corrected with prescription glasses. True or false?
2. Which of the following are problems associated with right hemiplegia?
   a. Speech disorders
   b. Paralysis on left side
   c. Paralysis on right side
   d. Perceptual problems
   e. Tremor
3. The proper sequence in self-care training is important because:
   a. It encourages the patient to become independent.
   b. It reinforces the learning process.
   c. It reduces patient frustration.
   d. It ignores the necessity for teaching simple tasks.
4. Which of the following self-help devices would you select for eating procedures for the left hemiplegic patient?
   a. Fork
   b. Plate guard
   c. Built-up spoon
   d. Suction cup
5. Which of the following problems might prevent the patient with left hemiplegia from combing the hair on the back of his head?
   a. Limited range of motion
   b. Perceptual problems
   c. Poor demonstration
   d. Patient's confusion
6. Mrs. K. is a right hemiplegic with severe speech impairment. You are planning to teach her dressing techniques. Which of the following techniques would you use first?
   a. Give her verbal instructions for dressing procedures.
   b. Explain the difficulties in putting on a shirt.
   c. Demonstrate the proper procedures to put on a shirt.
   d. Ask her to put on the shirt.
7. In putting a coat on a right hemiplegic, which extremity would you put in first?
   a. Right
   b. Left
8. A left hemiplegic with complete paralysis, hemianopsia, perceptual problems, and unawareness of the body and space on the left will have difficulties with:
   a. Eating
   b. Speech
   c. Shaving
   d. Dressing
9. Mr. A. will shave today for the first time after his stroke. What would you do?
   a. Ask the orderly to do it.
   b. Give him the electric razor and tell him that you will be right back.
   c. Shave him yourself.
   d. Observe him when he shaves and help when necessary.
10. A hemiplegic woman will not require help to put on her make-up since she is used to doing it. True or false?
11. You notice that the hemiplegic arm is bruised over and over again and that the hand gets caught in the wheelchair spokes. What would you do about it?
    a. Suggest an arm sling.
    b. Tell the patient to watch for his hand.
    c. Explain to him that he should watch where he is going.
    d. Attach a protective shield to the spokes.

12. Training the patient in self-care takes more time at the beginning of the program and less time after he has had the benefit of some practice and repetition. True or false?

13. Mrs. M. is very particular about her appearance. After assisting her in dressing herself, she asks you to comb her hair and put her make-up on. Would you:
    a. Let her do her best and assure her that you will finish so that it looks right.
    b. Hand her the comb and assure her that she can do a good job of combing her own hair.
    c. Fix her hair and make-up for her but tell her she will have to try to do it next time.
    d. Tell her not to worry about how she looks; she will eventually be able to do a good job herself.

14. A left hemiplegic is trying to feed himself for the first time. Which of these procedures would you follow?
    a. Give him a plate guard.
    b. Show him how to cut his own meat with a rocker knife.
    c. Prepare his food for him and hand him the fork.
    d. Give him a fork with a built-up handle.

15. Which are the most commonly used devices for dressing?
    a. Clothespins
    b. Shoe aids
    c. Elastic shoe laces
    d. Button hooks
    e. Stocking cones

16. Mrs. A. has had a light stroke affecting her right side. She is not aphasic. It is her second day in learning to dress herself. She feels she cannot do anything for herself and often refuses to try. How can you best help her?
    a. By refusing to help her with steps you know she can do.
    b. By pointing out what she did the day before and giving her an easily attainable goal for the day.
    c. By dressing her and telling her she will have to try it by herself tomorrow.
    d. By leaving her with her clothes and telling her you will help when she is ready to learn to help herself.

Answers:

1. False

2. a, c

3. a, b, c

4. b, d

5. a, b, d

6. c

7. a

8. a, c, d

9. d

10. False

11. a, d

12. True

13. a

14. c

15. a, b

16. b

If you missed any of the answers, review the appropriate sections. If there are still some confusing facts that have not been explained by this unit, make notes and ask for further explanation during the clinical experience. If, however, you answered all the questions correctly, you have accomplished the objectives of this unit. You are now ready to begin the unit on self-care training for patients with arthritis and Parkinson's disease.

ARTHRITIS AND PARKINSON'S DISEASE

The knowledge that you acquired from the unit on hemiplegia will be useful in teaching self-care to patients with other disabilities, since you can apply many of the same dressing, eating, and hygienic procedures and self-help devices. The following unit contains a discussion of the unique aspects of self-care training for two common chronic disorders: arthritis and Parkinson's disease. The additional concepts and technical knowledge to be learned here are applicable to arthritis, Parkinson's disease, and similar disabilities.

Unit Objectives

The goal of this unit is to prepare you in the use of basic techniques and procedures for training patients with arthritis and parkinsonism to perform self-care activities.

Specifically, once you complete the instruction in this unit, you should be able to

1. identify the major disabilities and problems faced by arthritic and Parkinson's patients
2. select appropriate self-help devices and schedules for use by patients in eating, personal hygiene, and dressing
3. identify and defend appropriate sequences and procedures for training patients in self-care
4. identify procedures to promote patient independence through the use of positive reinforcement and patience

Arthritis

The word *arthritis* means *inflammation of a joint*. The term is used for many different conditions that cause pain in the joints and connective tissues throughout the body. However, not all of these conditions involve inflammation.

The two most common forms of arthritis are *osteoarthritis* and *rheumatoid arthritis*. We will review both of these very briefly. Then we will discuss the self-care for rheumatoid arthritis, since it presents more clinical problems and its self-care techniques can easily be applied to other disabilities such as osteoarthritis, fractured hip, hip contractures, senility, different types of cancer, and general weakness.

Osteoarthritis

Osteoarthritis is a noninflammatory, nonsystemic disease. It most often affects the weight-bearing joints, such as the knees, hips, and spine, but it often involves the fingers as well. It is a "degenerative" process that begins in the cartilage. It can deform the joint but seldom is disabling, except when far advanced in the hips.

Rheumatoid Arthritis

Rheumatoid arthritis is an inflammatory, systemic, and chronic disease that occurs in three stages: acute, subacute, and chronic. It primarily affects the joints, but can affect the eyes, heart, lungs, spleen, liver, blood vessels, kidneys, and digestive system.

The acute stage of the inflammation of the joints is characterized by the typical symptoms of pain, local swelling, redness, restricted range of motion, and sometimes fluid in the joints. In the acute stage, complete rest is indicated. In the subacute stage, the symptoms begin to subside and the patient is permitted to function with the upper extremities within the limits of his pain.

In the chronic stages, there are no signs of acute inflammation, but three major disabling factors interfere with functioning:

1. *Pain*. This is caused by the inflammation and instability of the joint. The pain can be local or general. The severity of the pain can vary throughout the day and from day to day. The pain can exist throughout the three stages and can hinder the patient from functioning. You might find that the patient hesitates to function from fear of pain. Also aching and stiffness result from periods of inactivity.
2. *Joint Disorders*. After the acute stage is over, the limited range of motion (ROM) leads to contractures due to adhesions (scarring), and the process can end with complete loss of movement within the joint—ankylosis. Limitation in ROM will result from the ankylosis, subluxation, or dislocation. There is likely to be joint instability, too.
3. *Muscle Weakness*. This is the result of disuse caused by the pain and limited ROM.

For a short review, answer these questions.

1. *Which of the following are anticipated symptoms in arthritis?*
   a. *Pain*
   b. *Sensory loss*
   c. *Paralysis*
   d. *Muscle weakness*
   e. *Joint disorders*
2. *Rheumatoid arthritis affects primarily the joints. True or false?*
3. *Rheumatoid arthritis is a degenerative disease. True or false?*
4. *You would encourage independence in the acute stage to ensure a good start. True or false?*
5. *A fused joint is the result of inactivity. True or false?*

If you missed any questions, review this section again. If you answered all questions correctly, you are ready to proceed to the next section. You may also want to review Chapters 4 and 5.

Self-Care Training

In self-care training, the stage of the disease determines how much the patient should be encouraged to do for himself. The desirable amount of effort to be spent by the patient depends on the joint's condition and his general tolerance for pain.

Depending on the functional deficit, many of the procedures and self-help devices that you used for the hemiplegic can be applied to self-care training of the arthritic patient. In addition, there are some supplemental self-care techniques with which you should become familiar. They are as follows:

1. To avoid deformity, emphasize the correct positioning of the body at all times.
2. Emphasize the sequence of self-care procedures. The same concept and procedures you used with hemiplegia apply here with slight changes. These changes will be discussed throughout the remainder of the chapter.
3. Although self-care devices play the most important role in rehabilitating arthritic patients in self-care and ADL, the devices should be used *only if necessary* and should be kept to a minimum. The devices are used
   a. to contribute to a patient's independence in self-care when his ROM is restricted, hindering him from performing the desired activities
   b. to conserve energy
   c. to avoid stress on involved joints
4. Stress the use of proper body mechanics and the simplification of procedures used in the activities of daily living. This will help the patient conserve valuable energy and prevent further damage to the joint.
5. The arthritic patient requires a lot of empathy. You must realize that he faces constant pain, disability, and depression. Encouragement and prodding are necessary to help him become independent. You

must learn to determine when to prod and when to comfort the patient, since this is the key to maximizing his self-care capabilities and making him happy.

Self-Help Devices for Eating

Since the basic eating procedures are similar to those for the hemiplegic patient, only self-help devices and procedures unique to rehabilitating the arthritic patient will be presented in this section. If you would like to refresh your knowledge of basic eating procedures, refer to the unit on self-care training for the patient with hemiplegia.

1. In limited ROM of the shoulder and elbow, use long-handled, lightweight utensils that can be positioned at any desired angle* (Figure 13-40).
2. In limited ROM of the forearm, use swivel spoon* (Figure 13-41).
3. If the wrist is painful and unstable, consult with the physician about a wristlet or a wrist splint to reduce pain and stabilize the wrist.
4. In limited ROM or weakness of hand, you may use a
   a. universal cuff or utensil holder (Figure 13-42)
   b. built-up handle (see hemiplegic unit)
   c. interlace utensil holder*
5. For drinking, the patient can use two hands around the cup or a No Tip Glass Keeper with a straw holder.* The straw can be stabilized by a pencil clip fastened to a cup (Figures 13-43 and 13-44).

The patient may refuse to eat in the presence of other people but should be encouraged to do so. If possible, seat him with other physically disabled patients who have a positive outlook and attitude. It might help the patient accept the things he cannot change and direct his energy toward more realistic goals.

Self-Help Devices for Personal Hygiene

As you will notice, there is a slight difference in the sequence here, due to the fact that in arthritis the major problems are limited ROM and *weakness*, whereas in hemiplegia the major physical problem in self-care is *one-handedness*. Long-handled devices and special holders are used to overcome the limitation in ROM, to conserve energy, and to avoid stress on the joints.

*Available at Be OK Self-Help Aids and Fashion-ABLE.

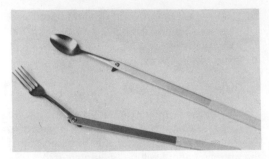

Figure 13-40 Long-Handled Utensils

Figure 13-41 Swivel Spoon

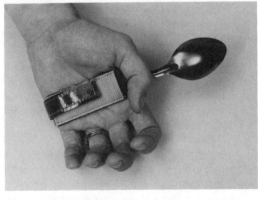

Figure 13-42 Universal Cuff

Temporary extensions can be made by taping a tongue depressor to an object and wrapping with a washcloth. If necessary, this extension can be attached at an angle.

1. Shaving:
   a. An electric shaver is preferable. If necessary, it can be provided with a holder for use by the patient with a weak grip.*
   b. A manual razor can be extended with a hollow metal or wooden attachment.
2. Make-up:
   a. If the patient has trouble reaching her mouth, the lipstick can be mounted on aluminum tubing.
   b. Use a mirror that can be hung around the neck by a plastic loop. These are available at most drug stores (Figure 13-45).
3. Oral-Hygiene:
   a. Use a toothbrush with a long or built-up handle when the patient cannot reach his mouth easily. A regular toothbrush can be modified with an extension.
   b. The toothpaste is not a problem unless the cap is screwed on too tightly.
4. Combing Hair:
   a. A long-handled brush and comb can be useful.* These can be purchased or made by adding a wooden attachment (Figure 13-46).
   b. Short hair is easier to handle.
5. Fingernails:
   a. Fingernails can be cleaned with a brush that fits over the palmar part of the hand (available at most stores) or a brush that attaches to the sink with suction cups (see hemiplegic unit).

*Available at Be OK Self-Help Aids and Fashion-ABLE.

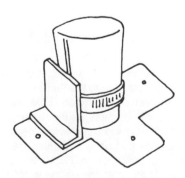

Figure 13-43 Glass Holder

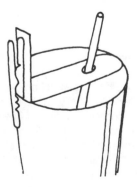

Figure 13-44 Straw Holder

b. Fingernails can be filed by using a nail file with a built-up handle made out of cork or a tongue depressor with a washcloth taped around it.

c. With toenails, the patient might require help.

6. Bathing: Bathing is among the most difficult tasks in self-care. You should be familiar with transfer techniques and be able to coordinate the patient potential with the proper techniques. (See chapter on Progressive Mobilization.) The assistive equipment and devices play an important role for energy conservation and safety. These include the following:

a. *Stable chairs* with backs and suction cups attached to the bottom of the legs. One chair beside the tub, another one with shorter legs in the tub. The seats should be even with the edge of the tub. For stronger, lower extremities, a bathtub seat that is adjustable in height would be adequate.

b. *Nonskid tape* with a rubber surface should be used for the bottom and edge of the tub.

c. *Grab bars* attached to the walls at the side and head of the tub to hold and push on.

d. A *portable shower hose*.

e. A *bathtub safety rail* to assist in getting in and out of the tub.

f. A *long-handled sponge and brush*.*

g. A *bath mitten* with a pocket for the soap.

A sponge bath by the sink will be the easiest for the patient to handle. The shower is less difficult and is safer to use than the tub.

Answer the following questions:

1. *It's most likely that an arthritic patient will require all the self-help devices mentioned above. True or false?*
2. *Generally, the same self-help devices are used for hemiplegic patients and for arthritic patients. True or false?*
3. *For limited ROM of the forearm, the patient requires a swivel spoon. True or false?*
4. *Conserving energy is an important consideration in the arthritis patient's life. True or false?*
5. *The arthritic patient will require the long-handled hair brush more often than the long-handled toothbrush. True or false?*

*Available at Be OK Self-Help Aids.

Figure 13-45 Around-the-Neck Mirror

Answers:

1. *False*   4. *True*
2. *False*   5. *True*
3. *True*

If your answers were correct, you should proceed to the next section on dressing.

Dressing Procedures

1. While dressing, the patient should be seated on a chair with his clothes in easy reach.
2. A stool will help when dressing the lower extremities by making it easier to reach the feet. This saves stress on the spine.
3. If one extremity is not very functional, the hemiplegic techniques should be applied for

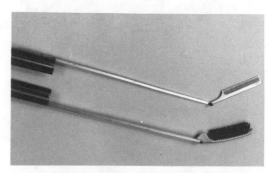

Figure 13-46 Long-Handled Comb and Brush

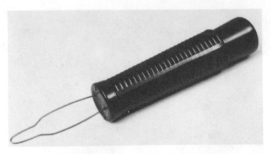

Figure 13-47 Button Hook

dressing the upper extremities. In order to avoid stress on the finger joints, do not use a clothespin when putting on a bra unless necessary.

Self-Help Devices for Dressing

1. The same styles of clothing suggested for the hemiplegic patient are suitable for the arthritic patient. The patient's needs will dictate the type of clothing he should wear, whether it be regular clothing, regular clothing with adaptations, or specially designed clothing.
   a. Regular or readymade clothing includes a wide variety of styles, fabrics, sizes, closures, etc. If carefully selected, it can save having to make adaptations or buying specially designed clothes.

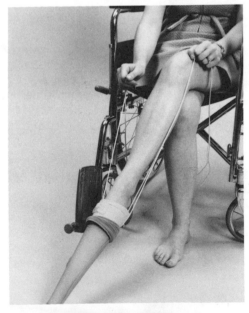

Figure 13-48 Device to Put on Stockings

b. Adaptation can be done on the patient's own clothes by converting buttons to Velcro or zippers, using elasticized bands for skirts, having dresses open all the way in the front, and changing zippers in pants to Velcro.
   c. Specially designed clothes with the easy-on—easy-off feature are available commercially at Fashion-ABLE and Vocational Guidance and Rehabilitation Services (see source list at the end of this chapter).
2. Button hooks make buttoning easier and are available in various shapes (Figure 13-47). To use one, grip the handle, push the wire loop through the buttonhole, catch the button by the wire loop, and pull it through the buttonhole. Release the button hook.
3. A stick with a clothespin taped to the end can be useful when putting on shorts. After hooking the clothespin to the shorts, the patient holds onto the other end of the stick while stepping into the shorts. He then pulls them up by means of the stick and unhooks the clothespin.
4. A device is available to aid in putting on stockings or socks. Below are step-by-step instructions on how to use this device (Figure 13-48).
   a. Sitting in a locked wheelchair or a stable armchair, extend the leg forward or place the leg on a stool.
   b. Insert the cone up to the toe of the stocking.
   c. Guide the cone over the toes so that the middle is aligned with the heel of the foot. Insert the foot into the opening and pull the straps up over the heel and into place (Figure 13-49).
   d. Repeat with the other foot.
5. To take stockings off: Use a long shoe-horn (Figure 13-50) to push the stocking or sock off the heel and off the foot. Repeat with the other foot.
6. To put on shoes, use a long shoe horn as described below:
   a. With the shoe on the floor or on a stool, place the long shoe horn in front of the shoe tongue; put toes in.
   b. Now place the shoe horn at the back of the shoe and press down on the knee.
   c. Fasten the shoe.
   d. Repeat with the other foot.

These procedures are designed to eliminate stress on the back, hips, and knees. The first attempts will be difficult for the patient, so be sure to encourage him and, if necessary, assist him.

Energy Conservation and Work Simplification

Most energy conservation and work simplification techniques apply to the patient in the home situation and are not among nursing objectives. Therefore, only a few useful suggestions will be made. The patient in need should be referred to an occupational therapy department.

1. In conversing with the patient, you will find that some of his routine activities can be simplified or eliminated. He should *avoid overfatigue* and have frequent, short rest periods during the day.
2. The patient should be instructed in the use of proper body mechanics when sitting, standing, walking, climbing stairs, pulling, lifting, or pushing weight (see Chapter 12).
3. Whenever possible, the patient should avoid lifting, pulling, or carrying heavy objects. A cart, a small table on casters, or any other device with wheels or rollers should be used. These aids should be used for food, dishes, laundry, cleaning supplies, books and newspapers, clothes, etc.
4. A Swedish Reacher* (Figure 13-51) will help the patient avoid bending to pick up objects.

Approach to Rehabilitation

Your approach and the patient's approach are very important in self-care training of the arthritic patient. You should not see the self-care training as merely a physical task on your part. The patient needs your constant support and reinforcement. Your encouragement of his independence and your praise for his efforts and successes, no matter how small, are extremely important. Emphasize the positive! Very disabled patients have proven that with positive attitude and motivation they can become independent with minimal adaptation.

Answer the following questions.

1. *The maintenance of improper body position for a short period of time will result in stiffness, limited ROM, and, eventually, deformities. True or false?*
2. *For a patient with trouble reaching his mouth as a result of restricted motion in the shoulder,*

*Available from J.A. Preston Corporation, 71 Fifth Avenue, New York, NY 10003.

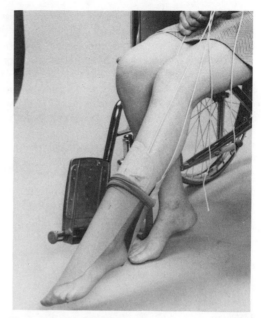

Figure 13-49 Pulling Stocking On

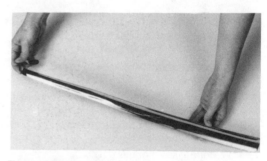

Figure 13-50 Long Shoe Horn

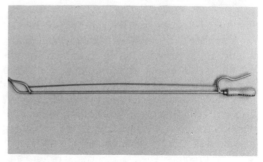

Figure 13-51 Swedish Reacher

which one of the following would you suggest?
a. *Built-up handle*
b. *Swivel spoon*
c. *Long-handled utensil*
d. *Utensil holder*

3. To gain strength, the patient should become overfatigued. True or false?
4. For the arthritic patient, the easiest task of personal hygiene is combing his hair. True or false?
5. Some of the hemiplegic procedures can be adapted for arthritics. True or false?
6. The nurse told Mr. G. that dressing should be done in bed. True or false?
7. Mrs. S. was told that she should eat lunch in bed, since she has to have rest periods throughout the day. True or false?
8. Mr. B. was pushing the armchair in his room; then he straightened up and held his back. It should not be the duty of the nurse who saw him to correct him. True or false?

Answers:

1. True   5. True
2. c   6. False
3. False   7. False
4. False   8. False

The following references could be of great value to every disabled homemaker:

1. American Heart Association, 44 E. 23 St., New York, NY 10036.
2. The Arthritis Foundation, 1212 Avenue of The Americas, New York, NY 10036.
3. *Mealtime Manual for the Aged and Handicapped*, Simon & Schuster, Inc., 630 Fifth Avenue, New York, NY 10020.

Parkinsonism

Although you are probably familiar with parkinsonism from Chapter 5, we shall review it again briefly. Parkinsonism, or the Parkinson's syndrome, is a chronic, slow progressing disease that is caused by damage to the basal ganglia in the brain. It is characterized by rigidity, tremor, and diminished automatic movements. Most cases are caused by an unknown factor. Others may be a result of postencephalitis or an arteriosclerotic process. The typical clinical picture that the patient presents is loss of facial expression, drooling saliva, slowing of functions, shuffling gait with no reciprocal movements, and trunk bent forward.

The three major disabling factors are as follows:

1. *Rigidity.* Rigidity is caused by the increased muscle tone that is equally present in opposing muscle groups. There is muscle stiffness, with resistance to both active and passive movements. The patient has trouble changing positions and in making starting and stopping movements.
2. *Tremor.* Tremors are involuntary movements which begin in one extremity and can gradually spread to the rest of the body and the head. The fingers and thumb move in characteristic motions called pill rolling movements. The tremor is present at rest, lessens during voluntary movements, and is absent at sleep.
3. *Lack of Automatic Movements.* There are no reciprocal motions, no blinking, and no expression on the face.

Answer the following questions:

1. Parkinsonism is characterized by joint stiffness, pain, and tremor. True or false?
2. The tremor in parkinsonism will increase with function. True or false?
3. The Parkinson's patient will have no trouble getting up from a chair. True or false?
4. Parkinsonism is a slow progressing, chronic disease. True or false?

Answers:

1. False   3. False
2. False   4. True

If your answers were correct, proceed to the next section.

Self-Care Training

The completion of self-care activities by the patient helps him to maintain his coordination, his ROM, his endurance, the level at which he functions, and his morale. As a result, performing self-care activities daily is of the utmost importance. There are very few specific devices and procedures for self-care activities in parkinsonism; therefore, the emphasis should be on

1. establishing a routine in the patient's daily activities
2. letting the patient do as much as he possibly can without getting frustrated
3. keeping the patient interested in social activities
4. supporting the patient's interests
5. encouraging the patient by praising his efforts (it usually takes a while before you can praise any success)

When the patient's performance is very slow, remember that is part of his disease. You will find yourself wanting to do it for him, but *don't*. You should have plenty of patience and allow sufficient time to promote the patient's independence. Ultimately, this technique will raise the patient's self-esteem.

The self-help devices for the patient with parkinsonism are used to help him perform his daily activities despite the tremor and rigidity and to assure the proper safety precautions. Weighted devices help to stabilize objects. Devices with extended handles help the patient reach the lower extremities.

Following are some suggested rules in self-care training:

1. Instruct the patient to make one continuous motion. For example, in trying to drink the patient finds that after he picks up the cup he cannot reach it to his mouth due to the rigidity and tremor. He should put the cup down on the table, then pick it up and reach to his mouth in one continuous motion.
2. While instructing in self-care you might find it helpful to point out the destination of the movement to be performed, or quote the estimated distance. Instead of saying "Let's shave now," say, "Let's shave now; pick up the razor." You let him pick it up, and then you say, "Reach the razor to your cheek."
3. Use self-help devices only when necessary.
4. If the patient's endurance is low, use a sequence of training in which the patient starts by doing the easier tasks and graduates to the more difficult tasks.
5. Be patient. Let the patient feel your genuine interest in him and in his progress.

Answer the following questions:

1. *Which of the following are characteristics of Parkinson's disease?*
   a. *Joint disorders*
   b. *Loss of sensation*
   c. *Tremor*
   d. *Rigidity*
   e. *Paralysis*
2. *Since the patient requires minimal assistance for his self-care but is very slow, the nurse should go ahead and do it all for him so that she can be available for other duties. True or false?*
3. *It is very important that the patient perform self-care activities and ADL daily to help maintain his endurance, ROM, and morale. True or false?*

Answers:

1. *c, d*
2. *False*
3. *True*

If you answered all the questions correctly, you are ready to proceed to the next section. Let us now look into the self-help devices used for Parkinson's patients.

Self-Help Devices for Eating

1. Use of unbreakable dishes is preferred.
2. A deep dish or a plate guard may be required.
3. If the plate has to be stabilized, use a suction cup or a wet washcloth placed underneath it.
4. If cutting the food is too difficult for the patient, it should be cut prior to serving.
5. For severe tremor, try a one-pound wristlet placed on the forearm while the patient is eating. Use it for about a week and then see if the patient can perform the task without it. Do not use it if it does not help the patient or it annoys him.
6. For drinking, use of a weighted cup or a cup holder will prevent the cup from tipping over (see subunit on arthritis).

Personal Hygiene Procedures

The procedures for hemiplegics and arthritic patients can be applied to the parkinsonism patient.

1. Use an electric razor for safety. Encourage the patient to move his head in all directions while shaving.
2. A wristlet might help for make-up procedures.
3. If the patient wears dentures and his coordination is poor, clean the dentures for him.
4. To avoid falls in the bath, the patient should be supervised, even if he is independent.

Dressing Procedures and Self-Help Devices

1. Recommendations concerning clothing:
   a. Have patient wear clothes one size larger than usually worn.
   b. Have patient wear clothes with roomy cuts.
   c. Use Velcro instead of buttons only if necessary. Buttoning and unbuttoning

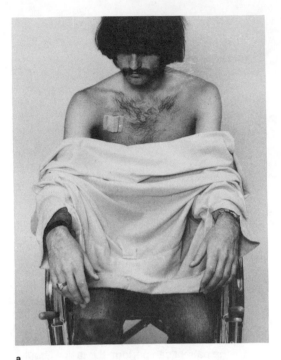
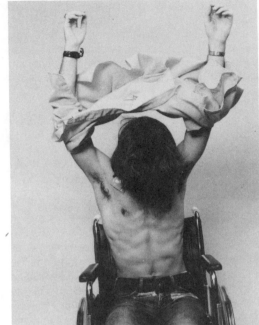
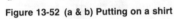

Figure 13-52 (a & b) Putting on a shirt

clothes is a good exercise (Velcro is available commercially).

d. Have big buttons rather than small ones.

e. On long-sleeved shirts, adapt the regular buttons on cuffs by sewing a piece of elastic onto the button and keeping the cuffs buttoned, or by using Velcro or cuff links.

f. Attach a fabric tie or a metal ring to zippers.

2. To dress, the patient should be seated in an armchair. The procedures for the hemiplegic will probably be the easiest ones to apply. There is an additional procedure that is not recommended for one-handed patients or for arthritic patients but can be useful for parkinsonism patients when putting on or taking off shirts, sweaters, or coats that have front openings.

a. Putting a shirt on (Figures 13-52 a & b):

(1) Put the shirt on your knees with the label facing down and the collar toward the knees.

(2) Place your hands in the sleeves starting at the armhole. Reach through to the cuffs and push the shirt up over the elbows.

(3) Gather the shirttail with both hands and pull the shirt over your head.

(4) Pull down on the shirttail and straighten it up.

(5) Button the shirt.

b. Taking a shirt off:

(1) Unbutton the shirt and sleeves.

(2) Raise your arms, bend your elbows, place your hands over your shoulders.

(3) Gather the shirt in back with both hands.

(4) Pull it over your head.

(5) Pull one sleeve off.

(6) Pull the other sleeve off.

3. In putting on socks and shoes, the patient might require help in the beginning due to his stiffness. Shoes with buckles, elastic laces, or Velcro fasteners are preferable (refer to unit on hemiplegia). The procedure for putting on socks and shoes can be done from a crossed leg position or using a foot stool. Procedures can be adapted from those for the hemiplegic or the arthritic patient, depending on the patient's potential.

Activities of Daily Living

As discussed previously, ADL have a tremendous impact on the person's interest and happiness in life. The patient should be encouraged to visit other patients, read the paper, listen to the radio, keep up with his hobbies, and, if feasible, go and get the newspaper or write a letter. For writing practice, the patient should start with large circles on large paper and continue with other prewriting exercises. As soon as this is managed, the same exercises should be done on lines one-half inch apart. The patient has to fill the entire space between the lines. The next stage will be writing in the space. You should make sure that the handwriting does not become smaller.

Answer the following questions:

1. *A hemiplegic patient could use a stocking device. True or false?*
2. *The Parkinson's patient should put on a shirt the same way the arthritic patient does. True or false?*
3. *A Parkinson's patient could probably put on shoes the same way the arthritic and hemiplegic patients do. True or false?*
4. *Mr. B., a Parkinson's patient, welcomes you every morning with a big smile. True or false?*
5. *The prewriting exercises for the Parkinson's patient are necessary because of the rigidity and tremor. True or false?*
6. *The benefits of performing self-care are not only independence or partial independence but improved endurance, ROM, and strength. True or false?*

Answers:

1. *False*	4. *False*
2. *False*	5. *True*
3. *True*	6. *True*

Unit Review Test on Arthritis and Parkinsonism

Please circle the correct answer or answers for each item. When you are finished, compare your answers with those given.

1. The arthritic patient told you that he didn't do well at all today. Choose one statement as your reply:
   a. "It's going to take time before you realize how well you are doing."
   b. "You did as much as you could."
   c. "We all have good days and bad days."
   d. "I noticed that today you put on your blouse independently; yesterday you still required my assistance."
2. Mrs. B. has severe arthritis and she can't reach with the spoon to her mouth; you solved the problem by handing her a built-up spoon. True or false?
3. You instructed Mr. S., an arthritic patient, in the use of a long-handled fork, but he seemed uncooperative. You assumed that the reasons were:
   a. He didn't understand the instructions.
   b. He didn't want to use his hand, since he was afraid of pain.
   c. He was afraid to fail.
4. The arthritic and Parkinson's patient should use an Insert-A-Foot Shoe Aid for putting on shoes. True or false?
5. Mrs. K., an arthritic patient, is a very active person. Yesterday you saw her pick up her glasses by using incorrect body mechanics. What should you suggest?
   a. Bend her back and reach.
   b. Use a Swedish reacher.
   c. Bend her hips and knees and reach.
6. The major disabling factors in Parkinson's are:
   a. Pain
   b. Perceptual problems
   c. Intentional tremor
   d. Rigidity
   e. Diminished automatic movements
7. The purpose of correct posture is to prevent pain. True or false?
8. The self-help devices for the arthritic patient have to be lightweight. True or false?
9. The Parkinson's patient requires a lot of self-help devices. True or false?
10. Mrs. G., a Parkinson's patient, is very slow in her self-care activities. It's probably due to pain. True or false?

11. Mrs. B. was admitted with the diagnosis of chronic rheumatoid arthritis for two weeks' observation. Which of the following, regarding self-care, should the nurse do?
    a. Obtain information regarding the physical, mental, emotional, and social aspects.
    b. Knowing that the patient will stay for only a few days, not bother with training.
    c. Evaluate the patient's potential and set realistic goals.
    d. Ask the nurse's aide to help the patient as much as possible to make her comfortable and happy.
12. You, the nurse, are very busy, but you should train the patient in self-care techniques to provide quality care and to promote the patient's maximal independence. True or false?
13. Before purchasing expensive devices, you should try using self-help devices constructed by modifying existing articles. True or false?
14. Arthritic patients will benefit from a weighted wristlet. True or false?
15. An arthritic patient should put his socks on the same way a hemiplegic does. True or false?

Answers:
1. *d*
2. *False*
3. *b and c*
4. *False*
5. *If you answered b and c, you were correct. If a reacher is not available, c will be appropriate.*
6. *d and e*
7. *False*

8. *True*
9. *False*
10. *False*
11. *a and c*
12. *True*
13. *True*
14. *False*
15. *False*

If you missed any of the answers, review the appropriate sections of this unit. Once you feel confident that you understand the material in this unit, please continue.

SPINAL CORD DYSFUNCTION

Spinal cord dysfunction is a very broad subject. This unit contains a very basic introduction and overview of the self-care training for spinal cord dysfunction.

The level of independence a person with spinal cord dysfunction can achieve depends upon the level of injury and whether the lesion is *incomplete* or *complete*. The readers should familiarize themselves with the disability syndrome of spinal cord dysfunction in Chapter 2. When a person suffers partial lesion the deficits can range from very minimal to those near complete lesion. The following practical suggestions may be useful in managing self-care for persons with complete lesion of spinal cord at various levels.

C_1 to C_3

The C_1, C_2, or C_3 quadriplegic is dependent on the respirator. He will require full-time attendants and is totally dependent in self-care, except for the use of an electric wheelchair. He may be able to propel the electric wheelchair using chin control. He may also be able to weight shift using chin control. With the recent advances in computers and telephones, he may be able to manage some communication activities.

C_4

The C_4 quadriplegic may not require a ventilator all the time. Some patients can be off the ventilator part of the time or even all of the time. The C_4 quadriplegic will need full-time attendant care; however, he may be able to use mobile arm supports to feed himself occasionally. In addition to mobile arm supports, he will need a wrist splint with a pocket to hold the utensils. Success in feeding varies.

The C_4 quadriplegic can type using a mouthstick and may be able to operate a computer using a mouthstick. He will be able to propel the electric wheelchair using chin control.

C_5

The C_5 quadriplegic has increased independence in self-care due to a motor control which allows hand-to-mouth activities. He can feed himself with mobile arm supports and/or a wrist brace. He can brush his teeth using the brace. He can propel an electric wheelchair using a joy stick or similar hand control. He can type, use a tape recorder, write, and use a phone by means of various assistive devices and adapted equipment. A strong C_5 may be able to dress the upper body with varying success. He needs attendant care for morning self-care and for transfers and homemaking; however, he can be left alone during the day if he is provided with appropriate assistive devices and occasional assistance.

C_6

C_6 quadriplegics have more independence, as more muscles are spared. They vary in their independence, depending on attitude and endurance. Some C_6 quadriplegics are able to live alone with morning and evening attendant care.

A C_6 can use a manual wheelchair with quad pegs, a good cushion, and other adaptations. He can manage wheeling on level surfaces and slight inclines. However, C_6 quadriplegics encounter difficulties with rough terrain.

A C_6 can feed himself with or without assistive devices and can manage simple hygiene using adapted equipment. He can dress the upper body but may need assistance with the lower body. He is independent in using a telephone, typewriter, etc. He can be independent in driving a car with a lift and appropriate adaptations.

A strong C_6 may become independent in transfers using a sliding board; other C_6s may need varying degrees of assistance.

C_7

The C_7 quadriplegic has the potential of living alone without attendant care.

He can feed himself, perform simple hygiene, dress himself, and manage bathing. He can also transfer using a sliding board. He can propel a manual wheelchair independently. He can drive a car and can manage simple cooking. Using assistive devices, he can manage a bladder and bowel program. He is independent in communication.

C_8

The C_8 quadriplegic should be able to manage his self-care independently from a wheelchair. He should be able to feed himself, dress, and perform hygiene activities. He can write, use a telephone, drive a car, and propel a manual wheelchair. He does need an elevated toilet seat for his bladder and bowel program.

Paraplegics

A paraplegic requires very minimal assistive devices and can manage some activities with braces and crutches. The major difference between various levels of thoracic and lumbar paraplegia is the presence of abdominal musculature. At T_4 there is no abdominal musculature, at T_{10} there is abdominal musculature, and at L_2 there is some lower extremity musculature.

However, all paraplegics should be independent in self-care from wheelchair level.

Persons with spinal cord dysfunction present a special set of problems and in teaching self-care training it is essential that appropriate wheelchairs, cushions, wrist braces, and assistive devices be used. Constant encouragement is needed, and setting the patients up for many small successes moves them a long way toward independence.

The reader is encouraged to review the excellent publications on spinal cord injury for further information.

Unit Review Test on Spinal Cord Dysfunction

For each statement, indicate whether it is true or false.

1. Weaning a C_2 quadriplegic from a respirator is a time-consuming but worthwhile process. True or false?
2. All quadriplegics at the C_5 level and above will require electric wheelchairs (the control device may depend on the level of injury). True or false?
3. Even a motivated "athletic" C_7 quadriplegic cannot be expected to live alone. True or false?
4. Excepting some aged and otherwise frail individuals, all paraplegics should attain "wheelchair independence." True or false?
5. Most spinal cord injured patients require a carefully thought-out assortment of assistive devices. True or false?

Answers:
1. False (the patient cannot be weaned).
2. True.
3. False.
4. True.
5. True.

SUGGESTIONS FOR ESTABLISHING A REHABILITATION PROGRAM

The following practical suggestions based on clinical experience should serve as a useful guide as you plan a rehabilitation program in your own setting.

1. It would be beneficial for the patients and nursing staff to *have a room appropriated for meals and recreation*. The patients with adequate sitting endurance would have a chance to socialize, get out of their rooms, and get into a routine. This would also allow nurses to supervise larger numbers of patients. In addition, patients with an hour and a half sitting endurance can use this period for meals, since it is easier to eat when sitting up.

2. *Wearing street clothes should be a routine* in a rehabilitation center and the preferred routine in a general hospital. Wearing clothes helps improve the patient's emotional condition, brings the patient back to a daily routine, and allows the patient to relearn to dress himself.

3. *Self-help devices should be part of the supplies kept on the ward*. Do not use them unless absolutely necessary, and keep them to a minimum. If a patient needs a device when discharged, he should be able to take it with him and the family should be instructed in its use.

4. Before attempting self-care training, *make sure that the patient has passed the acute stage of his illness* and is medically ready for the effort of taking care of himself.

5. *Know the patient diagnosis, cause, and prognosis,* and if possible, know the patient's background before admission.

6. *Routine procedures have to be done daily, the same way, and, when possible, at the same time.* Staff members will need to be able to apply the different procedures and devices. Make sure that the staff members who treat the patient are consistent in their use of techniques and terminology and are aware of the patient's level of performance.

7. *Encourage the patient to do for himself as much as he can.* Praise every interest, effort, and success. Approach the goal of independence slowly and realistically. In the beginning, help as much as needed; your help will decrease with progress. Use the patient's potential, no matter how limited, until he reaches his maximal level of independence. Don't frustrate the patient by letting him fail or become overfatigued. Don't handle him unnecessarily.

8. Prior to training, *explain to the patient*
   a. what you are going to do
   b. why you will do it
   c. what you expect from him
   d. how he should help himself
   Don't ask him what he can do, e.g., "Can you eat by yourself?"

9. The best way to evaluate the patient's abilities and limitations will be to *determine, through observation, the level at which the patient functions* and the problems he faces.

10. The training plan and goals will *start from the level at which the patient functions* and will be broadened according to the patient's progress. Small training groups and repetitions have been found to be efficient and more stimulating to the patient.

11. *Inform staff and family of the patient's progress and carry-over abilities* to avoid frustration for everyone concerned.

SOURCES

1. Be OK Self-Help Aids, Fred Sammons, Inc., P.O. Box 32, Brookfield, IL 60513
2. Fashion-ABLE, Rocky Hill, NJ 08553
3. Vocational Guidance Rehabilitation Service, 2289 East 55th Street, Cleveland, OH 44103
4. The Arthritis Foundation, 1212 Avenue of The Americas, New York, NY 10036

Catalogues are available on request.

REFERENCES

1. Bogen, J.E., and G.M. Bogen. "The Other Side of the Brain III: The Corpus Collosium and Creativity." *Los Angeles Neurological Society Bulletin* 37 (1972): 49–61.

2. Hurd, M. and G.W. Weylonis. "Shoulder Sling—Friend or Foe?" *Archives of Physical Medicine and Rehabilitation* 55 (1974): 519.

SUGGESTED READINGS

Burke, D.C., and D.D. Murray. *Handbook of Spinal Cord Medicine*. New York: Raven, 1975.

Donovan, W.H. "Spinal Cord Injury." In *Handbook of Severe Disability*. Washington, D.C.: GPO, 1981.

Ford, J.R., and Duckworth, B. *Physical Management of the Quadriplegic Patient*. Philadelphia: F.A. Davis, in press.

Hill, ed. *Spinal Cord Injury: Functional Outcome in Occupational Therapy*. Rockville, Md.: Aspen, 1987.

Hirschberg, Lewis Thomas. *Rehabilitation: A Manual for the Care of the Disabled and Elderly*. Philadelphia: Lippincott, 1964.

Hollander, Joseph H. *Arthritis and Allied Conditions*. Philadelphia: Lea and Febiger, 1986.

Larsen, George L. "Rehabilitation for Dysphagia Paralytica." *Journal of Speech and Hearing Disorders* 37 (May 1972): 187–93.

McCarty, Daniel J. *Arthritis and Allied Conditions*. Philadelphia: Lea and Febiger, 1985. This is the "Bible" for arthritis and is comprehensive.

Rodnan, J.P., and H.R. Schumacher. *Primer on Rheumatic Diseases*. Atlanta: The Arthritis Foundation, 1983. A somewhat less intimidating book.

Rusk, Howard A. *Rehabilitation Medicine*. St. Louis: Mosby, 1971.

Stryker, Ruth Perin. *Rehabilitative Aspects of Acute and Chronic Nursing Care*. Philadelphia: Saunders, 1972.

Swezey, R.L. "Rehabilitation in Arthritis and Allied Conditions." In *Krusen's Handbook of Physical Medicine and Rehabilitation*. Edited by F.J. Kottke, J.G.K. Stillwell, and J.F. Lehmann. Philadelphia: Saunders, 1982. A very good book for expanding your knowledge beyond what you learned in this chapter.

14 Wheelchairs: Selection, Uses, Adaptation, and Maintenance

Georgianna Burbidge Wilson, M.Ed., P.T.
Virginia L. Kerr, O.T.R.

INTRODUCTION AND OBJECTIVES

Which wheelchair is best for your patient?

If you can solve this problem, you can help to enlarge your patient's world; add to his independence, safety, and comfort; and save him money. Although there are numerous types of wheelchairs and accessories, we shall confine our discussion to a manageable few.

Our basic objective for this chapter is to teach you to evaluate a given patient's wheelchair needs and select the appropriate wheelchair for him. Specifically, once you have completed this package you should be able to

1. identify the basic parts of a wheelchair
2. identify several wheelchair accessories and their uses
3. properly measure a patient for a wheelchair
4. identify proper procedures for maintaining a wheelchair
5. adapt a given wheelchair to a particular patient problem
6. select the best wheelchair for a specific patient

THE PROBLEM

Picture yourself on 2-West of Ole Bloomin' Springs Hospital. You are facing 12 patients with different wheelchair needs and 12 wheelchairs. You must get every patient out of bed. Your problem is to select the appropriate wheelchair for each patient. If you select the wrong wheelchair, various problems may arise and some patients might not be able to get out of bed.

We shall begin by briefly describing each patient's condition; then we shall describe the 12 available wheelchairs. Please read these descriptions and become familiar with them. Once you have done that, complete the instructions in this chapter. At the conclusion of the chapter, you will be asked to select the proper wheelchair for each of the twelve patients.

These are the patients:

1. Mrs. H. has two long leg casts because of the arthritis in her knees. Her doctor is trying to straighten them out. She will be up in a wheelchair every day but will have to be lifted into it. She can walk a short distance with a walker.
2. Mrs. S. is a petite, 80-year-old woman. She weighs about 80 pounds and is very alert. She has some leg weakness and needs a wheelchair to get to the dining room.
3. Miss E. dove into a shallow lake and fractured her cervical spine at the C_4 level. She is now a quadriplegic and has been in bed for three months. This is her first time sitting.
4. Mrs. N. had anemia for two months. The doctors have it under control, but her legs are weak. She can get in and out of bed fairly well but tends to get confused and to get her feet tangled. This makes her stumble. She walks short distances with a walker.
5. Mrs. R. has breast cancer. She had surgery seven days ago and now has physical therapy treatments to loosen her arm. She has to go to the third floor for her treatments.
6. Mrs. A. had a cerebrovascular accident three weeks ago. She is five feet tall. She wants to wheel her own wheelchair. She has no movement in her left arm or leg. She

has a very large stomach and cannot wiggle very well.

7. Mr. W. is 11 years old and has a fractured left ankle. He was jumping a ditch full of water and twisted his ankle when he landed. He had to have surgery to correct the break.

8. Mrs. B. has had a total hip replacement. She cannot flex her hip beyond 45°. She has been walking with a walker.

9. Mr. L. is five feet nine inches tall and has a left hemiplegia. He wheels his wheelchair using one arm and one leg. He has hemianopsia, poor sitting balance, and poor head control.

10. Mr. G. is 20 years old. He fell off a telephone pole while at work and broke his back at L_2 and L_3. He is a paraplegic. He transfers independently by sliding from the bed to a wheelchair. He will be going back to school.

11. Mrs. O. fell over a cat at home and fractured her left hip. Since her hip surgery, she can only bend her knee to a 60° angle without a lot of pain. She weighs at least 250 pounds and loves to eat.

12. Mr. U. has a left hemiplegia and his leg swells. He is wearing an elastic stocking to decrease swelling. He stands up well and walks using a cane with minimal assistance.

These are the available wheelchairs:

1. Hemi wheelchair with removable legs and brake extension.
2. Full reclining wheelchair with elevating legs, removable arms, and headrest.
3. Semi-reclining wheelchair with elevating legs and removable arms.
4. Standard adult wheelchair with elevating removable legs.
5. Standard adult chair with hook-on headrest, toggle brakes, and hard roll insert.
6. Standard adult wheelchair with swinging detachable legrests.
7. Standard adult wheelchair with removable desk arms, regular removable legs, heel loops, pneumatic tires.
8. Standard wheelchair with removable arms and removable elevating legrests.
9. Narrow adult chair with removable legs.
10. Extra wide adult chair with elevating legs, removable arms, and brake lever extensions.
11. Junior wheelchair with elevating legs.
12. Standard adult chair with lever brakes.

The information you need in order to identify the appropriate chair for each patient is contained in the following pages.

THE STANDARD WHEELCHAIR

Standard model wheelchairs incorporate the wheelchair dimensions used most frequently by patients. The most commonly used standard models include the *adult, narrow adult,* and *junior chair.*

The standard dimensions need not be memorized since they are located in all wheelchair catalogs and manuals. When checking the measurements, be sure to note the overall width of the chair to determine if it will clear doorways. Also note that the wheelchair's turning radius is four and a half feet when maneuvered expertly and more when maneuvered less expertly (see Table 14-1).

Some wheelchairs with the above dimensions are available in a lighter weight. Have you ever

---

TABLE 14-1 Standard Wheelchair Dimensions*

	Adult	Narrow Adult	Junior
Width of seat at seat level	18″	16″	16″
Width overall (open)	26″	23″	23″
Width overall (closed)	10″	10″	10″
Seat depth	16″	16″	14″
Back height	16″	16″	16″
Arm to seat	10″	10″	9″
Seat to floor	20″	20″	18″
Overall length	42″	42″	39″
Overall height	37″	37″	37″
Seat to footrest (minimum)	15″	15″	13″
Seat to footrest (maximum)	20″	20″	17″
Net weight	47 lbs.	45 lbs.	45 lbs.

*All dimensions are to the nearest inch.

tried wrestling a wheelchair into a car? Sometimes this is quite a chore. Picture yourself as the elderly wife of a patient or as a partially disabled patient engaged in this struggle. Lightweight chairs are 50 percent lighter than standard chairs. They are a little less durable, but they are much easier to handle.

Wheelchair Parts

Correct identification of wheelchair features and components is essential when you wish to select a wheelchair (see Figure 14-1). *Right side* and *left side* refer to the sides from the point of view of someone sitting in the chair.

1. Arm
2. Armrest
3. Back
4. Seat
5. Skirt Guard
6. Footrest
7. Footplate
8. Brake
9. Wheel
10. Handrim
11. Caster
12. Handgrip
13. Tipping Lever

Study the wheelchair components as identified, then cover the numbered list of components and fill in the blanks with the correct numbers.

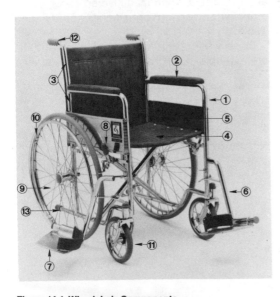

Figure 14-1 Wheelchair Components

_____ Arm	_____ Footplate
_____ Wheel	_____ Footrest
_____ Tipping Lever	_____ Caster
_____ Handrim	_____ Brake
_____ Handgrip	_____ Back
_____ Skirt Guard	_____ Armrest
	_____ Seat

If your numbers and components match up as follows, you have done well for the first time. If they do not match, study the diagram more carefully before you proceed.

1	Arm	7	Footplate
9	Wheel	6	Footrest
13	Tipping Lever	11	Caster
10	Handrim	8	Brake
12	Handgrip	3	Back
5	Skirt Guard	2	Armrest
		4	Seat

Function and Adaptation of Wheelchair Parts

Now that you know the names of the wheelchair parts, you need to know their functions and what you can do to adapt a given part to a particular patient problem.

Wheelchair Arms

There are three types of arms available:

1. Standard arms (pictured in Figure 14-1) come with most chairs.
2. Desk arms are shortened to allow the chair to fit under a desk, table, etc.
3. Detachable arms can be removed by pressing a release button. They are necessary when a patient cannot stand up to perform a standing transfer and must slide from the wheelchair to his bed. (See Chapter 12 for Transfers.) Patients requiring detachable arms are paraplegics, those with long leg casts, or those with limited ROM at the knees or hips. Detachable arms are also desirable when transferring a total care patient because you do not have to lift him over the wheelchair arms.

Wheelchair arm height is measured from the wheelchair seat to the patient's bent elbow plus one inch. Remember, if you use a seat cushion, its height should be considered when measuring for correct arm height. Thus, arm height is impor-

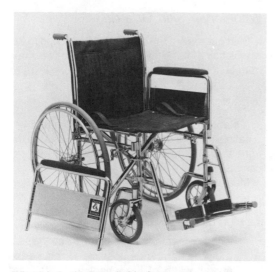

Wheelchair with Detachable Arms

tant if the patient will be confined to the wheelchair for life. Then the proper height not only adds comfort but helps to prevent deformities and aids the patient in doing adequate wheelchair push-ups. (See illustration below on measuring arm height.)

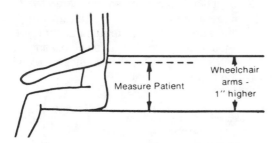

Measure Patient

Wheelchair arms - 1" higher

Refer back to the list of patients. For which of your patients should you be especially concerned about wheelchair arm height?

Answer _____

If you answered Miss E. (patient no. 3) or Mr. G. (patient no. 10), you were correct.

Wheelchair Backs

Four wheelchair backs are available:

1. Standard is the straight back pictured in Figure 14-1.
2. Semireclining backs recline from vertical to 30°. A patient with a hip prosthesis may not be able to flex past 45° and would require a semireclining or a full reclining back.

3. Full reclining backs or neurochairs recline to the horizontal. They are used to reduce frequency of patient transfers or to slowly increase a patient's tolerance to sitting erect.

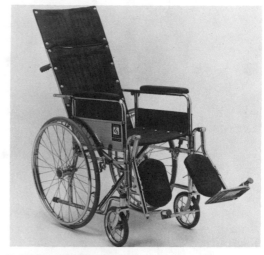

Full Reclining Back

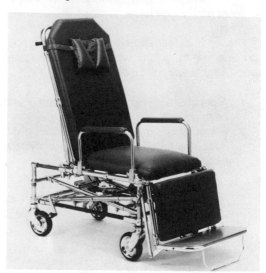

Neurochair

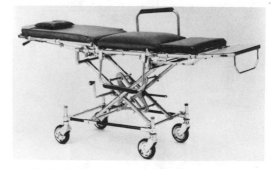

Horizontal Recline

4. Hook-on headrests can go on any of the above to support the head of a very weak patient or one with very poor head control. If a headrest is not available, use a padded backboard that extends to head level.

Hook-on Headrest

Which of your assigned patients needs the extra head support provided by a hook-on headrest? Answer: _____

If you wrote Mr. L. (patient no. 9) or Miss E. (patient no. 3), you were correct.

Proper back height helps to maintain proper posture and trunk support. But, again, standard back heights will do in most cases.

1. A patient requiring full trunk support would need a semi- or full reclining back.
2. For minimal trunk support, the wheelchair back should come to approximately four inches below the patient's armpit.

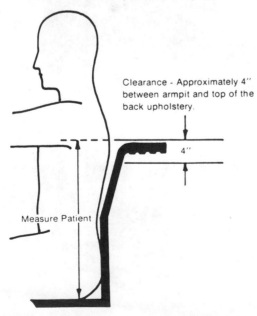

Clearance - Approximately 4″ between armpit and top of the back upholstery.

4″

Measure Patient

Wheelchair Skirt Guards

Skirt guards are the side panels attached to the wheelchair arms. They prevent a patient's clothes from becoming entangled in the wheels.

Wheelchair Seats

A standard sling seat (pictured in Figure 14-1) is satisfactory for most patients. *Note:* Be sure the upholstery is urine proof—naugahyde and not canvas.

Measurements are taken as follows:

1. Seat width is measured from the sides of skirt guards and is approximately two inches wider than the patient. Keep the seat width as narrow as possible to reduce the overall width of the wheelchair. Standard adult = 18″ seat width; narrow adult = 16″ seat width; junior = 16″ seat width. Which of your assigned patients could use a narrow adult chair?

   Answer: _____

   If you wrote Mrs. S (patient no. 2), you were correct.
2. Seat depth should be approximately two to three inches less than the patient's thigh measurement. Just remember that you should be able to place three or four fingers between the back of the patient's knee and the edge of the seat.

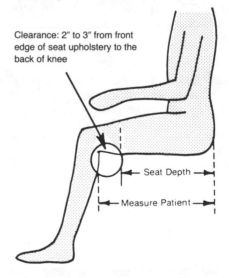

Clearance: 2″ to 3″ from front edge of seat upholstery to the back of knee

Seat Depth

Measure Patient

3. A hemi chair is of standard width, but it is set lower to the floor. This enables the short hemiplegic patient to touch the floor with his uninvolved foot and propel his chair (see Chapter 12 on wheelchair ambulation).

Additional Adaptations to Wheelchair Seats

Cushions. There are different types and sizes of cushions that aid comfort and help prevent pressure sores. Cushions also allow the patient to stand up more easily. However, if the cushion is too thick, your hemiplegic patient may not be able to touch the floor and will thus be unable to manipulate his wheelchair.

Hard rolls. Hard rolls can be rolled up bed pads; they can be used to aid the hemiplegic patient with very poor sitting balance who continually leans to his affected side. You may be accustomed to seeing such patients propped up with pillows stuffed between them and the wheelchair on their affected side (see illustration A below). Instead, place the hard roll you made between the patient's hips and the skirt guard on his *unaffected side* (see illustration B below). This prevents him from moving his hips up against the skirt guard and prevents him from leaning so far to one side.

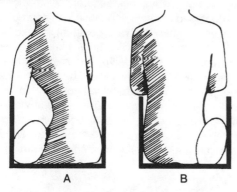

A   B

Which of your patients needs a hard roll?

Answer _____

If you wrote Mr. L. (patient no. 9), you were correct.

Seatboards. A seatboard is a solid insert placed on the wheelchair seat. It can be purchased or made from any padded board to assist the patient in maintaining a proper sitting position. Remember that this changes the seat height, just as cushions do. A cutout seatboard with a cushion on top may be used to help prevent pressure sores. (See also Chapter 9.)

Wheelchair Footrests

Footrests come in three types:

1. Standard footrests are attached to the chair, as shown in Figure 14-1.

2. Swing-a-way, detachable footrests lock into place or swing to the side by releasing a button. They can also be removed for close approaches to bed or tub and for easy loading into cars.
3. Swing-a-way, detachable, elevating legrests are recommended as an aid in lower extremity circulation or any lower extremity injury where edema is present.

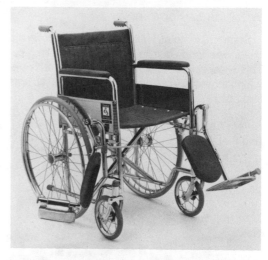

Wheelchair with Swing-a-way Footrests and Legrests

Measure the patient from the rear of the bent knee to the heel of the foot. All footrests are adjustable and should be adjusted properly for comfort and proper weight distribution on the thighs and buttocks. The patient's thigh must be elevated slightly (approximately two fingers width) above the front edge of the seat upholstery. Also the lowest point of the footplate should clear the floor by at least two inches. Some footrests

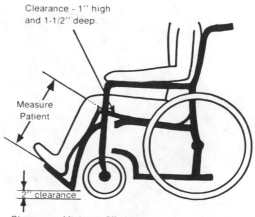

Clearance - 1″ high and 1-1/2″ deep.

Measure Patient

2″ clearance

Clearance - Minimum 2″ above floor for safety.

have a bolt on the bottom of the footplate and some have it on the side. To adjust the footrests, have the patient sit in the wheelchair with his feet in the middle of the footplates. Loosen the bolt and push in or pull out on the footplate to achieve the correct height. Tighten the bolt. Learn how to do this. It is not difficult to do and makes a big difference in patient comfort and functional position in the chair.

Wheelchair Footplates

Standard footplates flip up for safe exit from the chair. *Heel loops* help to hold flailing legs in place. This is especially helpful on wheelchairs with elevating legrests. *Toe loops* help hold spastic legs in place.

Safety Note: Be careful that the footplates are up and that they stay up before allowing a patient to exit a wheelchair.

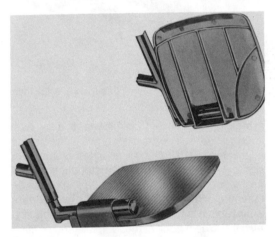

Footplates

Heel Loops

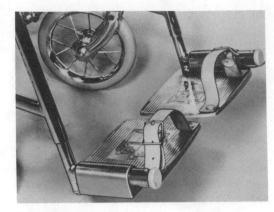

Toe Loops

Wheelchair Brakes

Standard *toggle brakes* are the safest and easiest to operate. Push-type locking action brakes are standard; however, pull action are available. *Lever brakes* have separate locking latches. These are easily bent out of shape, so they do not always lock securely. Also, elderly and confused patients and those with perceptual problems might not always get them into the last notch. For these reasons, lever brakes are not recommended. *Brake lever extensions* can be added to give better leverage. They require less strength and are helpful when you have a very weak patient or one with limited range of motion. They are also useful for hemiplegics who cannot reach over to the brake or who cannot find it. However, not all hemiplegics require them.

Toggle Brake

Lever Brake

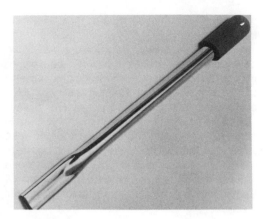

Brake Extension

Which one of your assigned patients could use a brake extension?

Answer: _____

If you answered Mrs. O. (patient no. 11) or Mrs. A (patient no. 6), you were correct.

Wheelchair Wheels

Standard wheels are shown in Figure 14-1. They are 24 inches in diameter. Notice that the wheel and hand rim are separate pieces. Lightweight wheels have the wheel and hand rim as one piece. Solid rubber tires are standard, but pneumatic tires 1-3/4 or 1-1/4 inches wide are recommended for patients who will be using their wheelchairs outside on grass, sand, or uneven surfaces. You should consider your patient's occupation before ordering tires. *Spoke guards* can be ordered on wheelchairs or they can be made by cutting a circle from plastic or cardboard and taping it to the spokes. These are helpful with

Pneumatic Tires

patients who have flailing arms or arms with poor sensation that might become caught in the wheel spokes and injured.

Standard *handrims* (shown in Figure 14-1) are chromeplated. There are rubber covers that slip on to improve friction; plastic coating also provides greater friction. Special handrims are available for patients who have difficulty grasping, such as quadriplegics, arthritics, etc. Handrims can be pushed with

1. rubber-tipped horizontal projections
2. rubber-tipped oblique projections
3. rubber-tipped vertical projections

Rubber-tipped Oblique Projections

Rubber-tipped Vertical Projections

The patient can push against the projections with the heel of his hand. *Note:* Special purpose handrims (chromeplated or plastic-coated) can be used depending upon the patient's needs. They are recommended when an individual has difficulty in grasping regular handrims.

Standard *caster wheels* are eight inches in diameter and are hard rubber, as shown in Figure 14-1. They come with the different tires discussed above.

Wheelchair Tipping Lever

Tipping levers are the horizontal projections at the bottom and back of the wheelchair. By placing your foot on one of them and pulling back on the hand grips, you can tip the front of the wheelchair up off the ground to move it over a door facing, electric cord, curb, etc. Never try to just push the chair over an obstacle—the caster can get caught and throw the patient out of the chair. If the chair does not roll easily over the obstacle, turn the chair around and pull the chair backward over the obstacle.

Tipping levers are also used to ascend and descend stairs. To ascend stairs, use the tipping lever to tilt the wheelchair backward onto the large posterior wheels. Instruct the patient to sit back in the chair. Maintaining this position, ascend the stairs backward, pulling the wheelchair gently up each step. Descending stairs can be accomplished by gently lowering the wheelchair forward to the next step while keeping the chair tilted backward onto its large posterior wheels. Always advise the patient to sit back in the wheelchair to prevent falling from the wheelchair. Please remember that ascending or descending stairs with a wheelchair is a difficult procedure and requires a strong person or two people for safety. See picture below for how to handle a patient safely.

Now for your big project.

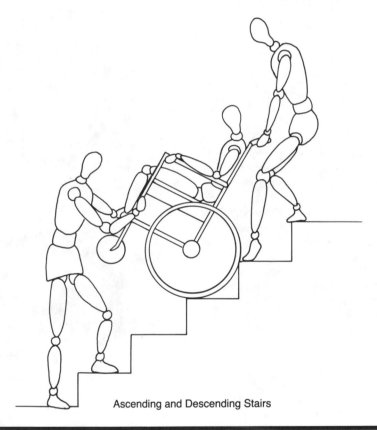

Ascending and Descending Stairs

CHAPTER REVIEW TEST

Directions: Repeated here is a list of the patients that have been assigned to you and the wheelchairs that are available to sit them in. Select the proper wheelchair for each patient (use the answer sheet) and then check your answers. Are you going to be able to get all of your patients out of bed?

These are the patients:

1. Mrs. H. has two long leg casts because of the arthritis in her knees. Her doctor is trying to straighten them out. She will be up in a wheelchair every day but will have to be lifted into it. She can walk a short distance with a walker.

2. Mrs. S. is a petite, 80-year-old woman. She weighs about 80 pounds and is very alert. She has some leg weakness and needs a wheelchair to get to the dining room.

3. Miss E. dove into a shallow lake and fractured her cervical spine at the C_4 level. She is now a quadriplegic and has been in bed for three months. This is her first time sitting.

4. Mrs. N. had anemia for two months. The doctors have it under control, but her legs are weak. She can get in and out of bed fairly well but tends to become confused and get her feet tangled. This makes her stumble. She walks short distances with a walker.

5. Mrs. R. has breast cancer. She had surgery seven days ago and now has physical therapy treatments to loosen her arm. She has to go to the third floor for her treatments.

6. Mrs. A. had a cerebrovascular accident three weeks ago. She is five feet tall. She wants to wheel her own wheelchair. She has no movement in her left arm or leg. She has a very large stomach and cannot wiggle very well.

7. Mr. W. is 11 years old and has a fractured left ankle. He was jumping a ditch full of water and twisted his ankle when he landed. He had to have surgery to correct the break.

8. Mrs. B. has had a total hip replacement. She cannot flex her hip beyond 45°. She has been walking with a walker.

9. Mr. L. is five feet nine inches tall and has a left hemiplegia. He wheels his wheelchair using one arm and one leg. He has hemianopsia, poor sitting balance, and poor head control.

10. Mr. G. is 20 years old. He fell off a telephone pole while at work and broke his back at L_2 and L_3. He is a paraplegic. He transfers independently by sliding from the bed to a wheelchair. He will be going back to school.

11. Mrs. O. fell over a cat at home and fractured her left hip. Since her hip surgery, she can only bend her knee to a 60° angle without a lot of pain. She weighs at least 250 pounds and loves to eat.

12. Mr. U. has a left hemiplegia and his leg swells. He is wearing an elastic stocking to decrease swelling. He stands up well and walks using a cane with minimal assistance.

These are the wheelchairs that are available:

1. Hemi wheelchair with removable legs and brake extension.
2. Full reclining wheelchair with elevating legs, removable arms, and headrest.
3. Semi-reclining wheelchair with elevating legs and removable arms.
4. Standard adult wheelchair with elevating removable legs.
5. Standard adult chair with hook-on headrest, toggle brakes, and hard roll insert.
6. Standard adult wheelchair with swinging detachable legrests.
7. Standard adult wheelchair with removable desk arms, regular removable legs, heel loops, pneumatic tires.
8. Standard wheelchair with removable arms and removable elevating legrests.
9. Narrow adult chair with removable legs.
10. Extra wide adult chair with elevating legs, removable arms, and brake lever extensions.
11. Junior wheelchair with elevating legs.
12. Standard adult chair with lever brakes.

Answer Sheet

Directions: Mark the appropriate patient's name and number on the line available, e.g., wheelchair no. 30 should be fitted to Mr. Z., patient no. 20.

	PATIENT NAME	NUMBER
Wheelchair no. 1		
Wheelchair no. 2		
Wheelchair no. 3		
Wheelchair no. 4		
Wheelchair no. 5		
Wheelchair no. 6		
Wheelchair no. 7		
Wheelchair no. 8		

Wheelchair no. 9   _____
Wheelchair no. 10   _____
Wheelchair no. 11   _____
Wheelchair no. 12   _____

When you are finished, check your answers with those given below.

Answers:

Wheelchair no. 1:	*Mrs. A., patient no. 6*
Wheelchair no. 2:	*Miss E., patient no. 3*
Wheelchair no. 3:	*Mrs. B., patient no. 8*
Wheelchair no. 4:	*Mr. U., patient no. 12*
Wheelchair no. 5:	*Mr. L., patient no. 9*
Wheelchair no. 6:	*Mrs. N., patient no. 4*
Wheelchair no. 7:	*Mr. G., patient no. 10*
Wheelchair no. 8:	*Mrs. H., patient no. 1*
Wheelchair no. 9:	*Mrs. S., patient no. 2*
Wheelchair no. 10:	*Mrs. O., patient no. 11*
Wheelchair no. 11:	*Mr. W., patient no. 7*
Wheelchair no. 12:	*Mrs. R., patient no. 5*

If you answered correctly, each of your patients will have the proper chair. If you did not, some of your patients will still be in bed! If some are "still in bed," rework the list and use the chapter as a reference. In a real life situation, it is very important to switch wheelchairs until the proper chair is obtained for each patient.

WHEELCHAIR MAINTENANCE

We have just discussed the most important aspect of wheelchairs, that is, matching the patient with the correct chair. But for that chair to continue to be good for that particular patient, it must be properly maintained. Basic maintenance involves keeping the chair clean, dry, protected from the weather, and repaired when needed.

To clean a wheelchair, use a mild soap and water solution and be sure to wipe dry. Never use an abrasive on the chrome, and pay special attention to the wheels and casters to keep them free of lint, string, hair, and dirt. Rub the telescoping parts with paraffin to prevent sticking. Do not use oil on these parts, because it collects dirt.

Never force a wheelchair to open or close. To close most wheelchairs, pull up on the seat by placing your hands on the front and the back of the upholstery. Some wheelchairs have upholstery handles provided on the sides of the seats; to close these wheelchairs, pull up on the handles. To open, push down on the sides of the seat. Never push *out* on the arms of the chair. This can "spring" the frame of the chair.

These simple measures, plus a yearly checkup by a reputable wheelchair dealer, can help prevent costly repairs.

PLACING A WHEELCHAIR IN A CAR

With some maneuvering, a wheelchair will fit either in the trunk or in the back seat of a car. If a wheelchair is to be transported often, it is recommended that you remove the back seat or remove the spare tire from the trunk to allow for more space and, consequently, easier loading of the wheelchair.

To load the wheelchair, first remove the armrests and/or footrests. This makes the chair much lighter and more compact. To load a wheelchair in the trunk, fold the chair and grasp it by the large posterior wheels and the anterior border of the frame. Using proper body mechanics, lift the chair into the trunk. Lay it down flat according to how it best fits in the trunk. Gently close the trunk lid. Be cautious never to slam the trunk lid down on a wheelchair, for it will bend the frame and cause costly repairs.

To load a wheelchair in the back seat of a car, fold the chair and back it up to the door. Move the front seat ahead so as to allow as much space as possible for the chair behind the seat. Lift or pull the chair onto the back floorboard. You will probably need to tilt the wheelchair in order to close the back door. Providing the car is wide, a wheelchair can fit in the front seat. With practice, some patients can learn to pull a wheelchair into the front seat of a car.

CONCLUSION

Which wheelchair is best for your patient? This chapter gives you the background to make a selection. There are more variations of wheelchairs and patients than this chapter can encompass. Collect catalogs and peruse them. The most important message of this chapter is that the wheelchair should fit your patient instead of the other way around. Pay attention to overall weight. These chairs must occasionally be lifted into cars,

often by elderly spouses or by the patients themselves. A heavy-duty wheelchair with all the
accessories may look good "on paper" but might
tend to make the patient stay home. Keep the
accessories to a minimum to decrease weight
and increase ease of travel and of maintenance.
Catalogs list weights, and the lighter of compara-
ble chairs should be chosen. Keep it light and
keep it simple.

SUGGESTED READINGS

Everest & Jennings, Inc. *Wheelchair Prescription Booklet
No. 1: Measuring the Patient*. Los Angeles: Everest & Jennings, 1983.

———. *Wheelchair Prescription Booklet No. 2: Wheelchair
Selection*. Los Angeles: Everest & Jennings, 1983.

———. *Wheelchair Prescription Booklet No. 3: Safety and
Handling*. Los Angeles: Everest & Jennings, 1983.

———. *Wheelchair Prescription Booklet No. 4: Care and Service*. Los Angeles: Everest & Jennings, 1983.

15 Methods for Effective Communication

Linda Jean Larson, M.A., S.P./C.C.C.

INTRODUCTION AND OBJECTIVES

An understanding of a patient's communication difficulty is necessary for performing adequate nursing care and for the patient's optimum recovery. In this chapter, general information concerning communication disorders will be provided, emphasizing the nurse's role and methods for effective communication.

Completion of this chapter should enable you to

1. recognize the presence of a communication disorder
2. identify some of the associated symptoms and characteristics of the patient who is experiencing communication problems
3. communicate more effectively with patients who are experiencing communication problems

COMMUNICATION PROCESS

Communication is the exchange of messages by verbal, written, or gestural expressions. Adequate execution of the communication process depends on reception, integration, and expression of messages. Reception of messages involves comprehension of spoken and written words and the interpretation of gestures. Three input channels are necessary for adequate reception: auditory, visual, and tactile. After messages have been received, the information must be integrated and processed for expression. The expression of messages is performed by speaking, writing, or gesturing. An impairment in either the reception, integration, or expression system results in defective communication. Many of the patients in a hospital setting have incurred deficits

from cerebrovascular accidents, head trauma, brain tumor, infectious diseases (encephalitis), cerebral atrophy, debilitating neurological diseases (Parkinson's disease), or surgical intervention. When the neurological impairment or surgical intervention involves any of the areas of the brain or the vocal system that specialize in communication, the patient may present various communication disorders. The most frequently occurring impairments will be discussed.

COMMUNICATION DISTURBANCE

One of the most devastating effects of stroke or brain damage is impairment of the ability to communicate. Such an impairment may result in speech difficulty, language disturbances, or both.

Speech is simply a motor act which involves the movement and coordination of muscles of the respiratory system, larynx, lips, palate, and jaw that form speech sounds and spoken words. Speech problems, therefore, involve motor and mechanical deficits.

Language disturbances involve the processing of symbolic material. This symbolic process includes the ability to understand the speech of others, speak, read, write, use gestures that are understood by others, understand the gestures of others, and perform mathematical calculations. An impairment in any or all of the systems results in a language disturbance called aphasia. In the majority of people the left side of the brain is the dominant side for speech and language. If the site of the brain damage is on the left side of the brain, the patient is likely to have not only right-sided weakness or paralysis, but also an impairment in his communication abilities.

Aphasia

Aphasia is the complete or partial loss of language, including the understanding of speech, reading, speaking, writing, and arithmetic. Depending upon the location and extent of the damage, patterns and severity of impairment vary. In some patients, the disturbance is so mild that it may be undetected. However, the patient may be aware of difficulty in recalling certain words, understanding lengthy reading material, or performing complicated mathematical calculations. In other patients, the impairments are so severe that the patients have no means of expression and their ability to comprehend messages is so poor that they appear disoriented or mentally incompetent.

Let us discuss some of the problems that the aphasic will experience in the reception and expression of language.

Understanding Speech

An important question is necessary. Can the aphasic patient understand you when you communicate with him? Most aphasic patients have some degree of receptive deficit. Therefore, the patient finds it difficult to understand what others are trying to communicate to him. The pattern of the receptive deficit and the degree of severity may vary. No matter how mild or severe the deficit is, this is not related to a hearing loss but to brain damage affecting the centers for comprehension of language. The aphasic hears you but cannot understand you. The level of comprehension may vary from difficulty with the retention of conversational speech, to comprehension of selective sentences or parts of sentences and isolated words, to a total loss of understanding of the spoken word. It is important that personnel associated with the patient understand the level at which he is comprehending. An aphasic's yes and no responses may be unreliable. Therefore, it is advisable to determine the patient's receptive level by asking him to obey certain general commands (e.g., "close your eyes," "shake my hand," "raise your leg," etc.) or to point to available objects in his room at your spoken word, first by name and then by general description of the object. These brief evaluation techniques will help you determine the level at which you should communicate with him, either by one-word responses or short phrases. If the patient does not respond to the spoken word, then new avenues must be explored. Possibilities include the use of gestures or the written word. It is important that in orally communicating with the patient, you speak slowly and distinctly in a normal tone of voice and use short, simple phrases, repeating if necessary.

Reading

How well can the patient read? Some patients can understand single words but not a whole sentence, while others can understand sentences but not paragraphs. Most aphasics are not capable of grasping or retaining the information in a newspaper or a magazine. Nurses must be aware that many patients can read aloud beautifully but are unable to understand what they have read.

Visual Problems

Some patients have visual problems not directly associated with reading comprehension. Patients who have a weakness or paralysis on the right side may have a right visual field deficit called right homonymous hemianopsia. These patients do not always see objects to their right and are likely to bump into objects and encounter difficulties in reading due to the decrease in the visual field.

Oral Expression

The most apparent and devastating impairment encountered by the patient and nursing is the disturbance in oral expression. The aphasic is no longer able to use words for totally effective communication.

The aphasic experiences difficulty with word-finding problems. This problem is common to most aphasics, but its characteristics differ depending upon the location and extent of the brain damage. The speech pattern may vary from gibberish to the use of the wrong word, the substitution of unintelligible responses for meaningful words, the repetition of one syllable of a word over and over, or incessant speech with little or no meaning. Depending upon his unique pattern of impairment, an aphasic may produce the sentence "I want a cup of coffee" in the following ways:

1. "Giddy giddy giddy."
2. "O.K. You bet O.K. You bet."
3. "Darn it." (Swear words)
4. "Coffee."
5. "I want cup."
6. "Coffee cup drink."
7. "I want the." "Darn it." "Uh, give me pot." "Oh, you know." "Forget it."

8. "Ba boo la cakka somma ba boo."
9. "I want a stack of dishes."
10. "Tup tah toppee."
11. "Need a deezer of sizzel now."
12. "I want a glass of water, no I mean hot pot."
13. "I want the silver setting for use with Folgers. You know. I want to make two spoon full and fill with water."

The nursing staff must be aware that many aphasics are unable to use any words at all except profane ones and are unaware of their meanings. Some aphasics use automatic or social speech, such as "Hi," "Hello," "How are you?", "I'm fine," "My name is Joe Doe," etc.

Communicating with an aphasic patient requires knowledge of the patient's level of comprehension and his present verbal capabilities. It should be remembered that the aphasic's intellectual functioning is intact and that he must be treated like an adult, not a child. The following list of suggestions should be helpful in the arduous task of understanding what the aphasic is trying to say:

1. Ask him short, direct questions requiring a yes or no answer. (Since many patients say yes when they mean no or vice versa, you must determine the reliability of his responses.)
2. Encourage him to use gestures, drawings, or writing as a supplementary means of communication.
3. Keep instructions and questions short and simple.
4. Rephrase the question, if necessary, to clarify the meaning.
5. Give the patient sufficient time to respond to your question, and then repeat the question and/or instruction if necessary, but do not frustrate him by continued repetitions.
6. Most importantly, be accepting and understanding with the patient and watch for signs of frustration and fatigue.

Gestural Expression

All of us use some form of body and facial gestures to communicate our thoughts. Many of these gestures are understood without the aid of speech. Therefore, when attempting to communicate with an aphasic patient, simple, specific gestures can help to clarify the message. A patient who can communicate his needs through gestures should be encouraged to do so. At times it will be necessary to stimulate the gestural system by demonstration and imitation of the action. The goal of language therapy is to stimulate and improve communication by any available means.

Written Expression

A frequent question asked by families is "Can't he write what he is unable to speak?" With few exceptions, all aphasics have writing problems, especially during the early stages of recovery. Writing limitations are frequently severe and usually the last skills to improve due to the complex symbolic process involved. Significant problems noted are the inability to recall the appropriate words, to retrieve the letters necessary for spelling the word, and, finally, to form the letters. These problems are further complicated by various degrees of paralysis in the dominant hand. However, writing should not be eliminated as an alternate avenue of expression unless the patient demonstrates agitation or a moderate to severe limitation.

Dysarthria

Dysarthria is a motor speech problem due to weakness, paralysis, or incoordination of one or more of the muscles used in speaking. This muscular weakness may result in an impairment in speech or voice, with associated problems in respiration, breathing, and/or swallowing. Due to the muscular weakness of the speech articulators (tongue, lips, palate, etc.), the speech sounds are produced imprecisely and words may be slightly slurred or totally unintelligible. Impairment to the vocal system may result in a hoarse, breathy, or strained vocal quality. Pitch changes may be noted, along with loudness variations, intonational deficits, and changes in the rate of speech.

A dysarthric patient must incorporate compensatory techniques to improve the overall intelligibility of the speech, including articulatory, vocal, and respiratory exercises specific to his articulation disorder. The nurse may be of assistance by carefully listening to the patient, eliminating outside noises, asking him to repeat the message if necessary, encouraging him to speak slowly and distinctly, and, if all else fails, providing him with materials for writing his message or a communication book using pictures of items needed for daily activities.

Verbal Apraxia

Apraxia is a motor speech problem, as is dysarthria, but occurs despite normal strength of the speech musculature. This patient has difficulty initiating and sequencing sounds for speech, although he can perform involuntary automatic acts such as eating, swallowing, and coughing. The apraxic patient is aware of what he wants to say but is unable to perform the movements necessary to produce the words with his mouth and tongue. The muscles are not paralyzed, but they no longer receive the correct information from the brain that enables the patient to articulate speech.

As in aphasia, the severity varies. A mild verbal apraxic can usually be understood, but his speech will contain mispronunciations. For example, the word *cup* may be spoken at different times by the same patient as *puk, pup, put,* or *tuk.* The severely involved apraxic may be completely mute or only produce nonmeaningful sounds.

Communication with a severely involved apraxic patient can be frustrating for nursing personnel, family, and the patient. It must be remembered that apraxic patients usually know what they want to say but are unable to express their desires. Families and nursing personnel can be of great help by reinforcing what the speech pathologist is working on in therapy. For example, if the patient has acquired a new word (e.g., *water*), it is advisable for those who come into contact with the patient to stimulate and reinforce this new word. Other methods for helping the patient and staff must be incorporated in his daily routine, such as

1. encouraging the patient to use gestures
2. providing the patient with a notebook or "magic slate" if he is capable of written expression
3. providing the patient with a communication notebook of pictures or objects for his immediate needs if he is unable to read (if he is able to read, a notebook arrangement of words that the patient is apt to use frequently should be available)

It is very challenging to find ways to communicate with an apraxic with little or no speech. For those patients who also have multiple aphasic problems, it may be impossible to find a reliable avenue of communication. As with aphasics, you should not pretend to understand what he is trying to say or ignore his attempts. Through the process of elimination or trial and error procedures, his desires may become evident.

Hearing Loss

When there is a question concerning a patient's hearing acuity, a referral for audiometric testing should be considered to determine the extent of the loss and the feasibility of correction with proper hearing aid fitting. Many elderly patients have hearing losses attributed to the aging process, and occasionally hearing loss is acquired through brain injury. Patients who were previously fitted for hearing aids should be encouraged to wear their aids at all times. Staff members should always communicate in a normal tone of voice without shouting. Face-to-face contact with the patient is optimum for a patient with a hearing loss.

LARYNGECTOMEE

The larynx lies in the upper front part of the neck, extending from the base of the tongue to the top of the trachea. The larynx contains the vocal system, primarily the vocal folds which are responsible for the production of human sound.

The laryngectomee has undergone surgical excision of the larynx and has lost the ability to produce phonation for speech sounds in the usual manner. These patients should be provided with alternate avenues of expression. Many laryngectomees can be trained to produce esophageal speech through vocal rehabilitation, but in the early stages of postoperative recovery the patient needs to be provided with aids for communicating. Pictures for indicating his needs and desires, paper and pencil for written expression, or specialized mechanical devices such as an electrolarynx or a handi-voice (computerized voice synthesizer) should be made available to the patient.

THE HOLISTIC APPROACH

In this chapter, the most frequent communication disorders encountered by nurses have been presented. A variety of methods to enhance communication attempts and to provide effective communication were also suggested. It must be remembered that a patient's communication problems are just a part of the total person. Each patient is unique, with his own behavioral needs and desires.

The inability of the patient to express his beliefs and feelings as he did before is devastating and creates many fears and frustrations known only to the communicatively impaired person. Just imagine your own reaction if you were unable to comprehend the world around you or express your most basic thoughts and wishes.

Each patient should be given your total care and consideration for optimum recovery. Total care requires not only the knowledge of communication disorders and methods of effective communication, but also the human compassion necessary to respond with sincerity and concern. The holistic approach to patient care should reflect your academic training and knowledge as well as your sensitivity concerning human needs.

A qualified speech pathologist will be a valuable asset in assisting you to better understand the level at which each patient is functioning and the proper methods for communicating with your patient. It is advisable to refer the patient with a communication disorder as early as possible to a qualified speech pathologist who is a member of the American Speech and Hearing Association and who has been awarded a certificate of clinical competence. If a speech pathologist is not available in your hospital or is not a member of your rehabilitation team, a qualified speech pathologist in your area can be located by contacting the American Speech-Language-Hearing Association, 10801 Rockville Pike, Rockville, Maryland 20852.

CHAPTER REVIEW TEST

Answer the following questions as quickly as possible:

1. Aphasia is the complete or partial loss of language, including the understanding of
   _____, _____, _____, _____, and _____.
2. A patient with the inability to voluntarily sequence sounds would be considered an
   _____.
3. A patient with a breathy voice, slurred speech, and respiratory limitations would be considered a
   _____.
4. What should be your first step if you suspect a patient has a hearing loss? _____
   _____
5. List three methods for assisting the laryngectomee in communication attempts: _____
   _____
   _____
6. The reception of messages includes the following abilities:
   a. _____
   b. _____
   c. _____
7. The expression of language involves the ability to
   a. _____
   b. _____
   c. _____
8. In order to communicate effectively with your patient, you must determine his level of
   _____ and his present _____.
9. Most aphasics' yes and no responses are reliable and dependable. True or false?
10. It is important that communication attempts with your patient be spoken _____ and
    _____ in a normal tone of voice, using _____ and _____ phrases.
11. List two alternate methods of communication if your patient fails to understand you:
    _____
    _____

Answers:
1. Speech, reading, speaking, writing, and arithmetic.
2. Apraxic.
3. Dysarthric.
4. Refer the patient for an audiological screening.
5. Pictures; paper and pencil for written expression; mechanical devices.
6. a. Speech comprehension.
   b. Reading comprehension.
   c. Gestural comprehension.
7. a. Gesture.
   b. Write.
   c. Talk.

8. *Comprehension; verbal capability.*
9. *False.*
10. *Slowly and distinctly; short and simple.*
11. *Gesturing to your patient; providing written instructions.*

If you missed any of the questions, please review the chapter so that you understand the correct answer.

SUGGESTED READINGS

American Heart Association. *Aphasia and The Family and Stroke*. New York: American Heart Association, 1969.

American Heart Association. *Why Do They Behave That Way?* New York: American Heart Association, 1974.

Baratz, Norma. *The Management of Patients With Aphasia: A Guide For Nurses*. Newton, Mass.: 1979.

Boone, Daniel R. *An Adult Has Aphasia*. Danville, Ill.: Interstate Printers & Publishers, 1976.

Broida, Helen. *Communication Breakdown*. Houston: College Hill Press, 1979.

Brookshire, R.H. *An Introduction to Aphasia*. Minneapolis: BRK Publishers, 1979.

Cohen, Lillian Kay. *Communication Problems After a Stroke*. Minneapolis: Sister Kenny Rehabilitation Institute, 1971.

Darley, F.L., A.E. Aronson, and J.R. Brown. *Motor Speech Disorders*. Philadelphia: Saunders, 1975.

Sarno, John E., and Martha T. Taylor. *Stroke*. New York: McGraw-Hill, 1969.

Sister Kenny Institute Staff. *About Stroke*. Minneapolis: Sister Kenny Rehabilitation Institute, 1975.

Taylor, Martha T. *Understanding Aphasia: A Guide For Family And Friends*. New York: Institute of Rehabilitation Medicine, 1959.

Waldrop, William F., and Marie Gould. *Your New Voice*. New York: American Cancer Society, 1969.

16 Psychological Responses to Disability

Mary Ellen Hayden, Ph.D.

INTRODUCTION AND OBJECTIVES

Robert is a 21-year-old man who, up until an automobile accident three months ago, was president of his senior class at a major university. He appeared to have a bright future as an engineer, and he was making plans to marry his girlfriend of two years. Now, because of a head injury, he has severe difficulty in talking and cannot move parts of his body. His family and girlfriend continually tell you how sure they are that he will "be just like he always was," but you sense a lot of fear in these statements. The family also is very critical of the nursing care, questioning your competence and complaining loudly whenever the least problem arises. The patient is very belligerent, fighting you angrily whenever you try to care for him.

Being a conscientious nurse, you find yourself feeling very upset over this case. The attacks on your competence are really disturbing. You work long hours and give each patient good care, and this family is becoming impossible!

The purpose of this chapter is to provide an understanding of how people react to physical disabilities—either their own or those of a significant other.

Specifically, the following objectives should be met by the end of this chapter:

1. Most people facing the loss of a significant bodily or mental function go through the same stages of grief as someone facing his own impending death. By the end of this chapter, you should understand the five stages of grief and have some idea how to handle each of them.
2. Most disabilities result in increased dependency upon other people and a loss of independence or control over one's own life. A person's previous experience regarding whether he basically controls his own life or whether he is at the mercy of others will significantly impact his ability to accept the more dependent role resulting from the disability. Your understanding of some of these issues is another objective of this chapter.
3. Several factors, such as age, premorbid personality, and particular kinds of brain damage, influence the manner in which individuals cope with disability. Your understanding of some of these factors is the final objective of this chapter.

STAGES OF GRIEF

Five stages of grief are usually seen in individuals facing their own death.[1] In the first stage, the person denies the reality of the situation. The patient might think, "The doctors are wrong, it is not cancer," or "Well, it may be cancer, but they will find a cure before it gets me." However, as the physical condition worsens, this first stage generally gives way to a second one in which the patient recognizes the probability that death may be approaching and becomes very angry. This stage usually involves questions such as "Why me?" and displacement of the anger onto other people. Some patients go through a third stage in which they "bargain" over some aspect of their condition. This bargaining may take the form of promising not to "ask for anything else if I can just live long enough to see my son married." Depression or a profound sense of loss is the fourth stage, and acceptance is the fifth stage.

Although these stages are conceptualized as being sequential, one following the other, people generally go back and forth among several of the stages for long periods of time. Thus a person who has been in denial for some time may show periodic states of anger, which increase in frequency. Gradually the anger is present more than the denial and the patient may start to make statements that sound much like bargaining. Or a person who has seemed to be accepting the inevitability of his condition for some time may appear extremely angry or depressed for several days.

These same stages that characterize grief over one's own impending death are found in people facing a significant disability, either their own or that of a loved one. Let's look at the manner in which the stages are manifested in such situations.

Denial

Denial is one of the most prominent aspects of coping with serious disability. One form that denial often takes is acknowledging the information being given but denying the implication. For example, a patient with transsection of the spine may acknowledge what has happened to him but deny that this will result in paraplegia. He may continue to tell you that he will walk again despite the medical evidence and despite his growing experience with other people on the ward with similar lesions. The family of a head trauma victim may stand over their loved one and talk about how "normal" he is despite the fact that they recognize that significant brain matter was surgically removed and that the patient is hemiplegic and has profound intellectual, memory, and personality changes.

One story is heard over and over from families of patients with significant brain damage: "When we got to the emergency room the first night, the neurosurgeon told us our son would not live, but he did. Then they said he was going to live but that he would be a 'vegetable.' Now he's talking, and he's obviously not a 'vegetable.' How do you expect me to believe what you tell me about his never returning to college? The doctors have been wrong in all their other gloomy predictions. I know he is going to be just like he was."

Another form of denial involves insisting that one has not been given significant information. For example, the effects of traumatic brain injuries are frequently so disturbing to families that they are essentially unable to process information they are given. Families have said very sincerely, many months after an injury, that they had never been told their loved one had permanent brain damage, despite the fact that the neurosurgeon, psychologist, and psychiatrist had told them several times.

A third form of denial often comes about much later during recovery when the patient and his family have accepted some of the deficits that appear to be permanent. At this stage you frequently start hearing that the patient really "never could write worth a darn." Despite the fact that he had a college degree and now is functionally illiterate, both the patient and his family may start to rationalize that there is really no great change from his premorbid level of functioning.

How do you deal with patients and families who are denying the realities of disability? Our first impulse is often to force acceptance on them. However, this is not always the wisest approach and it does not usually work. Denial is a way people protect themselves from the truth until they are able to accept it. If their denial is not hampering the rehabilitation effort, the best way to handle it is to be as honest as you can about the realities of the patient's condition but not try to force acceptance. If, on the other hand, denial is hampering the rehabilitation effort, advice should be sought from a mental health professional on how to handle the situation.

Anger

Anger is a natural consequence of the recognition that one's life has changed in dramatic ways because of a disability. Although a patient may deal with the angry feelings associated with his disability directly by verbalizing them or by angry outbursts whenever the disability prevents his doing something, very frequently the anger is displaced onto other people or seemingly unrelated situations. The family members are frequently the recipients of displaced anger and are often confused and hurt by it. They may come to you for support and/or explanations. One of the things you can tell families in such situations is that patients tend to displace anger onto people they can trust not to desert them as a result of their behavior. Therefore, the anger being received, painful as it may be, is a sign of confidence on the part of the patient and indicates a basic trust in the recipient. This frequently helps the family members become less threatened by the situation and allows them to help the patient express the anger more directly by talking about it.

The nursing staff is also a frequent recipient of displaced anger, both from the patient and from the family. Quite frequently on a rehabilitation service, a family will displace all their anger onto the nursing staff and a hostile relationship will be established. To understand how this might come about, put yourself in the situation described at the beginning of the chapter. Your son or boyfriend has survived a life-threatening crisis. You feel you should be grateful for that. On the other hand, you have begun to glimpse the fact that this survivor is considerably different from the person you loved so dearly. You have been told that his intelligence is seriously depressed, that he will probably always have a speech impediment, and that his potential for ever being an engineer or even being able to support a family is highly questionable. One of the things you have always loved about this person has been his quick wit. You loved to make puns with him, to discuss politics, to question the meaning of life. Now these things the two of you enjoyed seem unlikely to happen again. As a matter of fact, this survivor seems like a different person! You think about the fact that he will be highly dependent upon you for a long period of time—possibly permanently. You may have to seriously curtail your own activities to care for him. You tell yourself that such thoughts are selfish, that you have no right to feel angry toward your son or boyfriend, and that you should be grateful he survived. But inside there is an overwhelming conflict, and you feel intense anxiety and confusion. You certainly cannot be angry at the patient, but how can you keep from being angry at the nurses? After all, when was the last time they checked on the patient? And didn't you ring the bell for what seemed like two hours yesterday before anyone answered? And doesn't it appear that the patient is getting a skin breakdown, which they surely could have prevented? All the anger you are feeling about the disability suddenly is focused on the nursing care, and before you know it, the battle lines are drawn, with the hospital staff on one side, you and the family on the other. Obviously, this situation is not conducive to good rehabilitation.

How can you prevent this kind of situation? One of the most important steps has to be taken when the patient first is admitted to the rehabilitation ward. At that time, one member of the nursing staff needs to make contact with the family. In this initial interview, the nurse needs to find out what has been said by previous medical professionals about the extent of the disability and the prognosis. This gives the nursing staff a baseline for dealing with the situation. The nurse then explains the routine of the rehabilitation ward, including some statements which help the family recognize that the "emergency" or "crisis" period has been passed. Frequently a family comes to the rehabilitation ward still expecting "intensive care" nursing services and become very fearful when they do not find them. The necessary differences between intensive care nursing and the more independence-oriented rehabilitation nursing need to be detailed for the family. Ward rules, rehabilitation team members, and rehabilitation goals should be mentioned. As much as possible, this initial conference should serve the purpose of helping everyone feel a part of the team effort required for the maximum rehabilitation of the patient. The relationship between the patient and his family is one of the most important factors in determining rehabilitation success. Therefore, establishing rapport with the family is frequently as important as establishing rapport with the patient.

Many rehabilitation centers also have "rap groups" for patients and for families, which serve the purpose of helping them to recognize their anger and to deal with it more directly. These groups, if used effectively, can go a long way toward preventing the kind of battleground relationship described above. However, whether or not such groups are available, the rehabilitation nurse has the responsibility of understanding that displaced anger is a natural part of coping with disability and also the responsibility of finding ways to deal with it in a productive rather than a retaliatory manner.

Bargaining

Bargaining is a controversial method of coping as far as its impact on rehabilitation. One often hears a patient make a statement such as this: "If I can only walk again, I won't complain about my bum arm." The whole basis of the "bargaining" defense is usually the attitude that "If I am good, maybe I can change the situation for the better," and this attitude generally facilitates rehabilitation. However, some of the pitfalls of bargaining are revealed in counseling patients and families.

An example is the case of the devout Catholic father of a beautiful 22-year-old girl. When the girl had an automobile accident and he was told she would not live, he tried to strike a bargain with God by promising certain deeds if God would save the girl's life. The girl lived, but (as the familiar story goes) the father was told she had sustained such extensive brain damage she would be a "vegetable." He again promised God certain deeds if she were spared this fate. As a matter of fact, the girl turned out to have considerable residual intelligence. However, she was severely ataxic and could neither speak nor communicate manually because of the ataxia. The father then became severely distraught because he felt the actual outcome was the worst possible one—the daughter was essentially an intelligent prisoner in a body too impaired to allow her to communicate. The father went through a serious crisis regarding his feelings about a God who, he came to believe, plays cruel tricks. Thus bargaining, similar to the defenses used in the other stages, can be an effective method of coping with the disability or it can be overused and become a hindrance to eventual acceptance.

Depression

Depression is an emotion that everybody recognizes and most have experienced to some extent. For most people it is a less threatening emotion than raw anger. Whereas it is extremely difficult for most of us to say about a very angry patient, "Poor Mr. Smith is so angry today," we can become very sympathetic when a patient cries and talks about how terrible his condition is. However, most of us in the helping professions have the tendency to want to "make everything all right." We want to *stop* pain, physical or psychological. Therefore, our first impulse in the case of a depressed patient is to try to talk him out of his sadness, reminding him of all the things for which he should be thankful.

We are often amazed when we stop to think of our expectations of patients with physical disabilities. They frequently must use every ounce of energy they have to learn a technique that will make them only minimally more independent. We watch and expect them to continue working merrily along despite the heavy toll in energy and the minimal reward. Although this attitude on the part of rehabilitation professionals is to the patient's benefit, we need always to be sensitive to the extreme struggle we are requiring and to be supportive when the patient questions whether the entire effort is worthwhile. At those times, the patient most needs a quiet listener who understands the significance of the loss the patient has suffered, the enormousness of the struggle, and the resulting sense of hopelessness that comes periodically. The nurse who can listen and validate the reality of the struggle provides support for the patient at a time when support is needed. She is also able to be more effective with the patient when he needs firmness because she has established a rapport based on the sharing of a very human struggle.

Not infrequently, a patient in the depression phase of coping with physical disability begins to verbalize death wishes. Such patients frequently go through periods in which they question whether death is better than living with their disability or feel that they are now worthless to themselves and to their families and that everyone would be "better off" if they were dead. Again, these are natural reactions to serious disability, and the feelings being verbalized seem to involve the question whether the change in capabilities and the resulting loss of function and independence will be too painful to bear. Will life as a "cripple" be meaningful enough to be worth the fight? Although such a question is not uncommon, patients who have the physical strength and the means to commit suicide and who couple agitation and/or significant withdrawal with a stated death wish should be evaluated carefully.

Acceptance

The final stage of coping with the loss of a body part or function is that of acceptance. At this stage the patient can truthfully say, "I recognize my disability and feel able to live with it." However, most people, even after achieving this stage of coping, retain some hope for a change in their condition. A typical statement from a patient who is primarily in a stage of acceptance is as follows: "I know I won't be able to do the things I did before when I leave the hospital. I won't be able to be a perfectionist as a housekeeper from this wheelchair. But that's all right. I can live with that. But you just wait! Someday I'm going to walk again! It probably won't be this year, so I'll learn all I can about using this contraption. But some day I'm going to walk into your office. You'll see!" For a patient primarily in the *denial* stage, you would usually respond by saying, "I hope you are right, but what if you're not?"; at this stage you should feel comfortable in smiling *with* the patient and responding, "I hope you are right!"

The Five Stages: A Summary

Just as people who are facing their own impending death go through five stages of grief, people who are facing the loss of significant body parts or functions usually go through the same five stages. Several factors you should remember about this grief process are the following:

1. When we speak of grief over a "significant" loss of function, the degree of significance can only be defined subjectively by each individual. Because of individual differences, what one person may consider a severe loss may be only a minimal loss to another. Therefore, the rehabilitation spe-

cialist must respect the patient's evaluation of whether a functional deficit is "significant" to him.

2. Although the stages are conceptualized as being sequential, they overlap considerably and people usually alternate between two or more stages.
3. Families also go through the grief process in much the same manner as the patient, although the rate for each individual within a family may be considerably different. One important aspect of these individual differences is that two family members in different stages of coping may have extreme difficulty in communicating—because of the discrepancy between the stages. For example, if one family member is denying while another is depressed, the depressed member may find completely deaf ears when trying to express grief to the denying member.

Test on Stages of Grief

At this point you need to test your understanding of the material that you have read; therefore, please answer the questions that follow.

1. List in order the stages of grief identified in this section: _____, _____, _____, _____, _____.
2. In coping with a disability, the patient can be expected to go through the five stages of grief, but the family would cope in an entirely different manner. True or false?
3. Once a patient has gone beyond denial, you would not expect him to deny again, but would expect him to go through a period in which he would show only anger. True or false?
4. When a patient is in denial, it is the obligation of the nursing staff to force a more realistic outlook. True or false?
5. Denial is a very adaptive defense that allows the patient to avoid realizing his situation until he is psychologically able to cope with that realization. True or false?
6. Displacing anger onto the nursing staff, as well as onto family and friends, is a normal method of coping with disability. True or false?
7. Bargaining has only positive consequences for coping with disability. True or false?
8. A nurse should always take a "cheer up" attitude toward depressed patients, reminding them of all they have to be grateful for. True or false?
9. When a patient with a severe disability expresses the idea that he may be better off dead, this statement may be a fairly natural question about his ability to achieve a meaningful life despite his disability. True or false?
10. Even patients who have achieved a reasonable degree of acceptance of their condition continue periodically to express denial of its permanence. True or false?
11. A patient and his family can be expected to go through the stages of grief at essentially the same rate. True or false?

Answers:
1. *Denial, anger, bargaining, depression, acceptance.*
2. *False.*
3. *False.*
4. *False.*
5. *True.*
6. *True.*
7. *False.*
8. *False.*
9. *True.*
10. *True.*
11. *False.*

If you answered most of the questions correctly and understand the correct answers to the ones you might have missed, please move on to the next section.

LOSS OF CONTROL

Another way to conceptualize some of the difficulties involved in coping with physical and/or mental disability is to look at the problem from the standpoint of loss of control over one's life. One of the consequences of losing a significant body function is that it usually results in a period of relative helplessness in which one has to depend on others for basic needs. Some very interesting studies (conducted initially with animals) provide a model for looking at how people's coping styles can be biased through previous experiences.[2]

In 1967, some animal researchers[3] studied the effect fear had on the ability of mongrel dogs to learn new responses. To produce fear, they restrained the dogs in a hammock and, after sounding a warning tone, applied shock for several trials. Nothing the dogs could do would prevent the shock. They could struggle, whine, bark, etc., but they could not control the shock. They could not avoid it, terminate it, or escape it. The second step of the experiment called for putting these same dogs in a shuttlebox and training them to avoid the shock by jumping over a barrier. It has typically been found that dogs who have not gone through the fear conditioning of the first step very quickly learn to escape from and then to avoid the shock by jumping the barrier when they hear the warning tone. However, the researchers found that the dogs that had previously been given fear training never even attempted to escape or avoid the shock, nor could they seem to learn to do so. They just stood meekly and took it.

This phenomenon, which has been labelled *learned helplessness*, has been studied extensively since that time in several different animals (including humans) under many different conditions. In his book entitled *Helplessness*, M.E.P. Seligman summarizes the implications of the various studies, and these appear extremely relevant to rehabilitation patients.[4] Some of these implications are as follows:

1. The individual in a learned helplessness situation appears to learn that he is powerless to control his environment and that there is no connection between the effort he makes and the eventual outcome.
2. Learned helplessness is generalized from one situation to another, so that an individual who learns to be helpless in one environment tends to act as though he is helpless in other environments.
3. This helplessness takes the form of low motivation—the individual tends to make very few responses, even in situations in which these responses would result in control.
4. After helplessness training, the individual has difficulty learning that a response he makes *does* control a situation, even after experiencing this control. Thus, learned helplessness distorts the ability of the individual to perceive that he can control a situation.
5. Helplessness results in emotional disturbances such as fear and anxiety and psychosomatic illnesses such as gastric ulcers.
6. Learned helplessness can be "cured" in an individual by forcing him to respond repeatedly to situations in which his efforts effect a desired outcome until he has learned that he does have control.
7. Learned helplessness could be prevented if, prior to the helplessness training sessions, the individual was given a "dose" of control in the form of allowing him to learn, in traumatic or important situations, that he can control important aspects of his environment. Thus, a dog trained to escape or avoid shock *before* being given helplessness training was essentially immunized against learning to be helpless.
8. A kind of "reverse learned helplessness" can be produced by taking away the relationship between positive responses and rewards. Thus, feeding an animal without regard to his actions resulted in eliminating food-getting responses even when the previously unlimited, noncontingent food supply stopped.

Since we all have had experiences throughout our lives in which we have not been able to control the outcome of some important event, what keeps us from developing a generalized learned helplessness that paralyzes us? Seligman suggests three crucial factors:

1. We may have had enough experiences in our past, probably beginning relatively early in life, that our responses will exert some control over our environment. Thus, we have some immunity against generalized helplessness.
2. The limited experiences we have had that have involved loss of control have been discriminated from the more general experiences of being in control. Our immunity may not cover every specific situation, but it may be sufficient to help us discriminate the sit-

uations in which we are likely to have control from those in which we have no control.

3. Helplessness is generalized from traumatic or important events to less traumatic or important ones, but not vice versa. Therefore, what we have learned about our control or lack of control in traumatic or important situations will tend to influence our feeling of control or helplessness in relatively non-threatening, mundane situations. However, learning to exert control in unimportant, non-traumatic situations only may not be effective in immunizing us from helplessness in traumatic situations.

Patients undergoing rehabilitation subsequent to the onset of some physical disability appear to be facing a situation not unlike that of the dogs in the helplessness training stage of Seligman's experiments. The efforts they make may have little impact on their world. They may be imprisoned in bodies that are missing limbs or have limbs that are no longer functioning properly; they may be incontinent; they may be sexually impotent; they may be unable to remember or to learn; they may have visual or auditory deficits. Whatever the specific disability, it undoubtedly limits their ability to respond in ways that control their world as effectively as previously.

Based on the learned helplessness literature, we can predict that the way in which patients react to the new traumatic situation will depend upon what they have learned previously about their ability to control the important events of their world through their own actions. Those individuals who have experienced considerable amounts of control throughout their life, particularly in important situations, will probably continue to respond in their newly disabled state. Furthermore, the manner in which they have learned to respond is very important. Some may have learned to control their environment in direct, adaptive ways. Others may have found that direct responses were less effective than less direct, manipulative ones. Therefore, the manner in which people have learned to respond to their environment will influence the type of responses they make in their new situation.

It is suspected, however, that if an individual finds his condition drastically different from the old one, he may have difficulty finding the responses that will be the most adaptive. Thus, a patient who has learned that his responses are instrumental in controlling his environment may immediately make responses that are adaptive in his new situation or he may, either because of past learning or because of the drastic discrepancy between the old and new situations, persist in responding in maladaptive ways. For example, he may demand to make his own medical decisions despite a lack of training in that field. He may try to establish verbal control to replace the lost physical capabilities.

One example of this is the patient who continually orders the nursing staff around in a demanding, belligerent manner. This may well be an attempt to re-establish control by bullying the nurses into replacing the lost physical function with their own labors. This type of patient often generates real conflict with the nursing staff. They begin to feel as if they are being treated as slaves or servants and a battle begins in which the nurses try to show the patient "who really controls things around here!" This kind of conflict can quickly reach absurdity, as each side becomes more and more determined to show the other who is more powerful.

A more effective manner exists for dealing with a patient who needs to maintain control, even if this involves making maladaptive responses. First, the nurse needs to recognize that her patient's fight to maintain control is basically very healthy. The problem is to find more adaptive responses that will achieve control for him. Usually the whole rehabilitation team, including the nursing staff, can meet with the patient and let him be an integral part of the decision making about his own case. The patient can work with the team to set his own goals as well as the schedule and method for attaining these goals. This gives him an effective way of re-establishing some control over his life, even in the presence of loss of physical control, and will undoubtedly optimize the ultimate rehabilitation. The most important thing to remember in a case like this is that the nurse must not get into a power struggle with the patient. If the nurse should win, she may have taught the patient to be helpless in the new situation, which will certainly not facilitate the patient's ability to cope with the disability.

At the other end of the spectrum is the individual who has had little experience with control before the onset of the disability and who approaches the new situation as a "helpless" individual. In light of the experimental findings, we would expect such an individual to make very little effort toward his own rehabilitation. He would tend to be passive and would probably express the belief that his trying will not make any difference in the eventual outcome. Even when shown evidence that people can benefit from rehabilitation programs, such a patient would have trouble believing that this applies to him. He would not even tend to perceive progress when he made it, despite changes obvious to other people. His response rate, his ability to learn, and his perceptions would all be influenced by his previous history. He would also likely appear more depressed and show more anxiety, fear, and somatic symptoms than his counterpart at the other end of the "control" spectrum.

How do you handle such a patient? Seligman's work showed that the only way to cure learned helplessness was to force the individual to respond over and over again in situations in which his responses were effective. Similar treatment should work for the patient feeling helpless on a rehabilitation ward. He should be required to make responses over and over that are effective in exerting some control over some part of his existence. You may listen to and sympathize with his expressions of depression and worthlessness, but you must be firm in helping him make the *responses* required to demonstrate to him his own ability to control some aspect of his life.

Most patients will fall somewhere in between the two extremes of the control spectrum. However, the tendency to feel helpless and to perceive a loss of control will be an issue in every patient's rehabilitation. Anything you can do that will shift control of rehabilitation goals, treatment plans, treatment schedules, etc., to the patient will enhance his rehabilitation potential. On the other hand, anything you do that takes control away from the patient will increase his feeling of helplessness.

Test on Loss of Control

Let's test your understanding of the information you have just read. Please try to answer the questions which follow.

1. A person who has learned that he is helpless to control his environment would be expected to make very few _____, to have difficulty _____ that he could control a particular situation, and to show more _____ than a nonhelpless individual.
2. Which would be more damaging to an individual's coping skills: being made helpless in everyday tasks or being made helpless in a traumatic situation? _____
   _____
3. How can an individual be immunized against learned helplessness? _____
   _____
4. How can learned helplessness be cured? _____
   _____
5. Why is it important for a nurse not to get into a power struggle with a patient over control of the hospital environment? _____
   _____
   _____

Answers:
1. *Responses; learning; emotionality.*
2. *Being made helpless in a traumatic situation, because that would most likely be generalized to less important, nontraumatic situations.*
3. *By learning that his responses are instrumental in changing his environment in important ways.*
4. *By forcing the individual repeatedly to make responses that will exert some control over his environment.*
5. *Because she may, by winning, be giving the patient "learned helplessness" training.*

If you feel you understand the material, please go to the next section.

FACTORS THAT INFLUENCE COPING

We have now discussed the fact that most people go through five stages in coping with their disability and that their previous experiences in effectively controlling their world impact on their coping styles. Several other factors also influence the psychological reactions a person has to disability: age, brain damage, and life changes.

Age

The patient's age has a lot to do with the psychological issues that will be brought into play in the case of a significant disability. Let's look at some of the issues associated with different age groups.

Dependent Child

Whenever a dependent child has an acquired physical or mental disability, one of the most important psychological factors is the parents' guilt over the situation. Parents see one of their most important roles to be that of protecting their children, and if something happens to one, they feel that they have failed—that they were not successful parents. No matter how unavoidable an accident or illness may have been, a strong tendency exists to feel severe guilt. The guilt may not be at the conscious level, so that if questioned, the parents may insist that they did their best to protect the child. However, in all probability they are feeling some guilt at a deeper level. This guilt might manifest itself behaviorally through a deep depression and/or through a tendency to become overprotective of the child. As a matter of fact, one of the most common long-term pitfalls when a child has acquired a disability is that because of their own guilt, the parents will teach the child to be helpless. They will spend the rest of their lives trying to "make up" to the child for their failure to protect in the first instance. One of the tasks of a nurse in dealing with such a case is to help the parents understand that the primary goal of rehabilitation is to make the patient as independent as possible. If you can get the parents involved as members of the team focusing on this goal, perhaps you can help them shift from determining to protect to determining to support independence. If, on the other hand, you find them resisting the child's growing independence (either overtly or by providing verbal support while engaging in behavioral sabotage), then professional help should be requested. It is much easier to prevent the helplessness that would come from such overprotectiveness than to cure it at some later date. Also, if help can be obtained before maladaptive behavior patterns are established, the probability of a successful outcome is increased.

Older Adolescent or Young Adult

Frequently rehabilitation patients are in their late teens or early twenties. As a matter of fact,

individuals within this age group have the highest incidence of traumatic disability. Such patients probably were still partially dependent on their families premorbidly, particularly with regard to finances. On the other hand, they have probably attained at least some degree of independence in terms of their own identity. However, this independence, which is frequently achieved through great struggle, is still very tenuous, and any event that reverses the independence is seen as a serious threat. A patient in this age category would therefore be particularly sensitive to encroachments on his independence. Although in the early stages of recovery he would welcome being cared for, such dependency would soon be a real source of conflict for him. His parents, on the other hand, would be as likely to need to overprotect as parents of younger children. Therefore, at some stage of recovery a conflict between patient and family over lost independence is almost a certainty. Here again, if the rehabilitation team can begin early to help the family recognize that maximal independence is the first goal of therapy, some of this conflict might be avoided.

Adults in Childrearing Years

The problems for patients who are married and possibly parents of dependent children are somewhat different. Some of the same dependency issues that were a part of the child-parent relationship may be re-enacted between spouses, with the healthy partner trying to overprotect the patient. In addition to these issues, however, are myriad others, including (1) the fear of abandonment by the spouse, (2) the fear of being sexually unattractive or impotent (which, of course, is also an issue with the younger populations), (3) the financial burdens caused by having a wage earner or homemaker disabled, and (4) the children's feelings about the disability.

Quite frequently, patients are overwhelmed with fears about their condition and about whether their spouses and children can accept and love them as they now are. The spouses, on the other hand, have their own fears. They may have questions about their own ability to accept the changes, and then feel extreme guilt about these reservations. In addition, both spouses may be very upset over significant role changes. Perhaps the husband is the patient and the outlook is bleak for his being able to support the family again. If the marriage has been based on traditional role models, the wife may feel very confused about her new role as provider. She may be unprepared both educationally and psychologically, and she will undoubtedly feel angry about the changed circumstances. At the same time, the husband is feeling a sense of generalized impotence because he can no longer be the "man of the house" in the way he has always believed he should be. The scenarios are unlimited, depending upon the disability, the previous family structure, the flexibility of each member of the family to change roles, the communication skills of the family members, and the kind of support the family gets from the extended family and from friends.

However, one repeatedly sees families in which all members try to hide their feelings. How can the patient verbalize fears of being abandoned without seeming to have lost faith in the partner? How can the partner verbalize fears of being able to cope with the patient's disability without seeming to be a selfish brute? So, each family member hides deep feelings, sharing only trivia, and feeling more and more isolated at a time when he or she most needs to feel supported. As a rehabilitation nurse, you need to be sensitive to these issues and to provide a supportive stance for both the patient and his or her spouse. Sometimes it helps to say to one of the partners, "I would probably be feeling a good bit of fear if I were in your situation. I might feel pretty upset by this disability and would probably wonder if my spouse wouldn't be upset by it, too." Even if the listener rejects your statement as being irrelevant in the specific case, you have opened the door of acceptance for such feelings.

Older Patient

Although most of us are more prepared for the death or disability of an older spouse or parent than we are for disabilities in the earlier years, some very painful psychological issues arise when the patient is an older individual. One of the most common issues involves whether the patient can still live independently or whether he must now be taken to a nursing home. For the patient, going to a nursing home may be the psychological equivalent of preparing to die. For the family, sending the patient to a nursing home may be the psychological equivalent of abandoning him. Of course, many families do abandon patients to nursing homes although the patient may not really need nursing care. Other families, on the other hand, may unrealistically decide to manage a patient at home despite the fact that the patient needs skilled nursing care 24 hours a day. The nurse has a very important role in discharge planning in these cases. All other members of the

rehabilitation staff have their own perceptions of how independent the patient *could* be, but the nurse is the one who deals with the patient most extensively and knows how independent the patient actually *is* in caring for himself. She can therefore provide insight into whether a family can care for a patient. Here again she can also act as a supportive listener to both patient and family.

Brain Damage

Another factor in determining how a patient will cope with disability is the site of the lesion in brain damage. As is stated in Chapter 1, different effects are expected from damage to different parts of the brain. One of the most common examples of this is the effect of damage to the right hemisphere of the brain. Typically a right brain stroke results in left-sided motor problems (left hemiplegia), some tactile deficits, and a left visual field defect. A person with an equivalent lesion in the left hemisphere of the brain would probably compensate for the visual deficits almost immediately by turning his head to scan the side of the field defect. However, the left hemiplegic with a visual field defect (and some left hemiplegics without visual field defects) will tend to neglect the left visual field. He will not turn his head to the left to compensate. He will, in effect, ignore the whole left side of space, which results in his walking or wheeling into objects on that side, ignoring food on the left side of his plate, and trying to read starting in the middle of a line. The interesting psychological correlate of this behavior is that such a patient not only tends to neglect or "deny" the left side of space or the left side of his own body, but also will frequently deny that he has any of the very obvious difficulties just mentioned (or any other difficulties, for that matter). This denial makes the patient a great accident risk, because his denial results in poor judgment regarding his capabilities. The patient will have trouble understanding why the staff and his family do not give him more independence. After all, he has no major problems! Frequently the denial of deficits is so extreme that even when you set up situations that clearly demonstrate the deficit, the patient will believe he has been tricked. Time and persistence may help to overcome such denial, but in the meantime the patient must be protected against his own poor judgment.

Lesions to the frontal lobes of either cerebral hemisphere can also produce some fairly dramatic psychological deficits. Rate and speed of response may be impaired to the point where the patient can be said to be akinetic (without movement).[5] Such a patient may lie in bed without moving even to obtain food or drink. In severe cases, the patient would starve before he would make a response to obtain food. With the akinetic tendencies frequently come a very flat affect, little facial expression, and monotonic speech. In less severe cases or in recovery stages, the patient may simply move slowly, have extreme difficulty programming motor responses, and continue to show flat or inappropriate affect. You frequently find such a patient laughing when the appropriate response would be fear or sorrow. One patient laughed as he told about observing the futile resuscitation attempts associated with the death of his roommate a few minutes earlier. Inappropriate sexual behavior is also sometimes found in association with frontal lesions.

Lesions in the temporal lobes and some of the deeper brain structures are sometimes associated with angry outbursts and aggression. As a matter of fact, many patients with deep brain lesions go through a recovery stage that involves extreme agitation and aggression. During such a stage psychiatric help is often required to administer appropriate medications. Even under medication, however, many patients are unable to cooperate with structured therapies during this stage and attempts to force cooperation result in increased agitation and aggression. When this is the case, the rehabilitation team needs to minimize demands on the patient by requiring only those tasks that are absolutely necessary to the patient's safety and well-being and by dividing even those tasks into very short segments. Frequently a patient in this condition is aware of his agitation and is frightened by his own aggressive behavior. (I have had such patients ask me to stop an evaluation because they were afraid they would lose control.)

Life Changes

A final consideration in understanding how an individual copes with disability is that the disabling condition is only one event in his recent history. The patient under your care may have been in an accident in which other family members or friends were also disabled or were killed. Or the disability may have caused changes in the family such as financial difficulties, residential changes, and role changes. Other significant events in the family may not be causally related to the disability being treated. Some examples of this are births, deaths, and marriages within the family. Recent research has shown that the number of significant changes a person faces within a given time period will impact on his ability to cope with these changes.[6] A scale of life events has been devised in which 43 different events are empirically assigned a value (called life change units or LCUs) representing their relative degree of disruptiveness to coping mechanisms. According to this scale, for example, death of a spouse is worth 100 LCUs, pregnancy is worth 40 LCUs, outstanding personal achievement is worth 28 LCUs, etc. As these examples indicate, both positive and negative changes have disruptive value. Rahe has found that among Danish, Japanese, Swedish, and American samples, people who developed illnesses had accumulated up to 300 LCUs during the previous year, as compared with an average of 150 LCUs for patients who were healthy.[7] The implication of this research is that stress concentrated into a limited time span has a cumulative effect on the ability to cope. Thus, a patient's current disability must be viewed in the context of the other significant events in his life over the past year or two. If his life has involved many recent changes, you should be alert to coping difficulties.

Test on Coping Factors

Time for review again. Please answer the questions that follow.

1. What is the primary goal of rehabilitation that needs to be conveyed to families, particularly when the patient is a child? _____

2. What problem was mentioned as the most important psychological issue when the patient is a child? _____

3. List some of the special problems encountered by patients who are in their childrearing years.

_____

_____

4. What special help can the nurse give families who are considering whether or not to place a patient in a nursing home? _____

_____

5. Left hemiplegics often show an exaggerated use of one of the stages of grief mentioned earlier. Which stage is it? _____

6. Frontal lobe lesions often result in certain psychological problems. List some of them. _____

7. How would you suggest dealing with a patient with a deep brain lesion who shows severe agitation and aggression? _____

_____

8. According to the "life change" literature, would you expect a decrease in the number of fights in a family to disrupt coping? _____

_____

Answers:

1. *Maximum ultimate independence of patient.*
2. *The parents' guilt tends to result in overprotectiveness that sabotages independence of the patient.*
3. *Fear of abandonment by spouse, fear of sexual failure or unattractiveness, financial burdens, children's reactions.*
4. *Although the other professionals may know what the patient is capable of doing for himself, the nurse is the one who knows most realistically what the patient actually does for himself—how independent he actually is.*
5. *Denial.*
6. *Very slow movements, flat affect, inappropriate affect, inappropriate sexual behavior.*
7. *Request psychiatric evaluation for medication and then do not force the patient to participate in activities which he cannot tolerate at that point. Those activities he can tolerate should be broken down into tolerable segments.*
8. *Yes. Both positive and negative changes in life have disruptive value. As a matter of fact, a change in the number of fights between spouses is worth 35 LCUs regardless of whether the number increases or decreases!*

If you had trouble answering any of the questions in this test or the others, you should study this chapter again. If you feel satisfied with your understanding of the information, you should be able to help your patients cope with the psychological problems related to their disabilities.

NOTES

1. E. Kubler-Ross, *On Death and Dying* (New York: Macmillan, 1969).

2. M.E.P. Seligman, *Helplessness: On Depression, Development, and Death* (San Francisco: W.H. Freeman, 1975).

3. J.B. Overmeier and M.E.P. Seligman, "Effects of Inescapable Shock upon Subsequent Escape and Avoidance Learning," *Journal of Comparative and Physiological Psychology* 63 (1967): 23–33; M.E.P. Seligman and S.F. Maier, "Failure to Escape Traumatic Shock," *Journal of Experimental Psychology* 74 (1967): 1–9.

4. Seligman, *Helplessness*.

5. A.R. Luria, *The Working Brain* (London: Penguin Press, 1973).

6. R.H. Holmes and R.H. Rahe, "The Social Readjustment Rating Scale," *Journal of Psychosomatic Research* 11 (1967): 213–18.

7. R.H. Rahe, "Subjects' Recent Life Changes and Their Near-Future Illness Susceptibility," *in Advances in Psychosomatic Medicine*, ed. Z.J. Lipowsky (Basel, Switzerland: S. Karger, 1972), vol. 8, *Psychosocial Aspects of Physical Illness*.

Psychosocial Intervention and Discharge Planning

Frances Pendergraft, C.S.W./A.C.P
Barbara M. Henley, C.S.W./A.C.P.

INTRODUCTION AND OBJECTIVES

The overarching purpose of rehabilitation is to restore the individual to maximal functioning within physical limitations while promoting renewed feelings of self-worth and autonomy.

In view of the complex physiological and psychological changes that accompany severe disability, the ideal rehabilitation program should include a wide range of specialists working as a team for the purpose of accomplishing realistic, mutually agreed goals that will enable the patient to achieve maximal functional ability before discharge. In the "real world," this ideal is rarely achieved. Because of the nationwide necessity to contain the costs of health care, hospital stays have been shortened, and there is more reliance on outpatient and home care. From the first day of admission, there is a focus on what lies ahead for the patient after intensive hospital-level care. The process of assessment, intervention, and discharge planning is usually condensed into weeks rather than months.

Another institutional reality is the frequent absence of a full rehabilitation team (particularly in small or rural hospitals). Traditionally it is the social worker's responsibility to evaluate the psychosocial aspects of the patient's disability or impairment and to ensure that the patient and his family have all possible assistance at the time of discharge. However, any concerned professional may utilize those concepts which, when learned and skillfully applied, can help improve overall rehabilitation care. In the fast-paced hospital climate of today, all professionals are challenged not only to take on new roles, but also to accomplish more in less time.

The goal of this chapter is to help you become familiar with the process of psychosocial assessment, intervention, and discharge planning. After reading it, you should

1. understand the scope and process of psychosocial assessment and planning
2. know specific techniques to (a) enhance the patient and his family's hospital experience and (b) facilitate earlier discharge
3. have a working knowledge of activities and agencies that lead to successful discharge linked solidly to a community support system

PSYCHOSOCIAL ASSESSMENT AND PLANNING

Assessment Factors

To manage a severe impairment successfully, both in the hospital and after discharge, the health care team must take into account more than the patient's medical history and current pathology. Hence, the necessity for an ongoing psychosocial evaluation. *Psychosocial* is a useful term to describe factors "within" the patient (i.e., characteristic attitudes, defense mechanisms, aptitudes, and intelligence) as well as factors "outside" of the patient (i.e., people, equipment, shelter, and money) that impact on his current motivation and future adjustment. Starting at the time when a patient is being considered for admission and continuing through his hospitalization, information should be gathered in a conversational but systematic way. Gradually a picture emerges of the patient's internal and environmental strengths and weaknesses that will impact treatment and affect his ability to sustain the benefits of treatment after discharge. Following are some areas for sensitive exploration.

1. *Interpersonal Relationships.* Who are the most important persons in the patient's life and what is the quality of those relationships—conflictual or supportive, intimate or distant, dependent or cooperative? How available are those persons if the patient needs "hands on" assistance in the future? Who is the decision maker in the family? What have been past assigned roles and expectations? How will the circumstances created by the illness or disability impact the patient and the individual family members?

2. *Psychological Attributes.* How have the patient and family dealt with crises or severe illness in the past? What seems to be their reaction to and understanding of the current impairment? What characteristic attitudes may impinge on the rehabilitation process? How appropriate is the content and flow of the patient's verbalizations? Of his emotional reactions? Does the family report any uncharacteristic moods or reactions? What evidence is there to help evaluate judgment and intelligence?

3. *Cultural Factors.* What is the patient's ethnic, religious, and geographic background? To what socioeconomic class does he belong? How do these cultural factors seem to influence his values, lifestyle, pain behavior, health practices, food preferences, or language of choice?

4. *Environmental Factors.* What are the outstanding facts about the home and living situation prior to admission? How adequate may we expect this to be in terms of space, privacy, barriers such as narrow doorways or steps, and convenience to shopping and to medical facilities? What transportation is accessible to the patient and his family? Who has been responsible for cleaning, cooking, laundry, etc.?

5. *Financial/Vocational Factors.* What sources of income have been available to the patient's household? How are they affected by the current illness? In view of the patient's employment, age, dependents, degree of disability, and needs, what benefits might be expected to flow? (See the section below entitled "Community Agency Referral" for specifics.) How will his insurance, personal savings, benefits, or other resources affect the length of time he can remain in the hospital? What is the patient's recent work history, including the name of his employer and the length of time he has been at that job? What are his other skills and aptitudes and what other jobs, training, and education has he had?

Psychosocial Treatment Plan

From the wealth of information gathered, one can begin to form impressions about the problems and needs relevant to developing a psychosocial treatment plan for facilitating early discharge. These should be set down in the form of a concise summary, with an emphasis on salient facts and needs to be addressed. Clear plans to meet these needs should be stated and prioritized in terms of immediacy. For the sake of clarity and accountability, you should be as specific as possible about your roles and responsibility with respect to each identified need. Such plans should be modified as new information is gathered. Information obtained in the psychosocial assessment serves as a guide in planning services and treatment within the hospital environment as well as in planning for discharge. Appropriate information should be shared with the rehabilitation team so that they can view the patient in the context of his family, his environment, his past, and his future goals and expectations.

Test on Psychosocial Assessment and Planning

For each of the following, either complete the statement or indicate whether the statement is true or false.

1. Psychosocial assessment is useful to help plan for both _____ and _____.

2. Five important areas to include in the assessment are: _____, _____, _____, _____, and _____.

3. In gathering background information from the patient and the family, the interviewing style should be _____ yet _____.

4. Cultural factors can have an impact on such health-related behaviors as _____, _____, and _____.
5. A psychosocial treatment plan should be concise, should prioritize needs, and should be modified as new information arises. True or false?
6. Questions about the patient's financial status should not be asked, since this is highly personal and confidential information. True or false?

Answers:
1. *In-hospital management; successful discharge planning.*
2. *Interpersonal relationships; psychological attributes; environmental factors; cultural factors; and financial/vocational factors.*
3. *Conversational; systematic.*
4. *Pain behavior; food preferences; health practices; language of choice; life style; values.*
5. *True.*
6. *False.*

ENHANCING TREATMENT AND FACILITATING DISCHARGE

There are many issues in the rehabilitation process that require psychosocial intervention. (See Chapter 16 on psychological responses to disability for discussion related to this topic.) These issues include, but are not limited to, those discussed in the following sections.

Crisis Intervention

Physical illness or injury severe enough to warrant inpatient rehabilitation creates feelings of crisis for the patient and family. Research into theories of crisis intervention tells us that, unless handled well, crises can lead to lowered ability to function in the future. Specific strategies are necessary early in the hospitalization to reduce anxiety and encourage the development of trust. Some of these are as follows:

1. Provide basic information.
2. Honestly acknowledge questions you cannot answer and direct the patient or family to the appropriate staff member for a response.
3. Describe your role and the role of others who will be working with the patient.
4. Review the environment, explain any equipment and procedures, and let the patient and family know what to expect.
5. Explain how the rehabilitation process works in your hospital, how decisions are made and communicated, and how the patient and family will be included in those decisions.
6. Assist with such immediate family needs as locating convenient housing, transportation, and child care and making emergency financial arrangements.
7. Assess the extent to which the crisis may have temporarily immobilized the family and be prepared to step in to help them regroup.

Families differ in their capability to handle stress based on their inner resources, their support networks, and their past experiences with stress. Some will need more direct assistance than others in using community resources and in problem solving based on a logical review of alternatives.

The techniques listed above may reduce the fears that surface during the early stages of rehabilitation, but the major life crises will not be resolved during the span of a hospital stay. It requires that the individual be able to let go of past expectations and to accept and find value in a new identity. This takes time, and each patient works at it at his own rate. His ultimate success depends on his inner strength and external supports. The rehabilitation experience should provide the momentum for change by offering some of that support and by helping the patient understand the process and the goal.

Restoring Control to Patients

The return of control to the patient to the fullest extent possible should be the number one goal of the rehabilitation process. Patients should be included in the establishment of goals, in the making of crucial management decisions during their hospitalization, and in choosing among options available to them. The eventual transition back to the community will be infinitely easier if a patient has developed a feeling of autonomy and of confidence in his ability to manage his life with new coping skills and new routines. Trips outside the hospital as well as day and overnight passes are effective in helping patients and their families gain confidence and experience in developing autonomy in manageable steps while having the support of the hospital staff and the security of the controlled environment.

Encouraging Family Involvement

The importance of family participation in the rehabilitation process cannot be over-emphasized. (For purposes of this chapter, the term family is intended to include caretakers or significant others.) Too often, staff, in their focus on the patient, leave the family feeling isolated and helpless. An uninformed or discouraged family can consciously or unconsciously subvert the patient's progress. Once the patient no longer needs hospital-level care, the family usually replaces the hospital as the patient's major support system. In order to prepare for this, the family should be allowed to participate in care whenever possible. Regularly scheduled conferences between the physician and other members of the team, the patient, and the family can ensure that communication is clear and open. It is important that everyone be moving in the same direction with the same expectations. Rehabilitation professionals must accept and respect family members for who they are, valuing and building on their strengths. They must acknowledge the family's anxieties while conveying to them confidence in their abilities to manage future care. It is also important to emphasize the positive aspects and specific capabilities of each unique family system.

Providing Supportive Psychological Intervention

All members of the rehabilitation team should be aware of the common reactions to the trauma of major disability: feelings of loss, grief, anger, bewilderment, loss of control, sadness, and denial. Patients' feelings should be accepted as stated, allowed free expression when they are within normal limits, verbally acknowledged ("I know you're feeling frustrated today") and universalized ("Lots of patients going through this feel a lot of sadness before they start feeling better").

Denial needs to be responded to with delicacy and good timing. Not all patients move through the stages of loss and readjustment at the same rate and in the same way. Allow for individual differences, take your patient's "emotional pulse" frequently, and keep in mind the value of empathetic listening.

Limiting Disruption in Employment and Finances

The patient and family may need help in sorting out alternative ways of maintaining income during the rehabilitation process. Learning about special community resources that may be helpful (in the short or long term) in meeting financial obligations can reduce stress. The family and patient should be encouraged to maintain contact with the patient's employer. Keeping the employer informed of the patient's progress often keeps the door open to future job options.

Examining Changes in Roles and Relationships

Changes in the functioning of one family member frequently leads to imbalance in the whole system. This can result in anxiety, lowering of self-esteem, and difficulties in carving out new roles for all family members. Roles include *patient*, *lover*, *friend*, *breadwinner*, and *homemaker* as well as the more subtle ones of *decision maker*, *peacekeeper*, *tower of strength*, etc. Counseling should be directed at helping the patient and family to acknowledge these changes, consider new ways of fulfilling the old roles, and identify new ways of relating to each other within the family.

Exploring Issues of Sexuality

Typically, sexuality is a difficult area for health professionals to discuss comfortably with patients. Most patients are left to struggle with misinformation, damaged self-esteem, and a distorted image of their own body. Providing an atmosphere conducive to the discussion of sexual issues can help both a patient and the staff. The most knowledgeable team member should give specific information about the disability and sexuality. The patient and his sexual partner should be encouraged to talk both separately and together with this team member to explore the emotional issues related to sexuality.

Test on Enhancing Treatment and Facilitating Discharge

For each of the following, either complete the statement or indicate whether the statement is true or false.

1. Strategies to reduce anxiety and help build trust include _____, _____ and _____.
2. The number one psychological goal of rehabilitation is _____.
3. Techniques for psychological support include _____, _____, and _____.
4. One of the most difficult areas for staff to discuss comfortably with patients is _____.
5. The less one involves the patient's employer, the better the chance of his being rehired in the future. True or false?
6. Because of the patient's changed abilities to function, the whole family may need counseling in order to adapt. True or false?

Answers:
1. *Providing basic information, answering questions, explaining your role, reviewing the environment, explaining how decisions are made, assisting with immediate family needs, etc.*
2. *Returning control to the patient.*
3. *Accepting feelings and allowing them free expression, universalizing, handling denial tactfully, listening with empathy, etc.*
4. *Sexuality.*
5. *False.*
6. *True.*

DISCHARGE AND LINKAGE TO THE COMMUNITY

Discharge planning involves a great deal more than merely coordinating the transfer of the patient from hospital to home and connecting him to various community resources. It is a collaborative clinical effort that begins at admission and extends into follow-up. Emotional or psychological readiness is a major factor in the success of community reintegration. Attention to the issues discussed in the preceding section prepares the way for the most successful discharge outcome.

The idea of leaving the familiar, protected routine of the hospital is usually a frightening one. This is normal. Emotional issues dealt with in the patient's admission often resurface at this time. "How will I manage? Will my friends reject me? Will I get worse? How can I face the world like this? I kept telling myself I would get better, but now they say I have to leave and I *still* have no sensation in my legs!" Reality comes crowding in. Don't brush aside these feelings with easy reassurances. Instead, help the patient focus on the here and now, on immediate plans. Help him decide which of his many worries he will work on

first, second, and so on; then see that he sticks to his priorities. Emphasize the positives in his past progress and in his prognosis, but always be realistic.

A critical decision must be made by the patient or family as soon as it is possible to estimate the patient's functional status: Where will the patient reside when hospital-level rehabilitation comes to an end? The alternatives are numerous, depending on the motivation of the patient to help himself, the availability and zeal of caretakers, the amount and sources of funding, the availability of resources, and the creativity of the discharge planners. Don't be constrained by the simplistic idea that a patient either goes to a nursing home or goes home. Depending on factors mentioned above and on the realities of the patient's needs and preferences, the best plan might be (1) to start a new life in an apartment complex for the handicapped, (2) to return home with special helpers (e.g., home health aides), (3) to spend nights at home and days in a day-care program, (4) to take up residency in a special foster or boarding home or in a nursing home (temporarily or permanently). Each situation is unique and deserves a "customized" plan!

Discharge Planning Checklist

Some very specific, concrete discharge planning activities are necessary to effect a successful return to the community:

1. Assess the patient's ability to manage activities of daily living, taking into account what will be needed in the way of training a caretaker, using special equipment, or modifying the home environment. The purpose, of course, is to promote the patient's independence and assist and support the caretaker. A form like the one shown in Table 17-1 is helpful in this assessment.
2. Ensure that needed equipment and assistive devices are acquired. This entails locating funding (Medicare is often helpful; sometimes private insurance or state vocational rehabilitation agencies will pay). If possible, the patient and caregiver should be made familiar with new equipment before leaving the supportive environment of the hospital.
3. Train the patient and caregiver in all aspects of care, seeking to fit the patient's home schedule with the family's usual daily routine as much as possible. Allow sufficient training time over an adequate period so that information can be assimilated.
4. Help mobilize community agencies, a task more complex than it sounds! Some agencies require that the application process be initiated by a physician or hospital or require the transfer of detailed medical, social, or nursing information. A host of other community services should be approached by the consumer. The discharge planner's job is to provide education on what is available and how to make it "work." In addition to the name, address, and telephone number of a given service agency, clients need to know whether to apply in person or by phone, what information or paperwork is required to prove eligibility, the name of someone to contact (if known), what to expect in the way of possible services, and the hours the agency is open. (It is often best to provide such information in written form.) It may be useful to help the patient understand what rights and entitlements he can claim, and service agencies often have an appeal process if clients are denied assistance. The patient should be encouraged to let you know if the service is not provided as expected. As referring agents, discharge planners need to treat community resource directories with caution—agency information changes frequently. If you have not had contact with a resource for six months, check your information before you pass it on

TABLE 17-1 Assessment of Activities of Daily Living

	No	With Help	Independent	If Help Needed, Caretaker Is: Adequate	Inadequate	Equipment Needed
Feed self						
Get in/out of bed						
Dress/undress						
Bathe/shower						
Shave						
Use toilet (get to bathroom)						
Cook meals						
Light housekeeping						
Heavy housework						
Laundry						
Shop						
Take medicine						
Ambulate inside						
Ambulate outside						
Transportation						
Handle money						
Use telephone						

to a client. Finally, be aware that community agencies unfortunately often have waiting lists, complicated application guidelines, and poorly trained "gatekeepers" at the front desk. The best laid referral plans can go awry. Moral: Follow-up with your patients to ensure that they receive what they need.

5. Provide instruction about medical aftercare: When and where are patients to see their physician? How will they get supplies and medications? Who do they contact in an emergency? What are the exact transportation plans (routine and emergency) to link them to medical care? Who exactly do they call regarding maintenance of special equipment? Finally, Who do they "have permission" to call for reassurance and comfort during their period of transition?

Community Agency Referral

The following is a list of resources that exist in many localities.

1. *United Way* many times has listings of community agencies, eligibility requirements, and referral procedures.
2. The following *financial assistance programs* (income and medical) are useful:
   a. *Social Security Disability Income* (SSDI) provides income to persons with a disability that prevents them from working and is expected to last for at least 12 months. Disability benefits are payable on the basis of credit for work under Social Security. If eligible, benefits usually begin six months after disability. Application is made through the Social Security office.
   b. *Medicare* is a health insurance program for persons 65 and older and for disabled persons under 65 who have received Social Security disability payments for two consecutive years or more. Sponsorship for rehabilitation services is available under Medicare; however, the two-year wait imposes a considerable delay for a newly injured individual.
      (1) Hospital insurance. Part A helps pay for hospital care and for certain follow-up care after discharge.
      (2) Medical insurance. Part B helps pay for doctor services, certain outpatient services, and some durable medical equipment.
   c. *Supplemental Security Insurance* (SSI) provides monthly income to disabled persons of any age. Parents of disabled infants and children may apply for them, since it is not necessary to have worked under Social Security to be eligible. Eligibility is based on family income for minors and on the applicant's own income if he is an adult. Application is made through the Social Security office.
   d. *Aid to Families of Dependent Children* (AFDC) provides monthly income to families with needy children deprived of parental support because of the death, absence, or disability of one or both parents. Eligibility varies from state to state. Application is usually made through the local office of the Department of Health and Human Services.
   e. *Medicaid* is a medical assistance program which helps to pay for the medical needs of uninsured, low-income individuals. It is automatically available to persons eligible for supplemental security income and AFDC. Services available under this program vary from state to state and may or may not cover rehabilitation services. Application is usually processed through the Department of Health and Human Services.
   f. *State programs for crippled children* offer various resources related to medical services for injured or sick children. They often provide diagnostic services and treatment, including rehabilitation and equipment for children who meet their eligibility requirements (financial and diagnostic). Again, the programs vary from state to state, and the specifics as to services and eligibility should be obtained from your state program.
   g. *City and county social services* are present in many communities and may offer emergency or ongoing financial assistance to individuals with limited resources. Publically financed city and county hospitals also offer medical services to those individuals who meet their eligibility requirements.
   h. *Worker's compensation insurance* provides medical and rehabilitation services to individuals who sustain work-related injuries. It provides financial support to individuals during the recuperative or rehabilitation phase.

i. *Private insurance and disability benefits* should be thoroughly investigated to determine the financial, medical, rehabilitation, and home health services that are available to policy holders.

j. *Veterans benefits* include the following:

    (1) Monthly non-service-connected disability payments are available to disabled veterans whose military service occurred within certain dates (wartime) and who meet income requirements.

    (2) Medical assistance in VA medical facilities is available to all service-connected veterans and non-service-connected "indigent" veterans who have medical needs if the facility determines there is space available. The VA office can provide more specific information.

3. *State departments of human resources* manage programs that vary from state to state. Many times they are a source of funding for nursing home placement. Home attendant care and other services focused on assisting individuals to remain in their own homes may be available through these agencies.

4. *Home health services* provide home nursing care. Some agencies also provide homemaker services as well as physical, occupational, and respiratory therapy and social work intervention. Home health services are usually limited to several visits a week based on need. A physician referral is required. Although there are many such agencies in the private sector, many communities also have visiting nurses funded by United Way or the local health department.

5. *Accessible transportation* is one resource that can help prevent the isolation of a disabled individual. Public transportation meets this need in various ways in different communities via accessible buses, vans, etc. Modified automobiles (hand controls) and specifically adapted vans enable many disabled individuals to continue to drive themselves or be transported conveniently by caregivers. Handicapped stickers or decals for automobiles enable individuals to park in conveniently designated locations.

6. *Housing* that is accessible and affordable for disabled individuals is available in some areas. Local housing authorities are aware of these resources. Shared attendant services are sometimes available in group housing projects.

7. *Residential homes and nursing homes* are, in some cases, a necessary alternative at the time of hospital discharge. The health department frequently is responsible for licensing and setting standards for these types of facilities and can provide lists indicating the level of care provided. If possible, the family and the patient should carefully evaluate the various facilities available before making a decision.

8. *Day care* is a valuable resource if a patient must have supervision and the caregiver is employed. Adult day care is available in some communities and may be publicly or privately funded.

9. *Vocational rehabilitation agencies* provide vocational counseling, vocational placement, and, in some cases, education, vocational training, equipment, rehabilitation, and other types of medical treatment. Their goal is returning the disabled person to employment. Every state has a vocational rehabilitation agency with offices located throughout the state.

10. *Educational* opportunities are mandated for all school-age children (3 to 21 years), including children who are disabled. Local school districts can apprise you of their resources and programs (including homebound education, if medically recommended).

11. *Counseling services* in most communities are available privately and through public agencies. Social workers, psychologists, psychiatrists, and ministers are the traditional providers of psychological counseling. Agencies such as family service and community mental health clinics are available in many areas.

12. *Disease-related groups* such as the American Cancer Society, the Muscular Dystrophy Association, and the National Head Injury Association offer various services. Some have a fund-raising focus, whereas others provide direct services or support groups. Many patients and families find support groups very helpful and welcome the opportunity to share experiences and discuss emotional issues with others who have similar problems.

13. *Recreation* is available in many forms for disabled individuals, including participation in sports, opportunities to travel, etc. In

many communities, there are publications listing accessible parks, theaters, restaurants, etc.

14. *Independent living centers* are very aware of resources for disabled individuals. Information about accessible housing, transportation, and attendant care services are frequently available through these agencies. They are strong advocates for the disabled and are active in community action efforts.

A well-planned discharge is the key to successful community re-entry. We must recognize the extent of the responsibilities we are transferring to patients and families and ensure that they have appropriate support services that will enable them to manage home care. A hasty, ill-conceived discharge plan will almost certainly lead to failure and it may result in an unnecessary hospital readmission. The patient and family will feel defeated and lose confidence in their abilities to manage home care. A good plan should include respite and stress relief for caregivers so that they can continue in the caregiving role. These resources are not always readily available; therefore, your challenge is to assist the patient and family in creating the most effective plan, one that takes into account the needs of the total family system.

Test on Discharge and Linkage to the Community

For each of the following, either complete the statement or match the appropriate items.

1. Before discharge, the patient's ability to manage activities of daily living should be evaluated so as to increase the patient's _____ and provide _____ to the caretaker.
2. The best laid referral plans can go awry because of _____, _____, or _____.
3. To expedite medical aftercare, at time of discharge the patient should have information about _____, _____.

4. Match the list of discharge problems, with the community resource that might be of help:
   a. A patient could do light work if he had a special wheelchair and transportation.
   b. The patient's family feels isolated and overwhelmed.
   c. A young adult has no family but wants to live as independently as possible, with some attendant care.
   d. The patient's spouse needs help with wound care, seeks some respite, and feels insecure about nursing procedures at home.
   e. The caregiver must be employed during the day, but cannot afford to have adequate help at home.

   (i) Independent living centers.

   (ii) Adult day care.

   (iii) State department of vocational rehabilitation.

   (iv) Home health care agency or visiting nurse association.

   (v) Support groups run by disease-related organizations.

Answers:
1. *Independence; assistance.*
2. *Waiting lists, complicated application guidelines; poorly trained "gate keepers."*
3. *The acquisition of medication and supplies; return appointments; emergency contacts.*
4. *a(iii), b(v), c(i), d(iv), e(ii).*

SUGGESTED READINGS

Blazyk, Stan. "Managing the Discharge Crisis following Catastrophic Illness or Injury." *Social Work in Health Care* 2, (September 1986): 19.

Cornelius, D.A., S. Chipouras, E. Makas, and S.M. Danial. *Who Cares? A Handbook on Sex Education and Counseling Services for Disabled People*. Washington, D.C.: George Washington University, 1982.

Guidelines for Discharge Planning. Chicago: American Hospital Association, 1984.

Kahn, Elizabeth. "Disability and Physical Handicap: Services for the Chronically Ill," In the *Encyclopedia of Social Work*, vol. 1. Washington, D.C.: National Association of Social Workers, 1977.

Krueger, David W., ed. *Rehabilitation Psychology*. Rockville, Md.: Aspen, 1984.

18 Organizing and Conducting Effective Instruction in Rehabilitation

Robert E. Roush, Ed.D., M.P.H.
J. David Holcomb, Ed.D.

INTRODUCTION AND OBJECTIVES

The purpose of this chapter is to present an overview of educational theory and practice that can help you in one of the most important roles you can play—that of teacher. In this third edition, the focus is on planning and organizing, as well as presenting, inservice education programs that may result in improved care rendered on the rehabilitation nursing service. Thus, the goal of this chapter is to motivate you to plan, organize, and conduct such programs.

To achieve this goal, you should be able to

1. organize the appropriate features of effective educational programs,
2. apply ten principles of effective instruction,
3. incorporate essential elements of good lecturing and effective small group and one-to-one teaching, and
4. employ appropriate evaluation procedures.

This chapter is organized around content material related to these four objectives. The material presented is a synthesis of educational research findings from leading educational researchers, the coauthors' experience in health professions education, and portions of two of the coauthors' published works.[1] Much of the ensuing narrative material can perhaps be made clearer by examining the illustration of the complete instructional process shown in Figure 18-1.

Content, regardless of the scientific discipline, comprises subsets of knowledge, skills, and attitudes, which are related respectively to the cognitive, psychomotor, and affective domains of human learning. Once decisions have been made about the domain(s) to be addressed regarding the content that learners should know and use,

inservice educators should organize their instructional programs by developing appropriate educational objectives, choosing the desired teaching method(s), and designing a valid evaluation protocol to assess the effectiveness of the educational program to be conducted.

ORGANIZATIONAL CONSIDERATIONS

Regardless of setting, in the busy, sometimes hectic world of patient care, rehabilitation professionals are constantly teaching each other and their patients. Too often, these educational sessions or encounters are conducted without sufficient time spent on planning. While the focus of this chapter is directed principally to those who must conduct inservice education for their colleagues, much of the suggested methodology is equally germane to the process of direct patient education. Thus, the first step that health professions educators should take in organizing an educational program is to ask this fundamental question: *What* is the body of knowledge that should be taught given what I am attempting to accomplish (e.g., teaching rehab nurses a new method of quantifying patients' ADL or teaching patients how to use some assistive device)? The next step is to pose this question: *Who* will teach *whom, when,* and *where,* and with *which* methods and materials will the body of knowledge be taught? Obviously, (1) the *what* and *who* relate to teachers; (2) the *whom* implies students; (3) *when* and *where* connote facilities, scheduling, etc.; and (4) choosing *which* method and materials implies consideration of the above, plus format and protocol.

The following narrative focuses on a few points that should be considered in answering the ques-

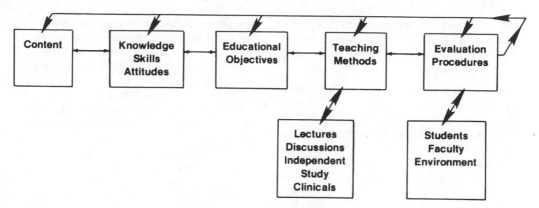

Figure 18-1 Instructional Planning, Implementation, and Evaluation

tions posed during your initial planning. Regarding *what* should be taught, rehab experts, curriculum committees, professional societies, and the appropriate body of literature are sources for determining what constitutes acceptable knowledge. You should use all of these resources to validate the content you want to teach. In the context of your objective, a situational analysis of the problem—whether it be to teach a patient a compliance protocol or to teach a group of nurses a new process—should guide further organizational attempts. Regarding patient education, this analysis assumes that patients present with certain problems that require certain tasks to be performed under certain conditions. With the focus on desired patient outcomes, the conventional wisdom and the customary practices that have proven to be effective for similar patients define the appropriate body of knowledge. Finalization of what should be taught must also include such professional, legal, and ethical factors as accreditation, certification, and licensure, all of which involve proscriptions determining what a health professional is allowed to do. For specific tips on one-to-one patient education, see the appropriate sections of the chapters on self-care and wheelchairs.

When considering *whom* (students, patients, and/or colleagues), think of the epidemiological principle of person, place, and time. With regard to *person*, what are the characteristics (age or experience, previous training, current knowledge, aptitude, cognitive and physical capabilities, etc.) of the recipient? With regard to *place*, where are the learners' loci on a career continuum or life span? With regard to *time*, how much time is available for instruction and practice as compared with what is needed; also, what are the work-related time commitments of the inservice trainees?

The other issues are *when* and *where*. Be sure to schedule classes at important times during the work day, not the last hours of a shift—breakfast and/or lunchtime classes usually work well. If possible, arrange classes in pleasant, comfortable surroundings, with as few distractions as possible. Remember, classrooms should be designed for learning to the same degree that operating rooms are designed for surgery.

Questions about *which* methods and materials require making choices. Should the instruction make use of lectures; small or large group discussions; case studies; mediated formats, e.g., trigger films, etc.; individual instruction; or computer-assisted instruction? Regardless of the choice, teachers and students should know what are the expected learning results at the end of a session, whether it be a class, course, or degree program. Also, behavioral theory defines learning as a change in behavior over time. Upon completion of an instructional session, it is up to you to determine what students should be able to do, as measured by appropriate standards.

Use of a planning and evaluation tool such as a Gantt chart (a task-by-time matrix) can assist you in determining if the actual results of your organized course differ from the original goals.[2] Assuming that there is no variance or that it is positive in nature, the final question to be asked is this: So what? Determination of what has been accomplished refers back to the goals and objectives of your instructional program and the definition of learning, i.e., change in learners' behavior.

PRINCIPLES OF EFFECTIVE INSTRUCTION

The concept of effective instruction implies that someone is teaching something that someone else is learning. There is also an implication that perhaps effective instructors do certain things that ineffective ones don't do. Therefore, the following ten principles can be taken to describe what good instructors do.

Principle 1: An instructor should have clearly defined instructional objectives.

As suggested in the model shown in Figure 18-1, the first steps in the teaching process involve the development of instructional objectives. Your first task as a teacher is to answer the following question: What should my students be able to do (specific behavior) as a result of the instruction I provide them? The specific behavior is an observable, measurable act students do as a result of your using active words or phrases such as *list, define, identify and describe, compute and solve.* As you answer this question, you will be defining the basic element of any instructional objective developed for your teaching assignment.

The second element of an instructional objective is a description of the condition(s) under which the student is expected to perform or demonstrate the behavior specified in the first or basic element of the objective. This can be expressed in a variety of ways depending on the actual setting or environment in which the teaching-learning encounter is to take place (e.g., "given a picture of numbered wheelchair parts"; "in a laboratory setting with a two-headed teaching microscope"; "on a rehab ward with a left hemiplegic patient presenting with aphasia").

The third element to be included in developing an instructional objective is the determination of the criteria you will use to assess the extent to which your students accomplished the objective. By formulating your evaluation criteria, you will be able to determine the suitability of the objective for the students involved and for the learning conditions of the teaching setting.

Based on the foregoing, instructional objectives should be written to include these three elements:

1. what students will know or be able to do following instruction,
2. the conditions or situation in which students will be taught and/or demonstrate the desired content or behavior, and
3. the criteria to be used in assessing whether or not students know or can do what you want them to.

The following is an example of an instructional objective written with all three elements: "Following the lecture on wheelchairs, all students, when given a picture of a wheelchair with its parts numbered, will be able to correctly match all the numbers to an accompanying list of wheelchair parts."

This objective has (1) what students will do—match wheelchair parts; (2) the teaching-learning conditions—a lecture followed by the matching exercise using a numbered picture and a parts list; and (3) the evaluation criteria—all students will correctly match all the numbers.

While it is not absolutely necessary for you to write instructional objectives using a 1, 2, 3 format, it is important to think of the triad of what, where, and when—*what* will students know, *where* or how will they know it, and *when* will you and they know they know it?

Finally, after you have determined the objectives of your program, they should be communicated to your students. If students understand the purposes of the instruction, they will be better able to accomplish the specified objectives.

Principle 2: An instructor should select teaching strategies that assist students in accomplishing the objectives.

After you have determined the objectives of your teaching activities, you are ready to select an appropriate teaching methodology. In making your selection, you should keep a number of considerations in mind. They are as follows:

1. *The objectives of the teaching session.* Are the students supposed to learn basic facts about a patient's condition or a management technique? Will the students be required to perform a skill? Are you providing information not readily available in textbooks? Are you trying to develop positive attitudes toward a specific concept or patient problem? Answers to these questions will help you select a teaching style which is appropriate for the objectives. For example, if you are teaching a specific skill, you may want to demonstrate the skill a few times and then have each student practice the skill until all of them have mastered it.
2. *The number of students involved.* If you are teaching a small number of students at one time, your teaching strategies can be more flexible. However, if your student group is large (more than 15 students), it may be very difficult to demonstrate a skill and then allow each student to demonstrate the degree to which mastery has been attained. If you are essentially teaching on a one-to-one basis, you will probably want to use an informal style of teaching.

3. *The time available.* The amount of time you have available for teaching may have an influence on your teaching strategy. Limited time may necessitate having your students learn the factual material outside of formal classes. If time is plentiful, you may be able to promote extensive skill development and do an extensive evaluation for every student.
4. *The learning environment and resources.* Where will you be teaching? Are appropriate audiovisual aids and equipment available? Does the medical library have the references you need? Will the hospital provide the patient education materials you need? Answers to each of these questions will have an influence on your selection of a teaching strategy. For example, if there is a film available which is an excellent instructional aid to students in accomplishing certain objectives, you may want to schedule time for your students to view it.

Principle 3: An instructor should strive for clarity and understandability in instruction.

Clarity and efficiency of presentation are essential to good teaching. Often clarity and understandability are based on organization. The unorganized instructor will have unorganized, confused students. Your ability to speak plainly and explain clearly and logically will determine, in large part, your teaching effectiveness.

Principle 4: An instructor should stimulate and motivate students toward independent learning.

The intellectual stimulation of students—motivating students to think rather than to memorize—and the ability to get more from them than merely what is expected or required are very important aspects of teaching. As a teacher, you should strive to motivate your students to want to learn more than what was merely presented in the classroom.

Principle 5: An instructor should concentrate on principles and problem solving rather than factual material.

The teaching-learning process should be primarily concerned with the identification of principles and the solution of problems. The mere presentation of facts or data can be done without the aid of a teacher. In many instances, a textbook or handout can present information considerably better than a teacher. You should spend your teaching time helping students with the integration and correlation of material, applying princi-

ples to solve problems, and determining the relevance of one situation to another. In short, the good teacher provides learning experiences that include the transfer of learning, the acceptance or rejection of concepts, and the drawing of conclusions. Ideally, you should be teaching students how to learn and how to prepare for a lifetime of learning.

Principle 6: An instructor should provide evaluative feedback to students concerning their progress in accomplishing the objectives of the course and help them understand their mistakes.

Determining whether a student has attained a set of defined objectives and providing this information to the student are essential to good teaching. These activities should constitute a continuous process that begins early in the course with the initial student-teacher contact.

Feedback is important if students are to get involved in the learning process. It will help you identify student problems and it contributes greatly to the interaction necessary to make the teaching-learning process optimally effective. In order to have the satisfaction that comes with achievement, the students must know they have achieved. In order to learn more, the students must know what they have learned and what more they need to learn.

Your constructive criticism, with helpful suggestions for improvement made at the time of the student's performance or activity, constitutes one of the most effective teaching methods that you can employ. In contrast, criticism without explanation and suggestions for improvement, as well as inconsistency or procrastination in explaining errors, probably will contribute as much or more to the failure of the teaching-learning process as any other factor. Use praise and encouragement frequently, even for small degrees of progress.

Principle 7: An instructor should be available to students for counseling and help.

Effective teaching is not limited to classrooms, clinics, and wards. The student who is trying to learn will have problems that need solutions and questions that need answers outside of formal class time. You should be willing to help your students when they seek help, whether it be in the classroom, in the corridor, or at the nurses' station.

Principle 8: An instructor should use fairness and tact in activities with students.

Among the optimal conditions for learning and teaching is an atmosphere of mutual respect between the student and the instructor. Your ability to respect your students' feelings and listen to your students will help create a climate that is conducive to learning and development. You should make your students feel that they are important to you.

Principle 9: An instructor should have regard for individual differences among students.

Good teachers make provisions for individual differences among their students. If you are aware of the differences among your students, your teaching will be more effective. You should appreciate the importance of recognizing and accepting the highly individualistic nature of the learning process and, where possible, allow your students to pursue their own special interests at their own rates.

Implicit in acknowledging students' differences is the exercise of patience in dealing with these differences. What is easy to some students may be difficult to others. To treat all students as having the same ability to learn is to ignore the genetic, environmental, and motivational differences that exist among humans. Unless the differences in student abilities are recognized and patience is exercised in dealing with them, an effective teacher for some students will be ineffective for others.

Principle 10: An instructor should be willing to admit shortcomings.

The extent to which an instructor can admit to error or lack of knowledge is an important factor in good teaching. The ability to admit errors or say "I don't know" is a reflection of self-security. It also indicates that you are not inflexible or dogmatic, characteristics which tend to block class discussion, minimize questioning, and form barriers to student thought. You should encourage rational opposition and spirited critical dissent by your students.

ELEMENTS OF INSTRUCTIONAL METHODS

Of the many types of instructional methods, the three most commonly used in the health professions are lecturing (didactic), small group discussion (clinical bedside), and one-to-one (clerkships, rotations, rounds, etc.). In this section, the coauthors have selected some tips to help facilitate improvement of your presentations when using these three methods.

Lecturing

The main criticism of this method is the poor use made of lecturing rather than the method itself. The following tips are offered as suggestions to alleviate this problem:

1. Know the subject thoroughly.
2. Explain the purposes, objectives, and relevance of the subject to the students.
3. Follow an organized and logical sequence.
4. Attempt to make the students feel at ease.
5. Maintain eye contact with students.
6. Speak clearly and with an appropriate vocabulary.
7. Appear to be enthusiastic about the subject.
8. Avoid stereotypical behavior.
9. Encourage student questions and opinions.
10. Highlight the main points of the lecture.
11. Use illustrations, audiovisuals, etc., where appropriate and where they enhance student learning.
12. Develop factual information into applicable concepts.
13. Summarize the main points as you lecture and at the closing.
14. Allow time for student questions and discussion.

Small Group Discussion

Before some practical information is presented on ways to improve the small group discussion of a clinical or medical-social-legal problem, it is appropriate to present here some theory to help in distinguishing between the efficacy of the lecture and small group methods.

The theory is Benjamin Bloom's now famous exposition of the hierarchical levels of learning called the Taxonomy of Educational Objectives.[3] This taxonomy is summarized as follows:

1. knowledge—recalling facts, terminology, definitions, etc.
2. comprehension—understanding material as evidenced by the ability to translate, interpret, and extrapolate into other forms of communication
3. application—using two or more generalizations to reach another generalization and/or using facts and generalizations to form a hypothesis

4. analysis—breaking down a concept into its constituent parts
5. synthesis—relating elements to create a whole
6. evaluation—judging the value of ideas, facts, and methods as well as standards for appraising the extent to which particulars are accurate, effective, etc.

Inspection of Bloom's levels of learning leads to the conclusion that lecturing is generally not the preferable method for content that requires learning above the first two levels, knowledge and comprehension. Therefore, when thinking about how to structure an effective clinical discussion, think about ways to facilitate students' opportunities to use levels 3 to 6.

There are techniques that will make a discussion more effective. Seven of them are as follows:

1. *Develop the discussion around objectives.* It is important that the students understand the purposes of the discussion.
2. *Make sure that the discussion is instructor directed but student centered.* Remember that the term *discussion* connotes two-way communication.
3. *Try to involve as many students as possible.* Do not let a few students dominate the discussion or prevent others from participating.
4. *Keep the discussion going by solving arguments and asking leading questions.* Questions should be planned before the discussion. They should require students to apply their knowledge to problem-solving activities.
5. *Give praise and encouragement to those who make meaningful contributions.* Verbal and nonverbal rewards promote student-teacher and student-student interaction.
6. *Make sure that the discussion ends with a definite conclusion.* Don't leave students hanging. Bring closure to the subject.
7. *Summarize the main points and make sure everyone understands the results.* Remember the beginning, middle, and end in light of the purpose of the discussion.

One-to-One Teaching Encounters

Now that you have been presented with information on the lecture and small group discussion methods, one other form of teaching should be considered. It comprises the single encounters that you as a mentor periodically have with others—staff and students—on your service when they ask you about a situation or problem that clearly requires your expertise.

Often, especially in a full-time hospital setting, informal one-to-one, teaching-learning encounters take up the major proportion of the time spent on teaching. If handled properly, they can also result in a great deal of learning. Things you can do in these one-to-one encounters include the following:

1. *Provide relevant information.* Give brief explanations, then ask the person to articulate a response that assures you that he or she knows the correct procedure or situation.
2. *Answer questions.* Give a specific answer, but inquire whether your answer actually provides the desired information as it is often the case that the wrong question is asked.
3. *Ask questions.* Pose questions in such a way that an open-ended response is required rather than a quick, simple answer, such as yes or no.
4. *Refer to another person.* Don't be reticent to defer to another person's greater expertise, particularly in the team-type setting of a rehabilitation service.
5. *Refer to the literature.* Where possible, refer individuals to appropriate journals and manuals, as you will not always be present.
6. *Conduct remedial tutoring.* Use Socratic inquiries, clear demonstrations, or any of the other techniques listed here to make sure your staff is providing the absolute maximum quality of care that can be rendered, given the facility and the patient's condition.
7. *Lead discussions.* Sometimes a question posed by a staff member indicates there is a problem involving several people on the service, particularly between shifts. When possible, you should call a group meeting to discuss and hopefully resolve the problem.
8. *Make assignments.* Use the technique of specific assignment in two ways. One is to have an individual who is experiencing difficulty complete a learning exercise that could remove the deficiency. The other is to assign topics to different staff members routinely in an effort to promote continuous inservice education, e.g., a journal club.

EVALUATION PROCEDURES

Thus far in this chapter, you have been presented with information on planning, organizing, and conducting inservice education programs for rehabilitation personnel. Now you must consider the fourth phase of teaching, that is, evaluation. While evaluation is normally thought of as a discrete phase, it is actually a continuous part of the process, beginning with the very onset of the idea for an educational program. For the sake of convenience, however, think of evaluation as comprising these two phases:

1. The formative phase: Formative evaluation begins with planning, is implemented soon thereafter, and assesses how well the plan is developed and what impact the plan itself has on the students (refer to Figure 18-1).
2. The summative phase: Summative evaluation is planned during the formative phase and assesses the outcomes of the program in light of the stated goals and objectives. It can be both short-term (assessing whether the students learned the material presented) and long-term (determining whether the students applied the material they learned).

While evaluation plans can be very complex, two simple ideas underlie any plan: (1) what went *into* the plan and (2) what comes *out*. Perhaps the single most important thing to remember about evaluation is that its purpose is to improve your program, not to prove something or someone was wrong. A well-designed evaluation plan provides for measurement of the input and output of your program, the results of which serve as feedback for you and your students regarding the degree to which your goals were the right goals and whether they were attained.

SUMMARY

The purpose of this chapter was to present you with some general ideas and suggestions on how to plan, organize, conduct, and evaluate inservice education programs for the medical, nursing, and other allied health rehabilitation professionals working on the ward.

You will meet the general goal and the objectives of this chapter if, in the future, you develop an inservice program based on instructional objectives; select and utilize appropriate teaching methods that effectively convey the knowledge, skills, and attitudes of the content information to be learned; and then afterwards assess the impact of the program. You will meet the goals and objectives of this *book* if you discharge your educational responsibilities in ways that demonstrably improve the care your patients receive and that result in patients returning to their homes and families as soon as medically feasible.

NOTES

1. J.D. Holcomb and R.E. Roush, "Methods of Evaluating and Improving Instruction," in *Improving Teaching in Medical Schools,* ed. J.D. Holcomb and A.E. Garner (Springfield, Ill.: Thomas, 1973), chap. 7.

2. D.L. Cook, *Educational Project Management* (Columbus, OH: Merrill, 1971).

3. B. Bloom, *Handbook I: Cognitive Domain* (New York: McKay, 1956).

SUGGESTED READINGS

Fuhrmann, B.S., and A.F. Grasha. *A Practical Handbook for College Teachers.* Boston: Little, Brown, 1983.

McGuire, C.H., R.P. Foley, A. Gorr, and R.W. Richards, eds. *Handbook of Health Professions Education.* San Francisco: Jossey Bass, 1983.

Mager, R.F. *Measuring Instructional Intent or Got a Match?* Belmont, Calif.: Fearon, 1977.

Morgan, M.K., and D. Irby, eds. *Evaluating Clinical Competence in the Health Professions.* St. Louis: Mosby, 1978.

Index

NOTE: Page numbers in italics indicate entries found in artwork.

Crisis intervention in rehabilitation process, 272
Crutches, 134, *135*
  measuring for, 139-140
  sitting down with, 149
  stairclimbing using, 125-126
  walking with, 142-146
Cultural factors in psychosocial assessment, 221
Cushions, wheelchair, 195

D

Day care, 227
Deconditioning in chronic pain, 28
Decubiti. *See also* Pressure sores
  pathogenesis of, 48
  treatable conditions predisposing to, 52, 55
Denial in grief process, 209
Dependence in chronic pain, 28
Dependent child, coping in, 216
Depression
  in chronic pain, 28
  in grief process, 211
Detoxification for chronic pain patient, 32
Devices, assistive, in gait training, 132-134
Diarrhea, 58, 59
Disability
  in chronic pain, 28
  psychological responses to, 208-218. *See also*
    Psychological responses to disability
Disability syndrome
  of arthritis, 18-21
  definition of, 3
  of hemiplegia, 3-9. *See also* Hemiplegia,
    disability syndrome of
  of parkinsonism, 22-23
  of spinal cord injury, 10-13. *See also* Spinal
    cord injury, disability syndrome of
Discharge planning
  checklist for, 225-226
  community agency referral in, 226-228
  enhancing treatment and facilitating, 222-223
  linkage to community in, 224-228
Disuse in chronic pain, 28
Ditropan for bladder problems, 45
Doctors in chronic pain, 28
L-Dopa for parkinsonism, 23
Dressing, self-care training for
  in arthritis, 179-181
  in hemiplegia, 163-170
  in parkinsonism, 183-184
Drug(s)
  for bladder problems, 45

  elderly rehabilitation and, 37
  misuse of, in chronic pain, 28
Dysarthria, 204

E

Eating, self-care training for
  in arthritis, 177, *178*
  in hemiplegia, 158-161
    left, 159-160
    right, 158-159
    self-help devices for, 160-161
  in parkinsonism, 183
Edema, decubiti and, 52, 55
Elbow
  flexion and extension of, range of motion
    activities for, 94
  supination and pronation of, range of motion
    activities for, 95
Elderly
  coping in, 217
  rehabilitation of, 35-40
  cardiovascular problems and, 36-37
  goals for, 39
  importance of, 35
  intercurrent acute illness and, 38-39
  mental problems and, 37-38
  musculoskeletal problems and, 38
  neurologic problems and, 37-38
  obstacles to, 36-39
Emotion, hemiplegia and, 7
Employment, disruption in, limiting, in
  rehabilitation process, 223
Environmental factors in psychosocial
  assessment, 221
Evaluation procedures for rehabilitation
  instruction, 236
Exercise for rheumatoid arthritis, 18-19
Expression
  gestural, in aphasia, 204
  oral, in aphasia, 203-204
  written, in aphasia, 204

F

Family involvement, encouraging, in
  rehabilitation process, 223
Family system in head injury, 16
Fearlessness of rehabilitation nurse, 66
Feeding. *See* Eating
Finances, disruption in, limiting, in
  rehabilitation process, 223

Financial factors in psychosocial assessment, 221
Finger, flexion and extension of, range of motion activities for, 97
Fingernails, self-help procedures for
  in arthritis, 178-179
  in hemiplegia, 161-162
Food
  cutting of, self-help technique for, in hemiplegia, 160
  spreading of, on bread, self-help techniques for, in hemiplegia, 160, *161*
Foot, inversion and eversion of range of motion activities for, 164
Footplates, wheelchair, 196
Footrests, wheelchair, 195-196
Four-person transfers in pregait training, 115-116
Frankel classification system for spinal cord injury, 10

G

Gait, normal, 131-132
Gait training, 128-136
  assistive devices in, 132-134
  backing up and sitting down in chair in, 148-149
  normal gait in, 131-132
  safety rules for, 128-130
  standing of patient from chair in, 137-139
  turning to sit in, 149-150
  walking aids in, 134-137
    measuring for, 139-141
    turning around using, 147
    using, 141-147
Games, pain, 30
Gestalt-synthetic ideation, hemiplegia and, 7
Gestural expression in aphasia, 204
Glasgow Coma Scale (GCS) in head injury assessment, 14, *15*
Grief, stages of, 208-212
  acceptance as, 211
  anger as, 209-210
  bargaining as, 210-211
  denial as, 209
  depression as, 211
Guards, skirt, wheelchair, 194

H

Hair combing, self-help procedures for
  in arthritic, 178, *179*

  in hemiplegia, 161
Hamstring stretching, range of motion activities for, 100
Hands, positioning of, in bed, 87
Head
  injury to, rehabilitation, 14-17
  positioning of, in bed, 85
Healing of decubiti, 55-56
Health care system in chronic pain, 28
Hearing loss, 205
Heel cord stretch, range of motion activities for, 103
Hemianopia, homonymous, in hemiplegia, 5-6
Hemi-inattention in hemiplegia, 5-6
Hemiplegia
  disability syndrome of, 3-9
    anatomy of, 3, *4*
    functional retraining in, 4-5
    homonymous hemianopia in, 5-6
    hemi-inattention in, 5
    paresis in, 4
    pathophysiology of, 3-4
    sensory loss in, 5
    spasticity in, 5
    specialized functions and, 6-8
    spontaneous neurological return in, 4-5
    verticality dysfunction in, 6
  lateralized stroke program for, 154-157
    severely paretic arm in, 155, 157
  self-care training in, 153-173
    for activities of daily living, 172-173
    for dressing, 163-172
    for feeding, 158-161
    for personal hygiene, 161-162
Hemi-somato-inattention in hemiplegia, 5
Hip
  abduction and adduction of, range of motion activities for, 101
  flexion of, range of motion activities for, 99
  internal and external rotation of, range of motion activities for, 100-101
Home health services, 227
Homemaking, self-help activities for, for hemiplegic, 173
Homonymous hemianopia in hemiplegia, 5-6
Hygiene
  oral, self-help procedures for, in arthritis, 178
  personal, self-care training for
    in arthritis, 177-179
    in hemiplegia, 161-162
    in parkinsonism, 183-184

Hypotension, orthostatic, elderly
   rehabilitation and, 36-37

I

Illness, acute, intercurrent, elderly
   rehabilitation and, 38-39
Immobility, decubiti and, 49
Incontinence. *See also* Bladder, problems with
   bowel, 59
   information gathering on, 43
   types of, 41-42
Independent living centers, 228
Instruction in rehabilitation, 230-235
   effective, principles of, 231-234
   evaluation procedure in, 236
   methods of, elements of, 234-235
   organizational considerations in, 230-231
Intermittent catheterization, 45
Interpersonal relationships in psychosocial
   assessment, 221

J

Jar opening, self-help techniques for, in
   hemiplegia, 160
Joint contractures in head injury, treatment of,
   15-16

K

Knee
   flexion and extension of, range of motion
      activities for, 102
   immobilizers of, in gait training, 133-134
   positioning of, in bed, 85
Knowledge of rehabilitation nurse, 66

L

Laryngectomee, 205
Lateralized stroke program, 154-157
Lecturing in rehabilitation instruction, 234
Left hemiplegic
   lateralized guidelines for, *156*
   self-care training for
      for dressing, 163-165
      for feeding, 159-160
Left hemispheric specialized functions,
   hemiplegia and, 6-7
Legs, positioning of, in bed, 86
Life changes, coping and, 218

Lifts in gait training, 132-133
Ligaments, contractures of, elderly rehabilitation
   and, 38
Litigation in chronic pain, 28
Loss of control, disability as, response to, 213-215
Lower extremities, range of motion activities for,
   99-105

M

Make-up, self-help procedures for
   in arthritis, 178, *179*
   in hemiplegia, 161
Medicaid, 226
Medical problems in head injury, 14-15
Medicare, 226
Medications. *See* Drug(s)
Mental problems, elderly rehabilitation and,
   37-38
Milk cartons, opening of, self-help techniques
   for, 160
Mobilizatlon, progressive, 69-152
   bed activities in, 84-109. *See also* Bed
      activities in progressive mobilization
   definition of, 69-71
   gait training in, 128-152. *See also* Gait training
   patient safety during, tools promoting, 72-81
      See also Safety, patient, during progressive
      mobilization
   pregait training in, 110-128. *See also* Pregait
      training
   starting point for, 81-83
Movement
   initiating, slowness in, in parkinsonism, 22
   in pressure sore prevention, 50-51, *52*
Musculoskeletal problems, elderly rehabilitation
   and, 38

N

Negative nitrogen balance, decubiti and, 55
Neglect in hemiplegia, 5
Neurogenic bowel, 59-60
Neurologic problems, elderly rehabilitation and,
   37-38
Neurological return, spontaneous, in hemiplegia, 4-5
Nursing homes, 227

O

Occupational therapy in chronic pain
   management, 32

Oral expression in aphasia, 203-204
Oral hygiene, self-help procedures for, in arthritis, 178
Orthostatic hypotension, elderly rehabilitation and, 36-37
Osteoarthritis, 19-20, 176. *See also* Arthritis
Osteoporosis, elderly rehabilitation and, 38
Oxybutynin chloride for bladder problems, 45

P

Pain
  acute, 29
  chronic, 27-33. *See also* Chronic pain
Pain behavior, 29-30
Pain games, 30
Pants, putting on/taking off, self-care training in, for hemiplegic, 167
Paraplegics, self-care training for, 187
Paresis in hemiplegia, 4
Parkinsonism, 175, 182-185
  disability syndrome of, 22-23
  self-care training in, 182-185
    for activities of daily living, 184-185
    for dressing, 183-184
    for eating, 183
    for personal hygiene, 183
Passivity in chronic pain, 28
Patience of rehablilitation nurse, 66
Patient-family ally, rehabilitation nurse as, 67
Personal hygiene, self-care training for
  in arthritis, 177-179
  in hemiplegia, 161-162
  in parkinsonism, 183
Physical problems in head injury, 15
Physical therapy in chronic pain management, 32
Planner, rehabilitation nurse as, 66-67
Positive thinker, rehabilitation nurse as, 66
Posttraumatic amnesia (PTA) in head injury, assessment, 14
Pregait training, 110-128
  assuming sitting position in, 110-111
  sitting balance in, 111-112
  stairclimbing in, 123-126
  standing in, 119-122
  transfers in, 112-117. *See also* Transfers
  weight shifting in, 118
  wheelchair mobilization in, 117-118
Pressure sores, 48-57
  healing of, 55-56
  pathogenesis of, 48

patient at risk for, identifying, 49
prevention of
  movement in, 50-51, *52*
  surface modifications in, 52, *53-54*
treatable conditions predisposing to, 52, 55
Progressive mobilization, 69-152. *See also* Mobilization, progressive
Pseudodementia, elderly rehabilitation and, 37
Psychological attributes in psychosocial assessment, 221
Psychological intervention, supportive, providing, in rehabilitation process, 223
Psychological responses to disability, 208-218
  coping as, factors influencing, 215-219. *See also* Coping with disability, factors influencing
  grief as, 208-212
  loss of control and, 213-215
Psychologist in chronic pain management, 32
Psychosocial assessment
  factors in, 220-221
  and planning, 220-222
Psychosocial treatment plan, 221
Pulse, monitoring of, progressive mobilization safety and, 74-77
Push-ups, wheelchair, in pregait training, 118

Q

Quadriplegic, self-care training for, 186-187

R

Range of motion (ROM) activities, 88-105
  importance of, 88
  performing, 91-105
    for lower extremities, 99-105
    for upper extremities, 91-99
  theory of, 88
  use of, 88-90
Reading
  in aphasia, 203
  self-help activities for, for hemiplegic, 172
Rehabilitation, 63-235
  head injury, 14-17
  instruction in, 230-235. *See also* Instruction in rehabilitation
  nurse's viewpoint on, 65-68
    atmosphere in, 67-68
    attitude in, 68
    impressions in, 65-66
    roles and attributes in, 66-67

Stance phase of normal gait, 131
Stand-up exercise, 119-121
Standing
    of patient from chair, 137-139
    in progressive mobilization, 119-122
Standing balance, 121-122
Standing transfers in pregait training, 113-114
Stockings, putting on/taking off, self-care training
    in, for arthritic, 180, *181*
Stress incontinence, 41
Stroke program, lateralized, 154-157
Supplemental Security Insurance (SSI), 2
Supportive psychological intervention, providing,
    in rehabilitation process, 223
Surface modications in pressure sore
    prevention, 52, *53-54*
Swing phase of normal gait, 132
Symbolic processing, hemiplegia and, 6-7

T

Teacher, rehabilitation nurse as, 67
Teaching encounters, one-to-one, in rehabilitation
    instruction, 235
Team approach to chronic pain management,
    31-32
Telephone, self-help activities for, for
    hemiplegic, 173
Thinker, positive, rehabilitation nurse as, 66
Thromboembolic theory of tissue death from
    infarction, 4
Thumb
    abduction of, range of motion activities for,
        97-98
    opposition of, range of motion activities for,
        98-99
Tipping lever, wheelchair, 198
Toe flexion and extension , range of motion
    activities for, 104
Toothbrushing, self-help procedures for, in
    hemiplegia, 161, *162*
Transfers, 112-117
    four-person, 115-116
    sliding board, 116-117
    standing, 113-114
Tremor in parkinsonism, 182

U

Underpants, putting on/taking off, self-care
    training in, for hemiplegic,
    166-167

Undershirt, putting on/taking off, self-care
    training in, for hemiplegic, 165, *166, 167*
United Way, services of, 226
Upper extremities, range of motion activities for,
    91-92
Urecholine for bladder problems, 45
Urethral obstruction, mechanical, incontinence
    of, 43
Urge incontinence, 41

V

Verbal apraxia, 204-205
Verticality dysfunction in hemiplegia, 6
Visual problems in aphasia, 203
Vocational factors in psychosocial assessment,
    221
Vocational rehabilitation agencies, 227
Voiding, 41

W

Walk, teaching patient to, 128-136. *See also*
    Gait training
Walker(s), 134
    measuring for, 139
    sitting down with, 148-149
    walking with, 141-142
Walking aids in gait training, 134-137
    measuring for, 139-141
    turning around using, 147
    using, 141-147
Weight shifting in wheelchair in pregait training,
    118
Wheelchair(s), 190-201
    arms of, 192-193
    backs of, 193-194
    brakes of, 196-197
    footplates of, 196
    footrests of, 195-196
    maintenance of, 200
    mobilization in, in pregait training,
        117-118
    placing of, in car, 200
    push-ups in, in pregait training, 118
    seats of, 194-195
    skirt guards of, 194
    standard, 191-198
    tipping lever of, 198
    weight shifting in, in pregait training,
        118
    wheels of, 197